Law and the Chinese in Southeast Asia

The **Institute of Southeast Asian Studies (ISEAS)** was established as an autonomous organization in 1968. It is a regional research centre for scholars and other specialists concerned with modern Southeast Asia, particularly the many-faceted issues and challenges of stability and security, economic development, and political and social change.

The Institute's research programmes are the Regional Economic Studies (RES, including ASEAN and APEC), Regional Strategic and Political Studies (RSPS), and Regional Social and Cultural Studies (RSCS).

The Institute is governed by a twenty-two-member Board of Trustees comprising nominees from the Singapore Government, the National University of Singapore, the various Chambers of Commerce, and professional and civic organizations. An Executive Committee oversees day-to-day operations; it is chaired by the Director, the Institute's chief academic and administrative officer.

Law and the Chinese in Southeast Asia

edited by
M. Barry Hooker

INSTITUTE OF SOUTHEAST ASIAN STUDIES

First published in Singapore in 2002 by
Institute of Southeast Asian Studies
30 Heng Mui Keng Terrace, Pasir Panjang
Singapore 119614

E-mail: publish@iseas.edu.sg
Website: www.iseas.edu.sg/pub.html

ISEAS Library Cataloguing-in-Publication Data

Law and the Chinese in Southeast Asia / edited by M. B. Hooker.
1. Chinese—Legal status, laws, etc.—Asia, Southeastern.
2. Citizenship—Law and legislation—Asia, Southeastern.
I. Hooker, M. B. (Michael Barry), 1939–
KNC145 C5L41 2002 sls2002010911

ISBN 981-230-125-9

Typeset by International Typesetters Pte. Ltd.
Printed in Singapore by Seng Lee Press Pte. Ltd.

CONTENTS

PREFACE

This collection of essays emanate from a conference held at the Australian National University in 1998 on the subject of "Law and the Chinese Outside China." As it happened, the majority of the papers were concerned with the Southeast Asian diaspora Chinese, particularly in French Indochina and Vietnam, Malaysia, Singapore, and Indonesia; these areas are the main foci of this collection.

Two things very quickly became apparent from the material. First, from the legal perspective, it falls into one of three classes. These are: (i) Chinese legal thought outside China, (ii) laws *of* the diaspora Chinese and (iii) laws *for* the diaspora Chinese. In chapter 1, I attempt a detailed description of this classification.

Secondly, the idea of "Confucian" or "neo-Confucian" appears in a number of guises. It may be that a more purely analytic rather than merely descriptive study of diaspora Chinese law could usefully concentrate on this usage.

The authors and I are well aware that this collection is a preliminary contribution to this subject and that much remains to be done, especially in the West and South Pacific. Do our initial three classes hold up, and what of "Confucian" in these areas?

Funding for the 1998 conference was provided by the Chiang Ching-Kuo Foundation to whom we express our thanks. Thanks are also due to Professor Wang Tay-Sheng of the National Taiwan University. We also acknowledge the Faculty of Law, Australian National University for providing the funding for the index done by Mr Alan Walker.

The contributors and I owe a huge debt to Professor Wang Gungwu, doyen of diaspora Chinese studies, for his valued support in this project. We are also grateful to our colleagues from the Asian Law Centre, University of Melbourne: Associate Professor Tim Lindsey, Professor Veronica Taylor, Mr Sean Cooney, Ms Sarah Biddulph and Dr Penelope Nicholson.

Finally I would thank Mrs Triena Ong and Mrs Roselie Ang of the Institute of Southeast Asian Studies for their help and efficiency in seeing this book to press.

M. B. Hooker
Faculty of Law
Australian National University
June 2002

CONTRIBUTORS

M. B. Hooker was formerly Professor of Comparative Law at the University of Kent at Canterbury, and currently Adjunct Professor of Law at the Australian National University. He is author of *A Concise Legal History of South-East Asia* (Oxford: The Clarendon Press, 1978); and editor of *Laws of Southeast Asia*, 2 volumes (Singapore: Butterworths, 1986–88). He was also a founding editor of *The Australian Journal of Asian Law.*

Melissa Cheung graduated from the Australian National University in 2000. Now working with Clifford Chance in Hong Kong, she is researching on Chinese law.

Esta Ungar is a lecturer in History at the University of Western Australia. Her primary research area concerns history, law and development with particular reference to land and gender issues in socialist countries in Asia. She also has overseas aid project experience under a number of international (UNDP, UNFPA) and local donor agencies (International Women's Development Agency, Quaker Service Australia). She completed her Ph.D. at Cornell University specializing in Vietnamese and Chinese history and the formation of the state in fifteenth-century Vietnam.

Charles A. Coppel is a graduate in law from the University of Melbourne. After practising as a barrister for five years, he began to take an interest in the modern history of Indonesia and its ethnic Chinese minority. His numerous publications include *Indonesian Chinese in Crisis* (Oxford University Press, 1983), which has been translated into Indonesian. He is also editor of the forthcoming *Violent Conflicts in Indonesia,* to be published by Curzon Press.

Daniel Fitzpatrick is a former solicitor and Federal Court judge's associate, and is currently lecturing at the Australian National University. He has published widely on Indonesian land law and corporate governance, most notably in the *Yale Journal of International Law*. In 1997, he was the inaugural recipient of the Merdeka Fellowship to research the Indonesian legal system. In 2001, he was a consultant to the United Nations Transitional Authority in East Timor. He was also a Visiting Professor at the University of Muenster, Germany.

Leo Suryadinata is Professor in the Department of Political Science at the National University of Singapore (NUS). He has published extensively on Southeast Asian politics and the ethnic Chinese in the region. His recent books include *Chinese and Nation-Building in Southeast Asia* (1997, 1999); *Interpreting Indonesian Politics* (1998); and *Elections and Politics in Indonesia* (2002).

1

LAW AND THE CHINESE OUTSIDE CHINA

A Preliminary Survey of the Issues and the Literature

M. B. Hooker

INTRODUCTION

"Law and the Chinese outside China" was the subject of a conference[1] held at the Australian National University on 1–4 July 1998. The focus was the laws relating to those of Chinese descent who live outside China, now often called the "diaspora Chinese". We have avoided the term "Overseas Chinese" which implies residence (longer or shorter) outside China. It is misleading because the great majority of the 20 million or so diaspora Chinese are, in fact, long-term citizens of the Southeast Asian and Western Pacific states in which they are concentrated. They are not citizens of China, and it is not uncommon to find many families who have resided for hundreds of years in Southeast Asia, and are loyal to those states.

For this volume a number of revised papers have been selected for publication.[2] The selection has been difficult because of the complexity of the subject. This introductory chapter will give a brief overview of the issues discussed in the following chapters. The study does not pretend to be exhaustive; as far as is known, law and the Chinese outside China has never before been approached as a single subject for extensive discussion.

The Geographical Area

In this volume we are concerned with that geographical area in which Chinese law, in one of its forms, has become a vital part of the legal heritage. Broadly speaking, there are two areas. The first consists of Japan, Korea and Annam (Vietnam). These are the modern states in which, historically, the Chinese legal legacy has played a determining intellectual role. Each state has taken elements of Ming and Qing legal thought and adapted them for its own use (see below).

The second comprises the states of what is now called Southeast Asia, where the vast majority of the diaspora Chinese now live and have lived for several hundreds of years. From west to east, the states are: Burma (Myanmar), Thailand, Laos, Cambodia, Vietnam, Philippines, Malaysia, Singapore, Brunei, and Indonesia.

The West and South Pacific (the United States and Canada, Australia and New Zealand, and the Pacific Islands) are excluded because at this stage this area probably replicates the trends already experienced in colonial and post-colonial Southeast Asia. The South and West Pacific Chinese legal diaspora may of course become a field for further study but for the time being, they are excluded here.

Law and Society

Much, if not most, of the material on the diaspora Chinese is to be found in the disciplines of history, sociology, and economics. These are valuable sources.[3] They often mention, explain, and to some extent summarize legal materials[4] but not in a systematic way. In addition, they tend to concentrate on the politics and economics of the diaspora Chinese, especially for the post-World War II period. Nevertheless, these studies are essential.

Concepts of Law: The Chinese Contribution

When we speak of the laws of China outside China, or the laws of the Chinese — Chinese law and custom, or laws applied to the Chinese — we are talking about hybrid or mixed systems. There is no one source for any of these laws. Instead, we have different sources, different ways of thinking about law, and different forms in which it has come to be expressed over six hundred years and in ten languages!

The form and expression of Chinese law is relative to time and place. There is no such thing as *a* diaspora Chinese law. Failure to recognize this has led to some confusion in the past, and nowhere more so than in the *forms* of law. From the fourteenth century to the end of the twentieth century, there have been much misunderstanding about Chinese law and legal thought. It is important to be specific as to time and place. Here, the more general questions will be examined. These include the subject of hybrid laws, of legal borrowing, and of the complex expressions of "right", "obligation", "wrong", and "duty". All of the Chinese diaspora laws are concerned with this and related issues, as will be shown later.

Hybrid Laws/Legal Pluralism.

The "laws of China" and the "laws of the Chinese" have existed outside China for the past millennium, if not earlier. They have not remained unchanged in their new homes in Southeast and East Asia. They have, instead, become "localized". To quote Professor Oliver Wolters:[5]

> The materials, be they words, sounds of words, books, or artifacts, had to be localised in different ways before they could fit into various local complexes of religious, social and political systems, and belong to new cultural "wholes".

Professor Wolters was actually speaking of Indian historical materials, but the proposition is equally true for law, including Chinese law.

The study of hybrid laws and legal pluralism has for the past twenty years or so become an important subject in its own right. It has today become central in the field of economic development in the newly developing countries and in the area of human rights. This is quite obvious to the legal observer. In their modern laws, the genesis of legal pluralism lies in the high imperialism of the nineteenth century when European powers reigned supreme. Not only were they supreme in politics, economics, and militarily but also intellectually, and this last is particularly clear in law. European laws were imposed directly (as in imperial possessions) or indirectly (as in demands made through treaties of extra-territoriality). The result was more or less the same in both cases; it was the subjection of the Asian law to European selection, validation, and indeed a new definition of law.[6]

There is a related issue which should also be mentioned here. This is extra-territoriality, the device by which European laws were imposed in Asia from the mid-nineteenth century onto ostensibly independent states. The examples are China, Japan, and Siam. The issue is one of sovereignty. There is no general history for the area.[7]

Legal Orientalism

This is a term used to describe the problems one faces in understanding "Asian law". As such, it begs the question: what (is) "Asian Law"? Various attempts have been made to answer this question in recent years, including the radical response which says that "Asian law" is merely a construct in the mind of a Western observer and so is subjective to a degree, which renders it without meaning. This issue has been discussed in detail elsewhere.[8] For now, we must recognize that the East and West have been in legal contact for the last two hundred years or more. There is no longer a "pure Eastern" or "pure Western" legal thought. To suppose otherwise is to fly in the face of the evidence. It is a fantasy to suppose that an "Asian" and a "European" legal system can be distinguished. We can, of course, point to cultural *elements* or culturally defined *forms* of law(s) but at the end of the twentieth century, there is now a common discourse about law.

Secondly, we must recognize the existence of legal and cultural pluralities. We have three for China and Chinese law, and these will be discussed now. First, let us list out some key terms: culture, historiography, re-definition of law, diffusion of law, sovereignty, and legal pluralism. These constitute "legal orientalism" and also serve as its antidote.

Chinese Diaspora Law(s)

These laws appear to fall into three groups, or approaches to the subject.

1. The law(s) of China outside China. This means the influence and effect of classical Chinese legal thought in Japan, Korea, and Annam. There is a secondary reference in the nineteenth century to Western imperial powers in which the British, French, and Dutch considered whether or not the laws of China had a part in the imperial possessions. In the event, the decision was that they did not and could not be relevant for nineteenth century imperial mercantilism.

2. Chinese law(s). This means Chinese "custom", "manners", "religion". "way of life", and other related terms. Essentially, it means those customs to which the Western powers were prepared to allow a legal effect as a law "personal" to the ethnic Chinese.

3. Laws applied to the Chinese. These are the regulations directed at the ethnic Chinese, which are mostly concerned with taxation, restrictions on immigration, travel, occupation, education, publications, and culture. In short, they include all of those matters which have a financial or

political aspect where the Chinese have been (and still are) seen to be a threat or competition to the established order.

LAWS OF CHINA[9] OUTSIDE CHINA

This is a large and complex subject area and I have divided it into two parts which are related but which must be kept separate for now. These are, firstly, on Chinese claims to suzerainty and its legal expression, and secondly, the adoption of Ming and Qing codes outside China.

Suzerainty

Imperial China's claim to suzerainty over its neighbours has been a consistent feature of Chinese history. It remains alive today well into the twenty-first century; the Chinese government's claims in the South China Sea are a current example. It is a complicated question in international law. While this is not a primary concern here, the Chinese official view, through history, of the legality of Chinese claims is also relevant because it indicates the Chinese view of law.

The literature in the European languages on this matter is rather sparse. The main evidence is in the Chinese sources. Perhaps a word of caution: the question of suzerainty, historical or contemporary, is always one of politics, and the literature is always interpreted in this light. Motives range from national prestige to calculated economics. The typical form in which this was expressed was through "tribute" and its commonest manifestation was in the receiving of a tribute mission by the Imperial Government. The mission would bring presents of varying value and, in return, would receive presents *and* an acknowledgment that the polity it represented was a legitimate one. From the point of view of the embassy, this served one purpose: legitimation by a highly formal and legalistic ceremonial. The best short general introduction is in Professor Wolfgang Franke's seminal paper,[10] published in 1989.

In this paper, Professor Franke makes two points. First, the acceptance of a barbarian (that is, non-Chinese) embassy was a confirmation of the superiority of China and a general suzerainty of the Emperor of China. This did not necessarily translate into actual rule over the embassy-giving states; indeed it was rather rare that this occurred. The objective was to overawe the border peoples and to attract them to the higher (Chinese) culture and, thus, neutralize any threat on the borders. The success of this policy varied from time to time. Secondly, the cultural superiority, even arrogance, historically shown by Imperial China, while quite understandable in a number of respects, also had its drawbacks. The most important, from our point of view, was the belief that Chinese legal thought, and legal forms could and should be transplanted in their pure forms to neighbouring cultures, especially in Korea, Japan, and Annam.

Serious attempts to do this were made from the thirteenth century until the early nineteenth century. It was never completely successful (see the section below on the classical texts outside China). However, suzerainty was from time to time a viable system for the control of the border areas.[11]

The contemporary version of suzerainty is to be found in modern international relations. This is outside the scope of this chapter but one should be aware of it. The example which comes to one's mind is the Chinese claim to the South China Sea and its islands and resources. The merits and demerits of these claims are secondary for us. The primary issue, and one around which an extensive and mutual miscomprehension arises, is the nature of international law itself.[12]

The Classical Texts Outside China

The reference here is to the Ming and Qing texts. The illustrious civilization of China had and still has a deep and abiding effect on the neighbouring civilizations of East and Southeast Asia.

Korea

The law, legal thought, and legal practice of pre-modern Korea are often described as "neo-Confucianism". The adjective obscures more than it explains but it appears to have an identifiable set of referents.

First, it is taken in the context of the adaptation of Ming codes based on the legislative and judicial records of the fourteenth to eighteenth centuries. These illustrate the status of the élite in society, the sovereign, and the law and duties of the population in rendering services — in short, analyses of the traditional polity and social structure.[13] Secondly, the adaptation of Chinese laws has become a feature of Korean legal-historical scholarship.[14] Finally, the issue of the "great" versus the "little" traditions has become an important topic in Korean legal studies. The debate over traditions first began in the 1960s, and has remained important in East and Southeast Asian studies generally.[15] The view that it is the "Great Tradition" which essentially determines the expression of the intellect, including the legal intellect, is still commonly held. The relationship between this position and the originality of the so-called "provincial" legal cultures is still much debated.[16]

Japan

The Japanese debt to Chinese legal thought is of course immense, and there is a huge literature in the Japanese language.[17] From the point of view of comparative law, a number of interesting topics have come to dominate the issue from the late 1980s. The first is the proposition that a major function of the imported thought was to provide stability through adopting the Chinese bureaucratic method. Perhaps the implication here is the precarious nature of government in pre-modern Japan. At the same time, Japanese practices and customs were not abandoned so that a complex set of rules developed from the interplay between Chinese and Japanese principles regarding the state, the individual, and the law.[18]

Secondly, modern scholarship is increasingly devoting attention to the vexed question of precisely what did Japanese scholars know of the laws of China in the pre-modern period(s). While the issue can be viewed[19] as simply an access to information, it is more likely to involve an investigation into how and why the Japanese authorities *chose* from the available Chinese materials. Professor Dan F. Henderson provides an especially valuable account[20] because it demonstrates three points, which can often be overlooked in the whole question of diffusion/borrowing from one legal tradition and settling its principles of reasoning into another. The first is that "Tokugawa borrowing was eclectic and subject to Japanese adaptation". This is now an obvious proposition but the complexity of the diffusion certainly went unrecognized for a considerable period of time. The consequences of this lack of recognition have been unfortunate. Secondly, borrowing from specific Chinese laws was not wholesale but rather narrow (penal laws), and even then it was confined to specific geographical areas rather than being Japan-wide. Finally, there are problems in dating the reception/diffusion/borrowing. These difficulties are real because they determined that which was translated. A result was that later developments, or reformulations in China, did not necessarily come through to Japan in the eighteenth century. Whether this is of any significance is yet to be determined.

Annam (in Vietnamese, Dai Viêt)

For many years, the study of Chinese legal thought in Vietnamese texts was conditioned by nineteenth century French colonial work.[21] Plainly, the assumption was that the historical materials — the Lê Code of the fifteenth century and the Gia-Long Code of 1813 — were "Chinese". This way of putting it is now known to be very misleading because it assumes the primacy of the "Great Tradition". However, the Annam case against this position is much weaker than the (now) contemporary Indian and Islamic histories.[22] For the 1813 Gia-Long Code, the written text is a plain copy of the Chinese. The fourteenth century Lê appears to have some indigenous features but one has to search hard for them.[23] Essentially it, too, is "Chinese".

LAWS OF THE CHINESE

The reference here is to the laws, practices, customary laws, and personal laws which the Chinese applied to themselves or were applied to them. The British and Dutch Chinese-customary laws are the best known. The immigrant Chinese took with them their customary practices, and these have both historical and contemporary significance. In the past, it was normal to treat these customs as only a part of colonial law, or as examples of the colonial legal policy. This is too narrow a view. My belief is that Chinese customary law, both within the Chinese community and as an aspect of the integration of the Chinese into the wider East and Southeast Asian world, is an essential part of diaspora history. In this respect, it has been quite neglected. In addition, it should be remembered that Chinese customary law persists (in concepts such as Li) despite attempts by various states to "reform" or limit its effects. There seems to have been a consistent movement in post-war Southeast Asia to really eliminate Chinese customary laws. These are mainly in the area of family law and charitable trusts, but also trusts involving "Chinese religion" about which there is no agreed certainty. The question is why the modern states, even those such as Singapore which have a Chinese majority population, wish to do this. If there is a new morality abroad, then this has yet to be explained. What about the much vaunted "Confucian values", or are these, whatever they are, inappropriate for Chinese customary law and the new nation states? Before we can answer this question, we have to know what these laws are.

It is the customs of the diaspora Chinese which have attained legal recognition in territories which, until recently, were the preserves of the British, Dutch, and French imperialisms in Southeast Asia and in Hong Kong. After the end of Empire and independence, these laws continued to be used in some places. However, the histories are varied. We can take the earliest date at about 1700 (in the Netherlands East Indies) and our latest in Malaysia in 1995. This spans three hundred years. There is no one "Chinese customary law". Instead, there are various versions conditioned partly by the legal policies of European imperialism and partly by the willingness of the Chinese diaspora leaders to take their communities into the public, legal arena. This was a difficult thing to do but it was done by a few outstanding individuals in Southeast Asia and East Asia who led their respective communities into the "modern" world.[24]

Chinese custom or personal law illustrates how this was done. It is one of the earliest examples of multiculturalism that we have. The law reports show Europeans and Chinese attempting to understand one another, and to come to some mutually intelligible understanding in the important fields of family law, property, and religious trusts. All these involved large sums of money.

The Recognition of Chinese Customs in British Colonial Law

The basic principle in all the British imperial possessions was that the law of general application was English law. However, from the late eighteenth century, it also became accepted practice that this general rule was or could be limited to some extent. The limitation, first put into written form in India in 1781, was that exceptions could be made in matters of "religion, manners and customs". During the succeeding two hundred years, this phrase was judicially defined as being applicable only to family law and some aspects of the law relating to charitable trusts. However, the exception was subject to a test — that it did not contravene "equity, justice and good conscience". This limitation allowed English judges unfettered discretion. Exactly the same approach was adopted in British India and, later, in British Africa.[25]

Singapore and Malaysia (formerly the Straits Settlements and Malay States).

The former Straits Settlements and Malay States were the oldest British possessions in Southeast Asia, dating from 1786. The population, even at that time, was heterogeneous and the Chinese had a strong social and commercial presence. The main centres — Penang, Malacca and Singapore — were Chinese cities built and maintained through Chinese effort. There were enough wealthy people to find the English courts an appropriate forum to settle disputes. It should be noted that these were all in the area of family law.[26] No Chinese ever brought a commercial dispute, *based on Chinese custom*, to the colonial courts. They were (and are) dealt with on a clan and commercial-association basis. The only partial exceptions were the money-loan associations (*hwai, bwei*).

The major issues in Chinese personal law up to the mid-1970s were as follows. First, what were the criteria for the recognition of Chinese law demanded by the dominant English system? There is a variety of answers. The initial answer and still the most persuasive is that the late eighteenth century policy for recognition (that is, "religions, manners, customs") was the basis and the precedent, which has since then evolved and taken on its own life. It could not be overturned except by very specific legislation (see below). Another basis was the local law/ordinance/Order in Council. There is only one example of this, the Perak Order in Council of 1893, amended in 1895. The third and final basis for recognition was the use of principles of the (English) Conflicts of Laws, also known as "private international law". This was a dismal failure, as was the same exercise in French Indochina and the Netherlands East Indies. The principles of Conflicts of Laws presuppose more than one *state*. It does not take into account more than one *religion* or *race*, which are the defining points for Chinese personal laws.

Secondly, what was the extent and scope of Chinese law? The answer for the Chinese of this area was the same as that for Hong Kong (below) and indeed for all "native" peoples of the British Empire. It was family law — that is, marriage, divorce, inheritance and custody. Particular problems encountered included whether the Chinese were "polygamous by nature", the position of Christian Chinese, and the validity of customary adoptions. In addition, Chinese custom in respect of "ancestor worship" and funds for the upkeep of temples raised difficult questions on the relation of law to religion and custom.[27] In British Borneo, complicated issues arising from interracial marriage remain.[28]

British Burma

The Chinese population was never large and was mainly concentrated in central and northern Burma. In 1948, its total was estimated at 300,000 out of a total population of 18 million. However, taken alone these figures are misleading. The Chinese easily assimilated into Burmese society, and the resulting "Sino-Burmese" regarded themselves and were regarded as Burmese. The figure above refers to "pure" Chinese. However, despite their tiny proportion of the population, the Chinese community generated a respectable judicial precedent.[29] The question was: to which religion did the Chinese belong; was Confucianism a religion? This had important implications for law. If a Chinese could be shown to be a Confucian, then the laws of China applied to him. The problem was that the British judges in Burma had little or no idea what this law was, either in the Qing or Republican periods. If, on the other hand, the Chinese were Buddhists, then Burmese (Buddhist) custom would apply. This, at least, was already known in various texts and in precedent. In addition, as a matter of policy, the courts were concerned with protecting the position and status of Burmese women who had married Chinese men. A finding that the Chinese were Buddhist, and hence fell under the British-Indian jurisdiction, was the practical solution. By the 1930s, this was in fact the established position. The current status of this complex precedent (1881–1947) is unknown.

For Hong Kong, the courts had to deal with the same issues as in Malaysia and Singapore.[30]

Chinese Customary Law in Dutch Colonial Law

The Dutch were quite exceptional in colonial legal history because they developed a policy of assigning peoples to legal regimes on the basis of race. The abhorrent apartheid in recent South Africa was a similar policy. Racial classifications, as such, do not work. There is plenty of evidence for this around the world. The classification always breaks down in the face of marriage, contracts, and property. As a matter of fact, it was meaningless, and this was true in respect of the colonial government in the Netherlands East Indies (NEI), and the administration of the Chinese. In effect, the Chinese were never really "Foreign Orientals". (See following sections.)

Colonial Legal Policy[31]

This can be summed up as racial and interracial law. The various populations of the NEI were legally defined as Europeans, or persons assimilated to that group, to which Dutch law applied; autochthonous peoples or "Natives", to whom customary law (*adat*) applied; and Foreign Orientals, that is, Arabs and Chinese. The Arabs were soon made to disappear into the Native group. The Chinese, however, were exceptional because successive Dutch administrations really had no idea of what to do about "Chinese law" or the "laws of the Chinese". This uncertainty was not confined to the Chinese. Muslims, whether Arabs or one of the races (*bangsa*) of Indonesia, were treated in a similar fashion.

Was There A "Chinese Law"?

Unlike the British colonies in Asia, this is a difficult question to answer for the NEI. Theoretically, as a class of "Foreign Orientals" some sort of Chinese law should apply. Up to 1824, the European courts (Raden van Justitie) dealt with civil matters for the Chinese, and applied Dutch law except in the case of inheritance. Criminal cases went to the Native Court of Justice (the Landraad) where some Chinese custom was admitted. By 1855, however, Dutch law was reconfirmed as applicable to the Chinese in civil matters and by 1918 the criminal law for all classes of the population was substantially the same. The Chinese had the option to assimilate with European law. In short, there was no "Chinese law" as such, with possible exceptions in the areas of inheritance and adoption, in which cases a modified Qing law applied.[32] In fact "Chinese law" meant the specific regulations for those of Chinese descent.[33]

Chinese Customary Law in French Colonial Law

There is no general history of French colonial law for the former Indochina[34] and this is a considerable obstacle to our understanding of the Chinese position. A more serious issue is the nature of French law itself. By the time of French occupation of Indochina (1868 onwards) the new laws of post-revolutionary France were only fifty years old. The laws of the French imperium were, in fact, very new, largely untried, and with no tradition of coping with legal pluralism. The Napoleonic Codes were a triumph of legal intellectualism. However, this was a self-contained, enclosed, and self-justifying system. The idea that the colonial subjects of France should have their laws and customs incorporated into the civil system was impossible. The best that the subject peoples could hope for was some administrative acknowledgment of their laws and customs.

This is one of legal history's great ironies. The best efforts of the intellectuals of France at the end of the eighteenth century, when put to the test in Indochina only seventy years later, failed badly and degenerated into technical obscurity, which the Age of Enlightenment was supposed to have swept away. In short, we had an immature legal culture facing legal cultures of great sophistication and long history. In Indochina, these were the laws of China (above), the oldest working legal culture in the history of law.

The authorities literally did not know what to do; nothing in their training had prepared them for the Annamite Mandarinate, nor for the increasing Chinese commercial and political presence. The Mandarinate was trying to implement the 1813 Gia-Long Code, a copy of the late eighteenth century Qing law. This was both the *Law of China* and also the laws *of the Chinese.* There was little distinction until the French imperium. The Gia-Long Code, as the law of Dai-Viet, remained in force in Annam until 1932.

The laws *of the Chinese*, however, were never clarified. In April 1871, the Chinese were classed as *asiatiques assimilés*, so that only the local customs were applicable to them. On paper, these laws/customs consisted of Annamite *statut personnel* (October 1883) which dealt with family law and some aspects of commercial law.[35]

In short, Chinese law was being defined as (a) the classical texts (Gia-Long after Qing) or (b) Vietnamese customs as codified in 1883 and later revised in the 1920s to 1930s. In fact, neither had anything to do with the actual practice of customary law in the Chinese community(s). We just do not know what it was and how it worked. The *jurisprudence* of the time tells us little or nothing.[36]

The fact is that the French were only interested in controlling immigration, Chinese commercial activity, and dealing with the governments of China on the northern Indochina borders. The actual administration of a "Chinese law for the Chinese" was not a priority until 1930. In that year, the Treaty of Nanking was concluded between France and the Republic of China. The result of this was a series of protocols which introduced the *laws of China*, that is, the Republican Codes, into French Indochina on a private international law basis.[37]

Perhaps a word about private international law, also known as conflict of laws: this is a special body of rules to determine which of two or more possible nation-state laws applies to a dispute between individuals. As far as the Chinese were concerned, it was only the French in the 1930s who really gave the problem the attention which it deserved. The question was: what was the appropriate forum for the choice of law? Between 1920 and 1942 the courts in Indochina spent a great deal of time and effort on this matter. The subject came to a head after the signing of the Treaty of Nanking in 1930 and the promulgation of rules to give effect to the Treaty provisions (which continued to be under negotiation until 1935). In practical terms, the Treaty was not effective until mid-1935. The result was that theoretically the Chinese in Indochina became entitled to the application of the *laws of China* in French territory. "Chinese law" became "the laws of China for ethnic Chinese" in Indochina.[38]

LAWS TO CONTROL THE CHINESE

This is a large subject and one in which historians and social scientists spend a huge amount of time and effort. The main areas pertain to control of immigration, financial and commercial activity, secret societies, education, the status of Chinese women and, of special importance at the dawn of the twenty-first century, nationality and citizenship. It will be obvious that many of the practices of the imperial powers in these matters have been carried on enthusiastically by successive independent states. It is appropriate, therefore, that we study the material on a state-by-state basis. The main historical and social science texts have already been indicated — that is, Purcell, Cushman and Wang, and Suryadinata.[39] These need no comment and the reader may indeed wish to add more recent works.[40] From the point of view of law, however, there is much material that is generally not known, and this has to be taken on a state-by-state basis.

The Philippines[41]

The "Sangley", as the Spanish called the Chinese, were in the Philippines before the Spanish imperium began. Relations between the two races were far from cordial, with repressive laws imposed by one side being met with violent resistance on the other. There were restrictions on residence and movement outside Manila, and the Chinese were forced to pay a variety of punitive taxes and supply personal services at the request of the authorities. This remained the position from the sixteenth to the nineteenth centuries.

There was one peculiarly Spanish use of law as a method of control over the Chinese. This was the place of religion (here Catholicism) in Spanish legal thought, indeed in the Spanish theory of empire. From the theological point of view, Spanish sovereignty could only be morally exercised over those who were Christian or were in the process of being converted. It was not open to the Indios/Sangley to resist the Truths brought by Spain. The legitimacy of this position of power over the Indios/Sangley was confirmed by a series of Papal Bulls. What then was the position of the Christian Chinese? Here is a perfect example from the early seventeenth century, which was consistently repeated into the late nineteenth century, often for the worst of motives.

> [The King] Fray Melchor Manzano, of the Order of St. Dominic, has reported to me, on behalf of the Sangley Chinese living in the Parian outside the walls of the city of Manila, that they experience much extortion and injury, on account of not only what pertains to the Christianity that they profess, but their liberty, possession, and honour, by making them cut their hair when they become Christians — a thing regarded as ignominious by their nation, and which is an obstacle to their conversion, and contrary to the orders of the decree of the king our sovereign and grandfather, who as in glory; as also that they pay annually sixty-four reals in silver, in addition to the ordinary tribute, or that they return to their own country, which means that they are forced

> to abandon the faith which they received with baptism. He declares that that tribute was never paid by the Christians until it was imposed by Don Alonso de Faxardo, my former governor of the Filipinas Islands, contrary to the advice of my Audiencia resident therein. Fray Melchor has petitioned me that, attentive to the above, I be pleased to order that those converted to our holy Catholic faith be not obliged to cut their hair, or pay the said tribute, or anything else besides the ordinary tribute paid by the natives of the said islands; or that it be moderated so that their conversion may not thereby be made difficult, and that those who once receive the faith be not obliged to abandon it by returning to their country because of their inability to pay so large a tribute — since the majority of those converted are poor labourers, who cannot earn that tribute. Having examined the matter in my royal Council of the Indias, I have considered it expedient to order this my decree to be issued. By it I order that for the first ten years after their conversion the said Sangley Chinese pay no tribute, and that none be collected from them, as I have commanded shall be done in regard to other pagan Indians who are converted. After ten years, the tribute shall be collected from them, as from the natives of the said islands. I order my governor and captain-general of the islands to see that the above is strictly obeyed and observed, and not to allow their hair to be cut, in observance of the decree that has been issued concerning this matter [Madrid, 19 November 1627].

In this one passage we have most of the themes of Spanish colonialism in the Philippines; the greed of the Spanish, the payment of tribute, the obsession with formal appearance, and the fact of religion. The question of whether or not the Sangley actually had souls and were, therefore, "human" was parallel to the issue in the celebrated "Trial" at Valladolid where the question was: did Indians have souls, were they in fact human beings and thus subject to the protection of the law?[42] In answering this question, religion was primary. The status of the Indios, which included the Chinese, depended upon conversion to Catholicism, as the passage cited above demonstrates.

However, the subsequent history of the Chinese up to the American period (post-1898) also shows continuing efforts at control, especially financial control in which religious adherence was not relevant. Instead, it was commercial jealousy on the part of the American and Philippine authorities which was decisive. From about 1910, there was a consistent policy[43] to exclude immigration and to limit Chinese commerce. A good example is the so-called "Chinese Bookkeeping Law" case (*Yu Cong Eng*) where the U.S. Supreme Court was required to pronounce on the validity of Philippine legislation directed against Chinese commercial interests. The Chinese were seen as "aliens", and as early as in 1912 the Philippine legislature attempted to pass laws requiring Chinese businessmen to keep account books in a non-Chinese language. The attempt failed. However, there were some successes. For example, an ordinance of the Manila municipal government requiring laundries to give receipts in English and Spanish was upheld on the ground that it did not conflict with any right or personal privilege. The Chinese Bookkeeping Law of 1921 was another example, but in this instance, it failed partly because of intense lobbying by Chinese interests in the United States as well as Chinese diplomatic pressure exerted there. In the event, the validity of the law was determined first in the insular Supreme Court and finally in the U.S. Supreme Court. The important point for us is that the arguments put forward to invalidate the law were founded solely in U.S. constitutional law cases.

Further matters of difficulty were immigration and, as always, education and commerce. A full account has yet to be written but it is worth noting that large parts of the Philippine legislation, from about 1910 or so, were based on U.S. immigration laws designed specifically to exclude the Chinese.

Full independence for the Philippines (in 1946) did little to change the pre-war policy or rather lack of policy. The Chinese remained entrenched in a somewhat ghetto mentality and the (so-called) native Filipinos in the legislature enacted a number of measures in the 1950s and 1960s, designed to exclude or offer considerable difficulty to the Chinese business community. These included Acts for the nationalization (that is, Philippine-ization) of public markets, and the retail trade and rice industries. Banking was also affected because large quotas (up to 80 per cent) of natural-born Filipinos were required to be in possession of bank capital. Naturalized citizen participation (the Chinese) was restricted to 20 per cent or even less.[44]

Indonesia

The Netherlands East Indies (c. 1640–1942)

The policy of the Dutch in the Netherlands East Indies period oscillated on a scale from oppression, to tolerance, and to positive encouragement. The gradations on this scale were determined by the financial and commercial interests of those in power. The policy towards the Chinese was rather inconsistent. The earliest mention of the Chinese was in *The Statutes of Batavia* (1642/50) which had extensive provisions on Chinese estates, Chinese debts (a debtor might be sold into slavery), the exemptions of Chinese from guard duty on payment of a special tax, and gambling where the Chinese were specifically licensed to keep gaming houses. None of these provisions gave an official status to Chinese law — indeed, in 1785 this was specifically denied. The reforms of the mid-nineteenth century legal system have already been mentioned, and by the end of that century, the Chinese had become legally assimilated with the European law group, with some exceptions (adoptions, the *kongsi*).[45]

However, one problem remained from the early years of this century. This was the vexed question of nationality and citizenship. A special feature has been the consistent claims by China of an interest in the Chinese outside China.[46] This was, and still is, based on the purely racial test — *jus sanguinis* (descent from a [male] Chinese). For the Imperial, Republican, and even Socialist governments, this was the essential principle which determined how an individual Chinese could or should or must be attached to a legal regime. The issue is one of international relations and law.[47]

Republik Indonesia

The nationality issue came to the fore immediately after World War II (1946–49), with the Indonesian Chinese caught between the two Chinas, the Indonesian nationalists, and the Dutch. Obviously, the issue was partly internal and partly within public international law (through treaties with the People's Republic of China), in private as well as international law with regard to the application of these rules.[48]

In addition to the nationality problem, the Chinese in Indonesia have been subjected to a complex and detailed array of control measures in the fields of economics and commerce, immigration, education, and publications in the Chinese language.[49] From 1965, assimilation of the Chinese has been a consistent and strongly enforced national policy.[50]

The Former British Possessions in Southeast and East Asia

British imperial history spanned about four hundred years and extended from the Americas to the Middle East, South Asia, Southeast Asia, and the Pacific. The law relating to the Overseas Chinese in Southeast and East Asia is but a part of a more general legal history and its main features are derived from principles established elsewhere.[51]

The Straits Settlements, Singapore and Malaya

The main issue in these territories was the imposition of public order onto a turbulent Chinese society which was male-dominated until well into the twentieth century. Initially, the Chinese were permitted an "*imperium in imperio*", ruling themselves through the institution of the "Kapitan China". However, clan and secret society rivalries made this impossible but it was not until 1877 in the Straits and 1889 in the Malay States that a Protector of Chinese was appointed to provide some effective control. Various ordinances followed, most notably the Registration of Societies Ordinance, the function of which was to control secret societies by dissolving them and repatriating the leaders back to China.

Another problem was the traffic in women and girls and the vexed questions of prostitution and *mui tsai.* It was not until the late 1930s that some order was brought to these issues.[52]

Education was similarly regulated from 1920, with a government-appointed inspectorate of Chinese schools designed to control and eliminate expressions of political opinion emanating from China. This was particularly important in respect of KMT (Kuomintang) politics from 1930 when China attempted to gain rights not just in education but also in the supervision of the Chinese in the Malayan peninsula. Finally, immigration and the movement of labour was a constant preoccupation of the colonial government, which initiated ordinances and regulations dating from 1823 when Raffles introduced an ordinance for the protection of immigrants to Singapore. More complex legislation followed from the 1870s and then became increasingly frequent. The Aliens Ordinance of 1933 was the most extensive.[53]

British Borneo (Sarawak and Sabah)

As in the Malayan peninsula, the main problem in Sarawak was the control of a turbulent male population many of whom were engaged in mining. There was a serious rebellion in 1856. In North Borneo (now Sabah), Chinese immigration was encouraged through generous land grants and passages from China to North Borneo. The government, however, retained, through the Protector of Labour, extensive powers of control, including deportation. Education and commercial activity (especially money-lending) were also extensively controlled.[54]

British Burma

There was never a large Chinese population in Burma except in patches in the north where Yunnanese traders and immigrants were active. The main controls over this population were found in various provisions of the Anglo-Chinese treaties dating from the late 1880s. They were either concerned with boundary matters or with Anglo-Chinese trade, including navigation rights on the Irrawaddy River. The Chinese government was permitted to open a Consular Office at Rangoon. Assimilation of the Chinese was quite easy and extremely common.[55] Religion no doubt played a part. The major problem since the war has been the control of immigration, and in recent years this has been complicated by the presence of KMT army remnants in the north and their involvement in the drug trade.

The Former French Possessions in Indochina (Vietnam, Cambodia, and Laos)

These states share a common legacy of civil law, although each also has had a version of Socialist law imposed for the last forty years or so. The political history of these states has been turbulent and this has naturally had serious effects on law, to the extent that one system — in Cambodia — was totally destroyed by the Khmer Rouge (1975–79). All have suffered grievously, and the legal position of the Chinese has fluctuated according to the politics of the day.

The politics of colonialism were decisive in the development of French colonial legal thought to an extent much greater than in the British or Dutch empires of the same period. The status of the "native" races was determined by everyday political expediency but also justified by reference to some "higher principle" — the "*mission civilatrice Française*"! A good example can be seen in the following:[56]

> The administration of native customary law is a branch of native policy and of territorial administration. The tribunal is an observation post from which the administrative officer who presides over it may study the effects of his own administration and the reaction of the people he governs, … And in pronouncing judgement he effects political actions; he maintains civil peace as well as public order; he recognises and observes native rights, and by pursuing justice he stimulates their evolution.

This proposition is true for all French possessions, including Indochina. The legal system here was technically very complex. Even today there is no proper history.[57]

The overriding principle was that French law was the determining law although its application as such was not straightforward because of the different status of the various populations — *sujet, asiatiques assimilés, protégé, assimilé.* It was further complicated by the different status of the various parts of which the Union Indochinoise was composed; Cochinchina and Laos were *pays de souverainete française* and the remainder were *pays de protectorate.*[58]

For the Chinese, the result was that in matters of private law they were classed as *asiatique assimilé*. On the public law side, which is our concern here, we have the function of the *congrégation* (association), and in international law their status was determined by treaty. In addition, there is a miscellany of further restrictions, and the ever-present nationality/citizenship issue.

The Congrégation (or bang)

This was an association based on the place of origin and/or dialect and was typically found in all Overseas Chinese places of settlement. The associations in Vietnam were early recognized by the nineteenth century Nguyen Dynasty emperors as the appropriate group for controlling the immigrant population. The French continued the practice.[59]

By the decree of 7 October 1871, all Chinese had to belong to a Congregation, and further regulations dating from 1890 laid down procedures for the election of heads, and other officers, and specified the duties which they had to perform for the French authorities. By 1906, there was a standard form of organization and it remained in force until the ratification of the Nankin Accords in 1935. The duties of the heads of Congregations were to keep a register of members, be responsible for debts and taxes of members, and to supervise government regulations over the Chinese. As far as civil law was concerned, they had full legal authority under the Civil Code.

The Congregation system was designed to cope with an immigrant population, and from the late nineteenth century to the 1920s it was a solution to the practical problems associated with the movements of the Chinese into Indochina. It dealt with a variety of requirements, such as contracts, medical expenses, taxes and identity cards, and must be judged to have been reasonably successful.

The Chinese in Public International Law

The first major treaty involving the Chinese in Indochina was the Treaty of Tientsin (June 1895), which was primarily concerned with commercial matters. It also gave China the right to set up consulates, although the actual establishment of these was postponed. This issue of consulates was not confined only to Indochina. Both the Dutch and the English were faced with the same requests from the late Qing China. By the Republican period, these requests had become more pressing, especially for the French who only among the colonial powers shared a common border with China. In 1935, the Treaty of Nanking between France and China was ratified.

The most important result[60] of the Treaty (or the various agreements which it comprised) was that the Chinese were now on the same legal footing as French citizens in almost all aspects of law. They were no longer *asiatique assimilé* but "privileged aliens"! However, they were, in theory at least, still subject to special taxes. This same position was continued after the war by the Treaty of Chungking (February 1946), but amounted to little as the first of the Indochina wars broke out.

Miscellaneous Restrictions

There are a number of works,[61] which taken together, refer us to the usual problems of immigration and visas, permissions/permits for internal travel, restrictions on occupations and professions, taxation, the keeping of accounts, acquisition of property, education, and gambling.

The post-1976 legal history of the Chinese in former Indochina has not been a happy one. There has been consistent restrictions and also periodic expulsion. The *jus sanguinis* and the *jus soli* remain as constant irritants, and recent events in Indonesia have done nothing to ease this tension.

Thailand (Siam)

Thailand has always readily assimilated its Chinese immigrants. However, despite this fact Thailand (Siam) has always had a consistent anti-ethnic Chinese policy. There is a long history of regulations, orders, laws, and procedures directed against the Chinese.[62]

The Chinese promulgation in 1909 of the *jus sanguinis* law[63] caused much difficulty with Siam as it did with the French and Dutch. Of course, it placed particular difficulties on the Chinese residents themselves and an obvious solution was for them to become or claim to be subjects of the European powers with which Siam had treaties. Their status, therefore, was governed by the then existing rules on extra-territoriality, and Thornley[64] gives a complete breakdown of the possible legal permutations as to status. The post-World War II era has seen a plethora of Thai legislation[65] affecting such matters as immigration, alien registration fees, citizenship and naturalization, franchise, education, reservation of certain occupations to ethnic Thai only, reservations to land ownership, and land taxes.

THE "CONFUCIAN" PARADIGM

The term "Confucian" is a much used, misused, maligned and debated one. Very often, it obscures more than it illuminates, but it does often appear in a number of contexts. We have seen it used in respect of the laws of China outside China (see the section on Japan and Korea earlier) and it may have proper reference in these instances. However, I leave that to the experts in the field to determine its appropriateness or otherwise. See also the debate in British Burma (mentioned earlier).

For contemporary affairs in relation to diaspora Chinese there are a number of references. An excellent introduction is in Professor Robert Hefner's edited volume, *Market Cultures*,[66] which consists of a number of essays. Of particular importance here is Part 2, especially the essay on business success among Southeast Asian Chinese[67] by Professor Jamie Mackie. He devotes some time to "Confucian values" as a purported explanation of Chinese business success, but he concludes that the phrase is "questionable", "confusing" and "best avoided". As an explanation for commercial practice, he is absolutely right.

There is strong support for this in Daniel Fitzpatrick's chapter in this volume where he discusses "Confucian Corporatism" in the light of evidence drawn from Chinese family firms in contemporary Indonesia. His question is whether "Confucian" can be said to be a cultural class, whether it has an identifiable reference, and whether it can, on its own, provide an explanation for the success of Chinese family firms. Fitzpatrick canvasses the options and finds that the Confucian cultural argument is not, on its own, a sufficient explanation. The so-called "Confucian" elements — paternalism, networking, mediation, family management — are outweighed by (or equally weighed against) the demands of modern corporate organization. The so-called "Confucian" elements are not a philosophy of management but are instead an easy rationalization of successful firms at a certain stage of *development* in certain *developing* countries.

The key word is *development*. For the Southeast Asian states in which 80 per cent of the Chinese outside China live, post-colonial economics has been a great success. This success has also transformed the "ten cent provision shop" into a limited liability company. The very large conglomerates were, of course, incorporated in the 1920s but *development* has also meant political linkage. None of this has much to do with "Confucian" which does not lend itself to any explanation of the institutional changes which have taken place.

"Confucian" cannot explain the transfer of shares, the grant of a licence or credit, or the nature of a contract, whether enforceable or not. The apparent "Confucian corporatism" is really a shorthand term for a complex of institutional practices engaged in by Chinese or Indonesian-Chinese concerned solely with economic practicalities. The fact that these are done (largely) by Chinese has nothing to do with "Confucianism". The same practices occur among Indonesian businessmen as well, but the focus is always on the Chinese as a race, and this is because the Chinese control large sections of the internal economics of Southeast Asia and the reputation they have for being "good with money". The parallels often drawn with the Jews of Europe are probably meaningless. The commercial practices are no more "Confucian" than they are "Halachic"! The point is that institutional factors determine the commercial practice.

However, commerce is not the whole experience of the Chinese diaspora. The "Confucian" reference has other aspects too although this is often forgotten in the rush to study/describe/look at economics and economic rationalism.

Esta Ungar's chapter in this volume is a good example. She deals with gender and how an ideology, such as Confucianism, can determine the definition of women in society. By "definition" I mean status and function. There is no doubt that Confucianism did do this from the fifteenth century until the recent past, if not to the present. The historical circumstances are explained by Professors Ta Van Tai and Nguyen Ngoc Huy[68] in their examinations of the Lê (fifteenth century) and Gia-Long (1812) Codes of Annam. This is an identifiable legal definition of "Confucian".

A third and final example is my description of Chinese Confucianism and Buddhism in British Burma.[69]

CONCLUDING REMARKS

These comments and the chapters which follow demonstrate a somewhat unsatisfactory state of affairs in Chinese diaspora law studies. There are no data for Burma and little for Thailand. Even in the Philippines, the subject appears not to have engaged recent attention by legal scholars.

The twentieth century has been a turbulent one for the diaspora Chinese and for the laws applicable to them. In China itself, the revolution of 1911, the Japanese war, and the advent of the PRC in 1949 have all contributed to immense legal change. The classical Qing was replaced by the KMT civil and criminal codes, themselves replaced by Socialist laws, and these in turn are now undergoing transformation in accordance with the dictates of a market economy.

For the Overseas Chinese, the relative stability of law provided by the colonial powers came to an end with World War II. Nationality and citizenship are now the dominant themes of discourse and, in the face of this, the former legal pluralism within which Chinese custom found a place is gradually losing ground. The "new" subjects are now in human rights (including race), the diaspora Chinese in Southeast Asian and international commerce, and the maritime regimes in the South China Sea.

Notes

[1] The conference was jointly sponsored by the Faculty of Law, Australian National University, the Asian Law Centre, University of Melbourne, the Centre for Southeast Asian Law, Northern Territory University, and the National Taiwan University. We acknowledge with gratitude the generous financial support of the Chiang Ching Kuo Foundation of Taiwan.

[2] For the full range of papers, see the conference programme.

[3] The main references include the *Annual Bibliography of the Journal of Asian Studies* but this is somewhat out of date and law is only a sub-entry under "Politics and Government". The Chinese outside China are not given a class. See also Victor Purcell, *The Chinese in Southeast Asia* (London: Oxford University Press, 1965). Although now more than thirty years old, this book is still the initial text for studying the Chinese in Southeast Asia. It has eight chapters with an extensive bibliography arranged by country. It is strong on history, politics, and economics. As far as law is concerned, it is weak on the purely technical side, but there are useful references to regulations and statutes where these directly concern control over the Chinese. Other references are:

Naosaku Uchida. *The Overseas Chinese: A Bibliographical Essay*, Series No 7 (Hoover Institute of War, Revolution and Peace, 1959); J-J Nevadomsky and Alice Li, *The Chinese in Southeast Asia: A Selected and Annotated Bibliography of Publications in Western Languages*, University of California Occasional papers (Berkeley, California: Center for South and Southeast Asian Studies, 1970); Leo Suryadinata, *Southeast Asian Chinese: The Sociological Dimension* (Singapore: Times Academic Press, 1995); Leo Suryadinata, ed., *Political Thinking of the Indonesian Chinese* (Singapore: Singapore University Press, 1997); Leo Suryadinata, ed., *The Ethnic Chinese in the ASEAN States: Bibliographical Essays* (Singapore: Institute of Southeast Asian Studies, 1989); Leo, Suryadinata, ed., *Pribumi Indonesians: The Chinese Minority and China*, 3rd ed. (Singapore: Heinmann Asia, 1992); Leo Suryadinata, ed., *Ethnic Chinese as Southeast Asians* (Singapore: Institute of Southeast Asian Studies, 1997); Jennifer Cushman, and Wang Guangwu, eds., *Changing Identities of Southeast Asian Chinese Since World War II* (Hong Kong: Hong Kong University Press, 1988); Robert W. Hefner, ed., *Market Cultures* (Sydney: Allen and Unwin, 1998) (Subtitled "Society and Morality in the New Asian Capitalisms", this book is an exemplar of rational scholarship and practical comment.); and J. A. C. Mackie, "Business Success among Southeast Asian Chinese", in Hefner, op. cit., pp. 129–46.

[4] Victor Purcell's work (see note 3) is particularly important in this regard.

[5] O. W. Wolters. *History, Culture and Region in Southeast Asian Perspectives* (Singapore: Institute of Southeast Asian Studies, 1982), p. 52. See also M. B. Hooker, ed., *The Laws of Southeast Asia*, Vol. 1 (Singapore: Butterworths, 1986), p. 17:

> The legal material seems to provide a particularly striking example of this process, whether one calls it "localization", "hybridization" or "re-definition". The emphasis in each case is on (i) an internal Southeast Asian intellectualism and (ii) process as opposed to something static. This last is particularly important because I believe the process is still going on, though now with reference to European laws in Southeast Asia. My own preferred term is "re-definition" because it emphasizes the element of originality which the Southeast Asian text writers and patrons brought to their formulations of law.

[6] The basic references are:

For Southeast Asia: M. B. Hooker, ed., *The Laws of Southeast Asia*, Vol. 2, (Singapore: Butterworths, 1988), pp. 22ff on new sovereignty, bureaucratization of law, and re-definition of law.

For Japan: D. J. Lu, *Sources of Japanese History* (New York: McGraw Hill, 1974); Annette Marfording, "Relocating Asian Legal Systems", in *Asian Laws through Australian Eyes*, edited by Veronica Taylor, at pp. 65–89, especially pp. 68–70. In her essay, Marfording demonstrates that the reception of European law in Japan (1868 – c.1926) does not mean that there is a "functional equivalence interpretation and application of laws". This is absolutely true but often ignored, even today. This essay is an exemplary example of plural law study.

[7] Cf. M. B. Hooker, "The Europeanization of Siam's Laws 1855–1908", in *The Laws of Southeast Asia*, Vol. 2, edited by M. B. Hooker (Singapore: Butterworths, 1988), pp. 538ff. This essay has references to China and Japan, as well as Siam.

[8] See M. B. Hooker, "Asian Law: The View From Australia", *Australian Journal of Asian Law* (in press) and the references cited there.

[9] The laws of China, as such, are not the subject of this study. However, the basic sources which have relevance are: Lin Fu-Shun, *Chinese Law, Past and Present* (New York: Columbia University, East Asian Institute, 1966); E. Balazs, "China", in *Bibliographical Introductions to Legal History and Ethnology*, (e/14), edited by John Gilissen (Brussels: Universite Libre de Bruxelles, 1972); and Jerome A. Cohen, et al., eds., *Essays on China's Legal Tradition* (Princeton, New Jersey: Princeton University Press, 1980). This collection of ten papers deal, between them, with Chou, Sung, and Ch'ing China as well as nineteenth century Taiwan, Tokugawa Japan, and the Yi dynasty in Korea. The bibliography (pp. 359–94) has works in both Western and East Asian languages. It is an indispensable reference.

For Southeast Asia, we are fortunate in having a number of comprehensive works collected in one place and accurate up to 1988. See M. B. Hooker, ed., *The Laws of Southeast Asia*, 2 vols. (Singapore: Butterworths, 1986–88). Vol. 1 has a comprehensive bibliographical reference (pp. 498–99), which is added to in Vol. 2 (pp. 609–15).

For East Asia (Japan and Korea) and Inner Asia, see M. K. Scheer, *Japanese Law in Western Languages 1974–1989* (Munich: Merkhaus, 1993); C. Steenstrupp, *A History of Law in Japan Until 1868* (Leiden: Brill, 1991); J. H. Wigmore, ed., *Law and Justice in Tokugawa Japan* (Tokyo: University of Tokyo Press, 1967–86); Ishii Ryosuke, "Japan", e/13 in *Bibliographical Introductions*, edited by Gilissen; and Lawrence Krader, "Mongol Law", e/15, in ibid.

10 Wolfgang Franke, "Some Remarks on Chinese Historical Sources ...", in *Sino-Malaysian ... Papers* (Singapore: South Seas Society, 1989 [originally published in 1972 in a *Festschrift in honour of Dr Hsiao Kung-ch'uan*]), pp. 476–88, especially pp. 478ff.

11 The best example is Annam. See Klaus Mading, "Suzerainty Over Annam ..." in *Historical, Archaeological and Linguistic Studies*, edited by F. S. Drake (Hong Kong University Press, 1967), pp. 150–52. This is still a useful short introduction. See also Nguyen Ngoc Nuy and Ta Van Tai, "The Vietnamese Texts", *The Laws of Southeast Asia*, Vol. 1, edited by M. B. Hooker, pp. 435–95 and 452ff. This is the standard work. Under the heading of "public law", which we would call international law/relations, the authors show the varying nature of the suzerainty and its equally variant manifestations over time (from the tenth to the nineteenth centuries). The strength of the relationship fluctuated according to the relative strengths of China and Annam. The title of the ruler of Annam varied in the same way, and ranged from "Governor" to "Prince" and "King". The use of these titles was, however, restricted to relations with China. Inside Annam and in relations with other Southeast Asian polities, the Vietnamese used the title "Emperor". For an example of the latter, see Nguyen Van Khuong-Hoai, "Assimilating the Distant Lands ..." (M.A. dissertation, University of Kent at Canterbury, UK, 1975). See also A. B. Woodside, *Vietnam and the Chinese Model* (Cambridge, Mass: Harvard University Press, 1971). We have a further example, this time involving the Melaka Sultanate as it appears in Ming dynasty texts. See Geoff Wade, "Melaka in Ming Dynasty Texts", *Journal of the Royal Asiatic Society Malaysian Branch* 70, no. 1 (1997): 31–70. This lengthy paper outlines textual evidence from the early fifteenth century, with a précis of references to Malacca in the Ming Shi-Lu, and an extensive glossary. On China-Malacca relations as seen from the Chinese suzerainty point of view, see especially p. 41ff. To this work should be added Liang Liji, *Lembaran Sejarah Gamilang* (Bangi, Selangor: Penerbitan UKM, 1996). Another example involving the Malayan peninsula is the Siam-Kedah/Trengganu relationship. Siam claimed suzerainty and this was expressed by the arrival of Malay embassies in Bangkok each third year bearing a small tree made of gold and silver (the *bunga [e]mas*). The significance of this was and remains a matter of dispute between Malay and Thai historians. There is also evidence of Chinese attempts to exercise some suzerainty over Burma between the late thirteenth and the

mid-fourteenth centuries. Tribute, where it was paid, was irregular and Chinese attempts to enforce it militarily usually failed and ceased altogether after the overthrow of the Ming dynasty in the seventeenth century. See Purcell, op. cit., p. 50, for references, including Henry Yule and Edouard Huber, *Bulletin Ecole Française d'Extreme Orient* (BEFEO) (1904): 142. For Burma, there is no evidence of a Chinese cultural and legal/philosophical legacy as in Annam. Indeed, Burma's inheritance is Indian. See E. H. Parker, *Burma with Special Reference to Her Relations with China* (Rangoon, 1893).

12 See J. Greenfield, *China's Practice in the Law of the Sea* (Oxford: Clarendon Press, 1992). This is a useful text because it demonstrates that the context of law and the nature of international law are not necessarily the same for China as they are for "the West". This is not an orientalist position but a statement of fact. If this book does not demonstrate suzerainty in the same way as the earlier examples, it does show disjunction, overt and covert, between Chinese and Western views of international law. The disjunction is in both theory and practice.

13 For references and analyses, see William Shaw, "Traditional Korean Law and Its Relation to China", *Essays on China's Legal Tradition,* edited by J. A. Cohen et al. (Princeton, NJ: Princeton University Press, 1980), pp. 302–26; and Hahm Pyong-Choon, *The Korean Political Tradition and Law,* RAS Korea Branch, Monograph No. 1 (Seoul: Hollym Corp, 1967). This is a somewhat eccentric overview of Korean law. The Chinese/Confucian issue is discussed in Chapter 1 and is well worth reading as a contemporary educated Korean view. See also Mark A. Peterson, *Korean Adoption and Inheritance* (Ithaca NY: East Asia Programme, Cornell University, 1996). The subject is inheritance and the rights of adopted children. These topics go to the heart of private law in fifteenth to nineteenth century Korea and define and re-define "Confucian" in Korea.

14 William Shaw, *Legal Norms in a Confucian State,* Korean Research Monograph No. 5 (Berkeley, California: Institute of East Asian Studies, University of California, 1981). This is the authoritative legal historical text and the Ming and Qing Codes are examined in detail. Chapter II on the Korean adaptation of Ming and Qing legal forms is especially important, as is Chapter V on Korean legal reasoning.

15 See note 5 above.

16 See William Shaw, "The Neo-Confucian Revolution of Values in Early Yi Korea", in *Law and the State in Traditional East Asia,* edited by B. E. McKnight (Hawaii: University of Hawaii Press, 1987), pp. 149–72.

17 Carl Steenstrup, "The Legal System of Japan at the End of the Kamakura Period ...", in McKnight, *Law and the State in Traditional East Asia,* pp. 73–110 (see especially the notes on pp. 99ff for sources).

18 See, generally, the essays in ibid.

19 Osamu Oba, "Edo Period Studies on T'ang, Ming and Ch'ing Law", in ibid., pp. 132–48. The material used here dates from 1603 to 1868 and is essentially a bibliographical survey. There is a valuable bibliography of Japanese sources, with

particular attention paid to the fluctuating access Japanese scholars had to Chinese materials in the century and a half under review.

[20] Dan Fenno Henderson, "Chinese Influences on Eighteenth Century Tokugawa Codes", in *Essays on China's Legal Tradition*, edited by J. A. Cohen et al. (1980), pp. 270–301.

[21] See notes 35–37 below for references.

[22] In these two cases, a high degree of originality in law texts is demonstrated. See M. B. Hooker, ed., *Laws of Southeast Asia*, Vol. 1 (Singapore: Butterworth, 1989).

[23] The standard accounts are in Nguyen Ngoc Huy and Ta Van Tai, "The Vietnamese Texts", in *Laws of Southeast Asia*, Vol. 1, edited by Hooker, pp. 435–96. This, together with *The Lê Code*, is now the standard study. For our purpose, the important part of this long paper is on pp. 449ff, where the authors discuss the "Vietnamese legislation [which] bore the marks of both legalist and Confucianist schools". As to the former, the authors find an excessive emphasis on punishment with a concomitant explosion of penal sanctions in a vast array of bureaucratic regulations. The standard formula was "... whoever does x shall receive the following punishment ...". The authors also demonstrate a Confucian element (on pp. 451ff). They also point to the late Gia-Long Code (1813) which is an almost exact copy of the late eighteenth century Qing law. See also Nguyen Ngoc Huy and Ta Van Tai, *The Lê Code: Law in Traditional Vietnam*, 3 Vols. (Athens, Ohio: Ohio University Press, 1987). This is the standard work on the subject and it is specifically written as a "Sino-Vietnamese legal study". Vol. I gives a brief legal history of Vietnam, outlines the special features of the *Lê Code* and gives a translation of the Penal Code. Vols. II and III then proceed with the rest of the *Lê* text, and each chapter is accompanied by detailed comparative references to Chinese codes, from which the extent of adoption may be gauged.

[24] See Suryadinata references in note 3.

[25] See M. B. Hooker, *Legal Pluralism* (Oxford: Clarendon Press, 1975).

[26] M. B. Hooker, ed., & comp., *A Source Book of Adat, Chinese Law ...*, Malaya Law Review Monograph No. 1. Part III (1967). "Chinese law" has over four hundred entries consisting of: A. Chinese law in Singapore and Malaysia; B. government regulation of Chinese affairs; and C. annotated judicial decisions up to 1967. There is no single source for later materials. However, the most important source for judicial decisions is *The Malayan Law Journal.* See also M. B. Hooker, *The Personal Laws of Malaysia* (Kuala Lumpur: Oxford University Press, 1976), pp. 124–46. This is a general survey incorporating material published earlier and all the judicial decisions up to 1974. There are a number of earlier studies referred to, of which the most important are by the late Professor Maurice Freedman. These are extremely valuable still, but it must be remembered that they were written in the late colonial period and for the purposes of colonial administration of the Chinese.

[27] See chapter 4 by M. B. Hooker in this volume.

[28] For British Borneo, see H. H. Lee, *Cases on Native Law in Sabah and Sarawak*, 2 vols. (Kuching: Government Printer, 1980).

[29] See M. B. Hooker, "The Chinese 'Confucian' and the Chinese 'Buddhists' in British Burma", *Journal of Southeast Asian Studies* 21, no. 2 (1990): 384–401.

[30] E. S. Haydon, "The Choice of Chinese Customary Law in Hong Kong", *International and Comparative Law Quarterly* 11 (1962): 231–50 This is an extremely good paper, though much of it is now out of date. The main issue dealt with is the reception of Chinese law and the choice of law rules. See also Leonard Pegg, *Family Law in Hong Kong*, 2nd ed. (Singapore: Butterworths, 1986). This book takes the reader through the reforms of Chinese family law in Hong Kong. Subjects include concubinage, the status of marriage under Chinese law, and matrimonial causes in the 1971 reforms. Adoption, including adoption under Chinese custom, is also dealt with.

[31] M. B. Hooker, *Legal Pluralism* (Oxford: Clarendon Press, 1975), Chapter VII on "Dutch Colonial Law".

[32] Peter Fromberg, *Verspriedle Geschriften.* This is a collection of Fromberg's vastly extensive writings on the Indonesian Chinese up to 1926. The main topic with which he was concerned was the status of ethnic Chinese in the NEI colonial state. From the work, it is apparent that the main concern of the Chinese was to achieve a footing of equality with the Dutch which the Japanese had achieved. By 1924–25 this had largely been achieved, though not fully in criminal matters.

[33] See *Nieuwe Regeling van den Privaatrechtlijken Toestand der Chineezen* (Batavia: Lardsdrukkerij, 1897). This is the last complete collection for the nineteenth century. It is concerned primarily with family law. Since the collection of the legislation in one place is quite rare, I give the Australian National University library catalogue number: (Menzies) JQ770.A3.N4. See also M. H. van der Valk, "De Rechtspositie der Chineezen in Nederlandsche-Indië", *Kolonial Studien* 5 & 6, "Foreign Orientals" (1936). Chinese who were not Netherlands subjects were governed by the law of their nationality, which means, after 1931, the Civil Codes of Republican China. How this worked in practice (if at all) has yet to be described.

[34] See M. B. Hooker, *A Concise Legal History of Southeast Asia* (Oxford: The Clarendon Press, 1978).

[35] See F. Lassere, *Cochin Francaise … Jurisprudence* (Saigon: Imp. Nationale, 1884); and E. A. F. Garrigues, *Rapport sur le fonctionnement de la justicie en Cochine* (Saigon: Imp. Moderne, J. Testelin, 1930).

[36] The best source is in the very valuable journal *La Revue Indochinoise: Juridique et Economique* (1928–1942).

[37] See G. Levasseur, "Les Repercussions…", *La Revue Indochinoise — Juridique et Economique* 1 (1937): 57–99; 2 (1937): 83–118. These two long papers are concerned with the repercussions of this Treaty.

[38] See G. Levasseur, "Les Conflits … les Chinese en Indochine", *La Revue Indochinoise — Juridique et Economique* 4 (1937): 42–134.

[39] See note 3 above.

[40] See Mary Somers Heidheus, *Southeast Asia's Chinese Minorities* (London: Longman, 1974); and Frank Golay, et al., *Underdevelopment and Economic Nationalism in Southeast Asia* (Ithaca: Cornell University Press, 1969).

[41] M. B. Hooker and John Villiers, "The Laws of Portugal and Spain", in *Laws of Southeast Asia*, Vol. II, pp. 27–147, especially pp. 86–88, and 107–8.

[42] See note 41.

[43] See generally E. E. Steiner, "Judicial Reinforcement of Empire: Philippine Law in the American Period", in *Laws of Southeast Asia*, Vol. II, pp. 447–529.

[44] See Antonio S. Tan, "The Philippine Chinese", in *Changing Identities of the Southeast Asian Chinese Since World War II*, pp. 177–203.

[45] John Ball, *Indonesian Law: Commentary and Teaching Materials* (Sydney: Sydney University, Faculty of Law, 1981).

[46] For NEI material, see Peter Burns, "The Netherlands East Indies: Colonial Legal Policy and the Definitions of Law", in *Laws of Southeast Asia*, Vol. II, pp. 147–297, especially pp. 262ff on "persons before the law", discussing the various categories of persons including Chinese.

[47] For references, see Fromberg, op. cit., Purcell, op. cit., and S. Pompe, *Indonesian Law 1949–1988* (Nijhoff, 1994), p. 144, for reference to the Chinese.

[48] D. E. Willmott, *The National Status of the Chinese in Indonesia, 1900–1958* (Ithaca, New York: Cornell University Press, 1961). Pompe, op. cit., pp. 480ff gives an outline of public international law and citizenship for the period 1949–63.

[49] See Suryadinata in note 3.

[50] Presidential Instruction No 14/1967, and Presidential Decision No. 240.

[51] For imperial legal history, see Hugh Jenkins, *British Rule and Jurisdiction Overseas* (Oxford: Clarendon Press, 1902); and Kenneth Roberts-Wray, *Commonwealth and Colonial Law* (London: Stevens and Sons, 1966).

[52] *Report of the Commission on Mui Tsai in Hong Kong and Malaya* (UK Colonial Office, 1936).

[53] V. Purcell, *The Chinese in Modern Malaya*, 2nd edition (Singapore: Oxford University Press, 1960). On the labour question, see W. L. Blythe, "Historical Sketch of Chinese Labour in Malaya", *Journal of the Royal Asiatic Society Malayan Branch* 20, no. 1 (1947): 64–114.

[54] See Purcell, *The Chinese in Southeast Asia.*

[55] Ibid.

[56] M. B. Hooker, *Legal Pluralism*, Ch. IV, p. 197.

[57] For a good short account, see H. Morché, et al., eds., *La Justice en Indochine* (Hanoi: Imp d'Extreme-Orient, 1931).

[58] For the legal significance of this distinction, see M. B. Hooker, *A Concise Legal History of Southeast Asia* (Oxford: Clarendon Press, 1978), Ch 6.

[59] See Nguyen Quoc Dinh, *Les Congrégations Chinoises en Indochine* (Paris: Recueil Sirey, 1941).

[60] See G. Levasseur, "Les Repercussions des Accords de Nanking …", *La Revue Indochinoise-Juridique et Economique* 2 (1937): 83–118; 4 (1937): 42–134.

[61] G. Levasseur, "La Situation des Chinoise en Indochine", in *La Revue Indochinoise-Juridique et Economique* 3 (1937): 96–149. See also Nguyen Huy Chieu, "La Statut des Chinoise en Indochine" (Paris: Faculte de Droit, 1939); and Alain Marsot, *The Chinese Community in Vietnam Under the French* (New York: Edwin Mellen Press, 1993).

[62] For general accounts, see Kenneth P. Landon, *The Chinese in Thailand* (New York: Institute of Pacific Relations, 1941), especially Chps II, VI, VII–X. For the position of the Chinese in relation to Courts of Extra-Territoriality up to 1930, see P. W. Thornley, *The History of a Transition* (Bangkok: Siam Observer Press, 1923); and Richard J. Coughlin, *Double Identity: The Chinese in Modern Thailand* (Westport, Conn: Greenwood Press, 1952). This book is now somewhat out of date as it was based on fieldwork conducted in the 1950s. However, in terms of its data, structure and organization, it is an exemplar for the subject. Unlike most social science monographs, it is both strong and accurate on the law.

[63] Fromberg, op. cit.

[64] See note 62.

[65] Standard accounts are in R. J. Coughlin, "Status of the Chinese Minority in Thailand", *Pacific Affairs* 25 (1952): 378–89; and G. William Skinner, *Chinese Society in Thailand* (Ithaca, New York: Cornell University Press, 1957).

[66] Robert Hefner, ed., *Market Cultures* (Sydney: Allen and Unwin, 1998).

[67] Ibid., pp. 129–46.

[68] Nguyen Ngoc Nuy and Ta Van Tai, "The Vietnamese Texts", in *The Laws of Southeast Asia*, Vol. 1, pp. 439–95.

[69] M.B. Hooker, "The Chinese 'Confucian' and the Chinese 'Buddhist' in British Burma", *Journal of Southeast Asian Studies* 21, no. 2 (1990).

2

THE LEGAL POSITION OF ETHNIC CHINESE IN INDOCHINA UNDER FRENCH RULE

Melissa Cheung

As in many parts of Southeast Asia, the Chinese community long played a prominent role in Indochinese society. Much has been written about the interaction between the Chinese and the local populace, their institutions and their culture,[1] and the influence of Chinese culture on the development of Indochina has been well noted.[2] However, how did they fare at the hands of the law during the colonial period? The changing attitudes of the French towards colonialization provided the framework for how they ruled the various parts of Indochina. Ruling Indochina became a balancing act between the French interest in developing it as a "back door" to China, the economic interests and power of the Chinese community, and the latent resentment of the local population towards the Chinese stranglehold over the economy.

The threshold question in examining how the ethnic Chinese population fared under French colonial rule is a question of identity: what was "Chinese" in the eyes of the law? Given the tradition of intermarriage with the local population, it was not always easy to delineate the Chinese as a specific legal subject. From the French point of view, the importance of controlling the Chinese lay mainly in their economic strength. As a consequence, it was largely in the public areas of law that ethnicity-specific regulation aimed at the Chinese was prolific. The French also saw a need for regulating the

Chinese in private law matters, such as property and contract, since these were integral to the economic role that they played.

This chapter gives an overview of the legal régime that governed the ethnic Chinese population in Indochina under French rule: how did the French colonialists use the law to control the Chinese? In what way did the Chinese legal position affect the relations between the Chinese and the local population? Lastly, what was the role of China as the "motherland" to the Chinese community, and how did the relations between France and China affect the Chinese community in Indochina?

THE POSITION OF THE CHINESE BEFORE FRENCH RULE

The relationship between China and what is now known as Vietnam can be described through time as both symbiotic and adversarial: while there was a desire to cultivate a concept of "our kingdom"[3] and numerous revolts against Chinese hegemony, at various stages throughout history, Indochina was also a tributary to China.[4] The development of native institutions drew heavily on Chinese theories of government,[5] as did various aspects of language and culture.[6]

The physical proximity of Indochina to the Chinese empire and the fact that for one thousand years it was under direct Chinese rule meant that it was an ideal destination for waves of Chinese immigrant-refugees, especially in times of dynastic change. While early immigration was mainly the result of political upheaval, the eighteenth century saw the beginning of Chinese immigration that was not explicitly fuelled by political factors.[7] While the majority of the Chinese immigrants settled in Cochinchina,[8] groups of Chinese also settled in Tonkin, Annam, and Cambodia. There were two different régimes to which the Chinese were subject, depending on their geographical location: that of Tonkin, Annam, and Cochinchina, and that of Cambodia.

In Tonkin, Annam, and Cochinchina, the Chinese were able to enter without difficulty and were subject to the laws of the kingdom.[9] While they enjoyed the same property rights as the indigenous population, they were subject to a special administrative régime and the imposition of specific personal taxes.[10]

Around 1787, the Chinese were allowed to form their own *bang* (society).[11] By allowing the Chinese a relative degree of autonomy, the local authorities sought to prevent possible challenges to their power.[12] Generally, a *bang* consisted of all the Chinese who originated from the same province in China. While there were no fixed territorial limits on the jurisdiction of the *bang*, it could encompass an entire province, a *phu* (district) or just a *huyen* (sub-district). The head of the *bang* was nominated by the elders of the group and approved by the *bo-chanh* (provincial head).[13] The head of the *bang* acted as an intermediary between the *bang* members and the local authorities. However, any power that the head of the *bang* may have had was counterbalanced by the allocation of legal responsibility for policing the Chinese to the mayor of the locality.

The head of the *bang* was responsible for the levying of taxes on the *bang* members. Taxes on the Chinese were levied on two different categories: on men with a family, property or an occupation, and on men without a fixed position. For the former, each had to pay 2 taels of silver, while the latter was taxed at a concessionary rate for three years, after which he had to pay the full tax.

The head of the *bang* was also responsible for the mediation of disputes between members of the *bang*. If the dispute was not resolved, the parties could resort to arbitration of the head of the canton, and finally to the tribunals of the *phus* and the *huyen*. Special punishments applied to the Chinese, including condemnation to military service and repatriation to China.[14] Generally, the Chinese were exempt from military service and corvée labour requirements, but were also barred from holding positions in the public service.[15]

The Chinese who lived in Cambodia prior to the creation of the French protectorate were subject to local laws and were not subject to any special legal régime.[16] In constrast, by the beginning of the nineteenth century, special rules were promulgated by the Emperor Gia-long to apply to all Chinese living in Cochinchina, Annam, and Tonkin.[17]

However, even if it was recognized that Indochinese culture was significantly influenced by Chinese culture,[18] this did not mean that the Chinese voluntarily assimilated into the local populations. While the Chinese were admired for their commercial acumen, their relationship with the local population was often antagonistic, and tinged with mutual fear and suspicion.[19]

THE CHINESE UNDER FRENCH RULE BEFORE THE CONVENTIONS OF NANKING

How the Chinese fared under French rule in Indochina was related to the French approach to colonialism generally and the pre-existing position of the Chinese in Indochinese society. Despite humanitarian ideals and initial disillusionment with acquiring overseas possessions, by the end of the nineteenth century, France joined the European race for colonies.[20] However, this did not necessarily mean that France implemented coherent policies in the regions that it acquired. Although policies tended towards assimilationist rather than associationist assumptions, in reality, French colonial officials were authoritarian and their policies highly variable and unsystematic,[21] often depending on the inclination of the individuals in charge. The inconsistent nature of French control was reflected in its attempt to control the Chinese population. Since much of the justification for the colonization of Indochina was economic in nature, it was important to deal with the economic power of the Chinese in Indochina.[22] While the French purported to promote assimilation of the Chinese into the local population, they found it impossible to treat the Chinese in the same manner as the indigenous population, as the special régimes which applied to the Chinese and the continued utilization of the *bang* system showed.[23]

Unlike the British, the French came late to colonization in Asia. This was a result of, among other things, the strong anti-colonization sentiment in France, which prevailed until approximately 1890.[24] Supported by philosophy,[25] economic beliefs,[26] and the political psychology of the times, to advocate colonization was tantamount to political suicide, as in the case of Jules Ferry, a strong proponent of colonial expansion.[27] However, the late nineteenth century quest for colonies among the other European powers and the increasing acceptance of the idea that colonial development was profitable[28] began a new phase of French colonial expansion. This new movement was primarily guided by the idea that colonies were to be acquired to strengthen France and serve its needs.[29] Consequently, in theory, the French adopted an assimilatory approach to colonization.[30] Assimilation meant that, not only was colonial economic organization assimilated to a form similar to a French *département*, but that the colony was seen as an extension of France itself rather than as a separate entity.[31] However, by the late 1890s, it was becoming apparent that assimilation was inadequate in the light of the increasing financial independence and economic desires of the colonies, which at times even conflicted with those of France.[32] As a result of these movements in French colonial policy, the early French acquisitions in Indochina, such as Cochinchina, were marked by colonial organization that involved the destruction of the native culture,[33] while later acquisitions such as Tonkin allowed a greater degree of native participation in matters of governance, at least in the early years.

The strongest and most coherent argument for the colonization of Indochina was the hope of opening the Southern Chinese market via a back door.[34] Even when trade with Southern China failed to eventuate in any significant volume, the belief that the Indochinese Federation as well as other French possessions should be economically beneficial to France still remained. In such a light, the French administrators had to come to terms with the Chinese residing in Indochina, as they played an important role on its economy.

In principal, foreigners resident in Indochina were divided into two juridical classes: Europeans/*assimilés* to whom French law applied, and Asian foreigners, who were subject to local law. The Chinese and the *métis*[35] were considered to be part of the latter class,[36] in contrast to the Japanese, who were treated on an equal footing to the Europeans.[37] However, there were specific regulations pertaining to the Chinese, which meant that the question of identifying the Chinese as legal subjects had to be broached.

Immigration: Laws Governing the Entry and Exit of Chinese in Indochina[38]

Of the special legal régimes promulgated to apply to the Chinese, the most direct in application were the immigration regulations. The French administration wanted to attract Chinese immigrants, but at the same time, wished to retain control over the process. Unlike Chinese immigration to other countries, their influx into Indochina was never arbitrary, as they were only allowed in as need or resources dictated.[39] To this end, each of the regions under French rule had a system of immigration checks that applied particularly to immigrants from China.

Tonkin

The Chinese coming overland to Tonkin were required to hold a passport in a diplomatic form agreed upon between France and China.[40] There were twenty-five restricted overland entry points into Tonkin. The French authorities issued these passports upon demand by the Chinese imperial authorities.[41] The superintendent of police who delivered the passport to its addressee was obliged to advise the authorities of the applicant's destination province.[42] The passport gave the holder the right to stay for two months in Annam and Tonkin,[43] and had to be stamped by the administrative authority of the holder's destination in Indochina.[44]

The Chinese entering Tonkin from the sea, in contrast, did not need a passport. Instead, upon arrival, they had to present themselves to a representative of the Protectorate's Administration and declare their occupations. The authorities would then issue the immigrants with an acknowledgement of their declarations.[45] The person responsible for the expedition also had to present the Chinese crew members to the same authorities who would issue them a special entry permit that lasted no longer than two months, and had to be surrendered upon departure.

Special passports were given to Chinese traders by the French authorities at five points of entry with the aim of improving commercial relations between France and China.[46] Holders of such passports were allowed liberty of movement within the French protectorate of Tonkin for two months from the date of entry, and were exempt from entry tax.[47] However, if the holder wished to stay beyond two months, he/she would have to go through permanent immigration procedures.

Just as entry was restricted, so was movement within the territory. The Chinese who registered in Tonkin and wished to change their residence or temporarily depart from Tonkin were required to obtain a pass for the price of one piastre.[48]

Contravention of the immigration regulations resulted in a fine of between one and fifteen francs, or one to five days imprisonment, or both of these punishments.[49]

Annam

The regulations governing the entry of Chinese immigrants into Annam were the same as those for Tonkin with respect to the need for passports for those coming overland, and the issuance of special passports to traders. However, all Asian foreigners in Annam were issued with a pass for a fixed registration price of one piastre. This pass enabled the holder to obtain a permit in a province other than that which effected his/her original entry. In Annam, departing Asian foreigners were entitled to a passport from the Resident Administrator upon payment of six piastres.[50]

Cochinchina

Chinese immigrants who arrived in Cochinchina through Saigon were subjected to a medical examination. Those who were guaranteed by the head of a *congrégation* (a *bang*)[51] were immediately given a pass that was valid for thirty days. The immigrant could then exchange this pass for a one-year permit. Those who were not guaranteed by a *congrégation* were asked to apply for acceptance into a *congrégation*, and given a pass. Persons not accepted by a *congrégation* were immediately repatriated.[52]

Chinese immigrants arriving in Cochinchina at points other than Saigon were required to be accompanied by the head of a *congrégation* to present themselves to the Administrator. Upon payment of the requisite taxes,[53] the Administrator would issue a permit if the immigrant wished to be resident in the province, or a pass valid for thirty days if s/he wished to reside in another part of French Indochina.

The Chinese who only wished to pay a brief visit were issued with a three-month, non-renewable permit upon payment of fifty piastres. This permit allowed the holder to travel freely throughout French Indochina.[54] Chinese holders of passports issued by French overseas authorities were also liable for a fifty-piastre tax if they declared that they did not intend to stay for more than six months.[55]

Cambodia

The central offices of immigration at Phnom Penh, the Residents and delegates concurrently with the governors of Cambodia in the interior of Cambodia, were in charge of immigration affairs in Cambodia.[56] Chinese immigrants were required to be part of an established *congrégation.*[57] An annual fee was payable by the members to the head of the *congrégation* for services rendered. Chinese residents of Cambodia who wished to temporarily leave the province were issued with a pass by the head of the district at no charge.

Chinese residents of Cambodia who wished to go to Cochinchina were required to obtain a three-month pass, which could be renewed for another three months. Those with more permanent interests in Cochinchina could obtain one-year passes. These passes were issued free of charge.[58]

Registered Chinese residents of Cambodia could not leave the territory without having paid the year's duties[59] and obtaining a one-year passport, the price of which was fixed at four piastres.[60]

LEGAL POSITION DURING RESIDENCE IN INDOCHINA

Systems of Collective Responsibility and Control: The *Congrégations* and the Sponsorship Requirement

The pre-existing formation of the Chinese communities into *bangs* was conveniently adopted by the French, who renamed them "*congrégations*". The *congrégation* had more than an administrative function; it was a socio-economic unit. As in a number of provinces, acceptance into a *congrégation* was a prerequisite to immigration into Indochina;[61] it was an effective way of controlling immigration. The *congrégation* was like a state within a state,[62] which although administratively convenient, was always an uncomfortable political force for the French.[63] However, the Administration derived some comfort from the mutual antagonism between the Chinese and the local population, which in effect prevented either group from becoming a real political threat.[64] The regulation of the *congrégation* varied from province to province, depending on local conditions as well as the status of the territory as a protectorate (*pays de protectorat*), where French control was indirect, or colony (*pays de souveraineté française*), where control was exercised directly.[65] In some cases, French control was such that it significantly altered the structure of the existing *bangs*.

Tonkin

Although designated as a protectorate,[66] the French in Tonkin exercised more direct control over it than its other protectorates, and aimed to reform the existing laws.[67] Legislative and administrative power was distributed between French delegates and local ministers, with overall control resting in the hands of the *Résident général*.[68]

In Tonkin, all Asian foreigners in a province were to form one *congrégation*.[69] The chief and sub-chief of the *congrégation* were elected by the *congrégation* every two years,[70] and acted as intermediaries between the French administration and the Chinese community.[71] For performing such a service, they were exempt from personal taxes.[72] However, their responsibilities were great, and punishable if not performed.[73] The chief and sub-chief were directly responsible for public order within the *congrégation*, and were obliged to make monthly reports on the movements of their members and the number of members.[74] The chief of the *congrégation* also carried the responsibility for the total sum of duties payable by its members. As an intermediary, the chief received all communications from *congrégation* members which were addressed to the administration.[75]

Despite the original idea of having one *congrégation* of Asian foreigners for each province, the administration later allowed a separate *congrégation* to be formed by Fujianese speakers,[76] and specifically mandated Chinese *congrégations* in all mining areas, to which all workers or coolies had to belong.[77] In fact, in relatively influential provinces, a number of *congrégations* were allowed to co-exist in the same manner as they did before the French conquest.[78]

In Tonkin, it was held that the *congrégation* was not a moral person (*personne morale*) but a simple association that existed and functioned by the force of custom and according to tradition. The *congrégation's* civil actions were carried out by the chief, or by persons designated by mandate. Consequently, in carrying out actions on behalf of the *congrégation*, such representatives had standing to claim redress for damage done to their prestige and authority, which derived from the *congrégation*.[79]

Annam

Of all the French-occupied territories, Annam was unique in the virtual lack of French intervention in the existing legal and administrative structure up to 1930.[80] However, French awareness of the strength of the Chinese communities led them to regulate the *congrégations* closely, although the Chinese population was relatively small.[81] The *congrégations* in Annam were established according to the place of origin[82] and, as in the other French territories, headed by a chief and sub-chief who were primarily responsible for the collection of taxes. Negligence on the part of the chief or sub-chief was punishable by a fine of two to twenty piastres, and fifteen days' imprisonment for repeat offenders. Members of *congrégations* in Annam were required to carry identification cards, and those who carried cards that did not belong to them were liable for a fine of ten piastres. As in Tonkin, in 1895, *congrégations* of workers or coolies were formed in mining areas.[83]

Cochinchina

As a colony,[84] Cochinchina was made subject to French law,[85] which was later modified by laws and decrees promulgated in and for the colony. While its inhabitants were all subject to French tribunals, the Chinese were, unlike French citizens, Europeans and later, the Japanese, subject to local law (*statut annamite*).[86]

The Chinese in Cochinchina were grouped into five *congrégations* according to their place of origin, or their spoken dialect.[87] These *congrégations* were presided over by a chief and sub-chief who were nominated by the Lieutenant-Governor, and elected for a term of two years. As in Tonkin, they were responsible for the taxes payable by their constituents. To cover general expenses, the chief of the *congrégation* was allowed to exact taxes[88] and also received 12 per cent of the personal taxes collected from the members of the *congrégations* on behalf of the administration. The *congrégations* in Cochinchina could admit or expel members at will, and the Chinese who were expelled from a *congrégation* were not allowed to stay in the colony.

In Cochinchina, unlike in Tonkin,[89] it was held that *congrégations* were moral persons (*personnes morales de droit public colonial*) rather than associations voluntarily formed by its constituent members. As a consequence, in carrying out actions as an entity they were afforded administrative protection, although they were still required to obtain the requisite authorization (either express or implied) to carry out such actions.[90]

Cambodia

Unlike the other French possessions, Cambodia did not have a pre-existing special régime for governing the Chinese. Upon becoming a French protectorate, *congrégations* in Cambodia were established according to the number of Chinese in the district, categorized according to their place of origin.[91] While they generally centred around the county towns, this was dependent on the number of Chinese in the district: when there was a large number of Chinese in the district, they formed a number of *congrégations*, while districts with few Chinese would join other districts to make up a *congrégation*.[92] Like the other French possessions, the *congrégations* elected a chief and sub-chief, but since Cambodia was a French protectorate rather than a colony, these elections were subject to approval from the *Résident supérieur*. The chief and the sub-chief were able to delegate their functions to delegatees approved by the administration, but retained ultimate responsibility for the collection of taxes. Chiefs who failed to perform their obligations were subject to penalties of between two and twenty piastres and up to fifteen days' imprisonment for repeat offenders. Chiefs in Cambodia who accepted into their *congrégation* an Asian foreigner who had been expelled from the Kingdom were liable for a fine of fifty to two hundred piastres.

Employment

Although the French were often wary of the Chinese community, they saw that it was to their benefit to create favourable working conditions for the Chinese, who were renowned for their commercial expertise. The Chinese were more knowledgeable about local conditions than the Europeans, yet were more sophisticated in commercial matters than the local Indochinese, thus making them indispensable in the commercial development of Indochina. Given that one of the aims of acquiring the Indochinese territories was to provide markets to fuel French industrialization, it was beneficial to France to sign the Franco-Chinese Treaty of Tianjin (1885), granting the right of free entry and of commercial operations in Indochina.

The freedom of the Chinese to carry on commercial operations was implemented generally in the protectorates and colonies with little circumscription. Certain areas of commerce were barred from native Indochinese as well as the Chinese, and these included activities with respect to arms and munitions[94] and, to a lesser extent, the exploitation of forest resources.[95] In contrast, they were allowed to own and operate mines and quarries.[96]

Although most occupations were open to them,[97] the Chinese remained most prominent in the retail trade[98] as well as holding a virtual monopoly over both the wholesale and intermediate trading of rice.[99] Few Chinese were actively involved in agriculture, with the exception of the Kejia people.[100]

Special Taxes

Of all the regulations that the Chinese were subject to, the system of taxes was the most controversial. The incidence of tax varied between the jurisdictions and was levied in addition to various general direct and indirect taxes.[101]

Tonkin

Chinese immigrants to Tonkin had to pay a registration tax every quarter, that is, at the same time as they paid for their residence cards.[102] The registration tax was levied according to five categories,[103] the first category paying the most, while the fifth category paid the least. The first category encompassed those holding first and second-class trade licences and trade licences exempt from duty, as well as landowners paying tax of sixty piastres or more. The second category consisted of those holding third, fourth and fifth-class trade licences and landowners paying tax of between twenty to sixty piastres. The third category included all Chinese not covered by the preceding two categories except those living in nine designated provinces.[104] The Chinese living in these nine provinces were instead subject to registration tax at the fourth and fifth category rates.[105] The fifth category of registration tax applied equally to all Asian foreigners employed by Europeans in agricultural capacities, public works, and mining operations.[106]

The registration tax was only levied on men aged between fifteen and sixty years of age; children, the elderly, women and invalids were exempt from the requirement of holding residence cards and paying registration tax.

Instead, for a nominal sum, they were issued with passes which were renewable annually.

Annam

By virtue of the same *Arrêté* of 1 June 1897 that set up the system of registration tax in Tonkin, the Chinese in Annam were also subject to a registration tax imposed according to same five categories as in Tonkin.[107]

Cochinchina

Chinese residents of Cochinchina between eighteen and sixty years of age were subject to three types of taxes which were additional to the general taxes: (1) a direct personal tax; (2) an indirect tax imposed by the municipality and province; and (3) a direct allowance tax. The personal tax was levied according to five categories, which were proportionate to the amount of licence-holder or landowner tax that the individual paid.[108] Females, the elderly, invalids, *congrégation* chiefs, and certain low-income earners who had been in the colony for fifteen years or more were exempt from paying this personal tax.[109] One per cent of the profits made by the municipality and province was also payable to the government. In addition, the Chinese were subject to an allowance tax by which they had to pay the municipality and province in which they resided the equivalent of five days' allowance. Persons who were fifty-six years and above and persons exempt from personal tax did not have to pay this allowance tax. The task of collecting these taxes fell on the chief of the *congrégation.*

Cambodia

Initially, the Chinese in Cambodia were subject to a regressive head tax of five piastres and fifty cents, payable annually before 31 March.[110] Upon payment, a residence card would be issued. However, this was changed in 1897 to a progressive system of registration tax similar to that in the other French possessions.[111] The tax was levied according to three categories, and was proportionate to the amount of licence-holder tax that the person was subject to. In 1902, the Chinese in Cambodia were also made to pay a levy equivalent to ten days' allowance, with each day being redeemable at the rate of 30 cents per day. For persons of between fifty-one and fifty-nine years of age, the rate was reduced to 10 cents per day. Those exempt from tax were children under fifteen, women, persons over sixty, and disabled persons unable to work.

Representation[112]

It was in the area of political representation that the divergence of French ideals and administrative reality was most prominent. Given the French tradition of democracy (albeit with a limited franchise), it was of ideological importance to set up a system of representation that encompassed the economically important Chinese community. However, the administration was less enthusiastic about the implementation of these ideas. While many of the special regulations applicable to the Chinese also applied to Asian foreigners, in the area of political representation, the Chinese were distinguished from other Asian foreigners, signifying their comparative economic importance.

Tonkin

In Tonkin, the Chinese were meant to be represented at three levels. A commercial convention between China and France[113] envisaged Chinese consuls being installed at Hanoi and Haiphong, among other places. In the municipal council in Hanoi, there was to be one Chinese or Asian foreigner, while in Haiphong, there were to be two. Such councillors were to be elected by Chinese or Asiatic constituents enfranchised by virtue of their age, property holding, or licence fee liability, and domicile.[114] A third tier of representation was the Chamber of Commerce, which was to include one Chinese businessman in each of the Hanoi and Haiphong Chambers.

However, administrative reality differed somewhat from the original plans. The consular posts to be established under the 1886 treaty were not created by the Chinese government.[115] By 1908, the Chinese or Asian seat in the municipal councils had been replaced by indigenous candidates.[116] When the composition of the Chambers of Commerce were fixed, despite the original reference to Chinese members, the statutory provisions relating to non-European members included only indigenous members.[117]

The cautious attitude of the administration towards the potential power of the Chinese as a group can be demonstrated in their regulation of the *Cercles Chinois.* As an association of Chinese persons set up to insulate themselves against the punitive effects of the administration's financial régime, among other things, it would pay a substantial guarantee to the administration for the protection of its members. While such associations were allowed,[118] they were closely monitored. In numbers, they were limited to not less than ten and not more than forty members.[119] In 1890, the head Resident of each province was given the power to provisionally close a *Cercle Chinois* for breach of regulations.[120]

Annam

In Annam, the situation was better than that of Tonkin. The commission of the municipal council of Tourane provided for a delegation from the Chinese *congrégations.*[121] The Chamber of Commerce and Agriculture in Annam had a Chinese member, who was appointed by the Résident Supérieur.[122] However, this member fulfilled only a consultative, rather than a truly representative function.

Cochinchina

Similar to the situation in Tonkin, the Saigon municipal council initially planned to have representation from the Asian sector, but the representative would be appointed by the Lieutenant-Governor after closed-door consultations.[123] The municipal council was to be made up of a mayor, two assistants, and twelve municipal councillors. Of the twelve, there were to be eight French, two indigenous, one non-Asian, and one Asian councillors. However, when the Saigon municipal council was set up in 1881, an indigenous candidate replaced the Asian representative.[124]

In Cholon, the municipal council comprised of a president, three European members, three foreigners, four indigenous representatives, and four Chinese representatives.[125] Three assistants nominated by the Governor (a European, an indigenous person, and a Chinese person) assisted the president. The European and foreign members were appointed by the Lieutenant-Governor, while the indigenous and Chinese members were elected. To be eligible for election, a Chinese person had to be of at least 27 years of age and pay 400 francs or more in direct contributions. Enfranchised Chinese included those of at least twenty-one years of age, were domiciled in Cholon, and paid at least 200 francs in direct contributions.

The Chamber of Commerce in Saigon and the Chamber of Agriculture of Cochinchina did not include Asian representatives among their members, although the contrary had been anticipated.[126]

Cambodia

There was no actual municipal council in Cambodia. Rather, the administration instituted a consultative commission at Phnom Penh. This commission was made up of eight members: five French, one Cambodian, one indigenous and one Chinese. All members were nominated by the Résident Superieur for a term of three years.

The consultative Chamber of Commerce and Agriculture at Phnom Penh consisted of eight French members, two Asian members, and one Cambodian member. The Asian members were elected by Asian and *assimilé* merchants who were twenty-one years of age or more who had been resident in Phnom Penh for two years or more and were liable for payment of a third-class licence fee or above. To be eligible for election, an Asian or *assimilé* person had to be on the Phnom Penh electoral role as being a first or second-class licence holder.[127]

Property

In the protectorates before French occupation, all land belonged to the sovereign. As a consequence, the subjects only had the right of using the land and were not able to acquire the full title to land within the kingdom. This right to use the land was acquired by virtue of nationality, and as such, foreigners could not acquire even this right. Since land ownership was not possible, ownership of real property on the land was also not possible.

However, two modifications to this general rule were made: prior to French occupation, in favour of the Chinese, and after French occupation, in favour of the French and the Spanish. The difference in the real property rights accorded to the Chinese and those that were accorded to the French stemmed from the fact that the rights of the Chinese were rooted in tradition and only formalized by treaty, while those of the French were entirely reliant on legislation.[128] Given that Annam and Tonkin were the most populated of the French possessions and that the legal developments regarding these two protectorates are well documented, the following discussion will focus on these areas.

Prior to the French occupation of Annam, the Chinese and the *métis* (of mixed race) held a traditional exemption from the general prohibition against holding real property rights. This did not change upon French occupation in 1884, but in fact, was formalized in 1886 by the commercial treaty between China and France,[129] Article 4 of which proclaimed that: "the Chinese have the right to possess land, build buildings, set up firms and to have shops in all of Annam".

It would seem that the indigenous laws rather than French law governed such ownership, although the official view seemed to express the contrary.[130] This special right of the Chinese was alluded to in the peace treaty and commercial arrangements entered into by France and China at Tianjin (Tietsin) the year prior to the 1886 commercial treaty,[131] and officially acknowledged by the consultative committee of the legal department of the general government of Indochina, which stated that: "the Chinese in Annam and Tonkin receive privileged treatment and may become real property owners".[132]

The only other foreigners in Annam and Tonkin who were able to own real property were the French and the Spanish. However, when compared with the concessions gained by the Chinese, these rights were limited. For example, initially, the French were allowed to possess (*posséder*) commercial and industrial operations in three designated towns, while French and Spanish[133] missionaries were allowed to purchase and rent land for religious purposes.[134] Such concessions were subject to the indigenous laws. Later, the geographical scope of the property rights conceded to the French and the missionaries was enlarged,[135] and such real property transactions became governed by French law.[136] However, the concessions granted to the French and the Chinese were not transferable to other foreign nationals.[137]

Contract

While generally the Chinese were subject to indigenous law, given their importance in commercial matters, the French saw it fit to subject them to French law in certain circumstances. However, this can be seen as a matter of practicality rather than as a concession, as indigenous law rarely provided for commercial contracts of the size and nature often entered into by the Chinese.

Cochinchina

In contractual matters, the law that was to be applied depended on the nationalities of the contracting parties. When the Chinese entered into civil or commercial relations with indigenous parties, indigenous law would govern the relationship. However, in such situations, the parties could also choose French law to govern the relationship.[138] In contracts between Chinese and Europeans, French law was applicable.[139] In Cochinchina after 1881,[140] French courts had jurisdiction over all matters,[141] whether they were civil, commercial or criminal, and applied either French law or indigenous laws, as the case required. Chinese businessmen who came under the jurisdiction of the French courts had to make a declaration at the local townhall or the inspection office as well as to the clerk of the court before they could start business.[142] If these formalities were not completed, the penalties consisted of imprisonment of up to six months or a fine of between 16 and 1,000 francs.

Cambodia

In Cambodia, all matters to which a Chinese person was a party were governed by the laws of Cochinchina.[143]

Annam and Tonkin

Similar to the situation in Cochinchina, the general rule was that indigenous laws applied to all Chinese in Tonkin.[144] While no such rule was promulgated in Annam, in the early 1900s when the French undertook a general reorganization of the judicial system in Annam and Tonkin, the juridical position of the Chinese was declared to be the same in both places.[145] Indigenous laws governed civil and commercial relationships between the Chinese and indigenous parties, while French law governed those between the Chinese and Europeans. In civil or commercial transactions involving the Chinese and indigenous parties, the parties could agree to be justiciable in French courts rather than the indigenous tribunals. However, in transactions involving Chinese and Europeans, the parties could not elect to be under the jurisdiction of an indigenous tribunal.[146] All actions involving a Chinese person were subject to the jurisdiction of the French tribunals, which would apply indigenous or French laws as appropriate.[147] However, if the dispute was one that involved a Chinese and an indigenous party, the court would follow the procedure used by the Cochinchina tribunals in respect of indigenous persons. In Tonkin, as in Cochinchina, Chinese businessmen were subject to a régime of mandatory declarations under the French Commercial Code.[148] This régime was not imposed in Annam.

THE EFFECT OF THE NANKING CONVENTION OF 1930

In 1925, as a result of its participation in World War I, membership in the League of Nations and its transformation into a republic, China declared a unilateral repudiation of treaties that it considered "unequal".[149] One of these treaties was the commercial treaty of 1886 between France and China, which was soon due to expire. In 1928, France entered into negotiations with the new government of China. The result of these negotiations[150] was the Nanking Convention, a complex document[151] that was not put into effect until 1935[152] because of the reluctance of the French parliament to ratify it.[153]

The benefits of the Nanking Convention were to apply to all Chinese nationals in Indochina. However, since the Convention was entered into by the Nationalist government in Nanking, it could only apply to the residents of those provinces that recognized the Nationalist government's sovereignty.[154] The provisions of the Convention were extended to persons from Guangxi, Xinjiang, Ningxia, and Qinghai where the sovereignty of the Nationalist government was tacitly accepted, but were not applied to the provinces that had formally rejected such authority.[155] As a matter of application, the term "Chinese nationals" was given a broad interpretation.

The Nanking Convention covered a wider range of matters than the preceding 1886 convention, and was intended to regulate the relationship between the two countries in respect of French Indochina and certain Chinese provinces. The key principle that resulted from the Nanking Convention was that the Chinese ceased to be classed as Asian foreigners[156] regulated by the *Arrêté* of 1871,[157] and were to enjoy the same treatment as that accorded to nationals of other countries. However, this does not mean that the Chinese automatically moved to the juridical class of Europeans and *assimilés*; and because the Chinese insisted on retaining their traditional advantages[158] they became the subject of a new category of foreigners[159] who were entitled to a privileged status.

Questions of Nationality: The *Métis* and Mixed Marriages

As a result of the juridical change in status, the Convention had a significant effect on questions of nationality in situations involving the Chinese in Indochina, especially the issues of the nationality of the *métis*, and marriages between Chinese and French citizens, subjects, or *protégés*. By the time of the implementation of the Convention, there were a considerable number of *métis* in Indochina.[160] Since their juridical status was often the cause of considerable confusion among members of the judiciary and the administration, in 1933, it had been declared that all children, legitimately or naturally born in Indochina within the following categories were either French subjects or *protégés* according to their place of birth: (1) children of indigenous parentage; (2) children born of an indigenous (or assimilated) parent and a foreigner; and (3) children born of an Asian foreigner and an indigenous parent.[161] However, the question was whether France could, by such a unilateral decree, determine the status of the *métis* born in the protectorates (as opposed to the colonies, where France's sovereignty and right to determine such matters was clear). It would seem that the 1933 *Décret* could not be applied in the protectorates until it had been legislatively promulgated in such protectorates.[162] To clarify this point, the sovereigns of the protectorates amended their legislation to conform to the provisions of the 1933 *Décret*.[163]

The manner in which the Nanking Convention affected marriages between Chinese and French citizens, subjects or *protégés* depended on the law governing the marriage, the nationality of the parties and, in some cases, the choice of the female party to the marriage. When a French citizen married a Chinese national to whom the Convention applied, a *Décret* dated 4 December 1930 applied.[164] As the 1930 *Décret* was not applicable[165] to indigenous persons and "assimilated foreigners",[166] the Chinese were only subject to the 1930 *Décret* after the Nanking Convention conferred on them the status of foreigners entitled to a privileged status. In the areas where France exercised direct rule, that is, Cochinchina, Hanoi, Haiphong and Tourane, French law[167] dictated that certain provisions of the pre-existing Civil Code continued to apply. In the protectorates (Annam, Tonkin and Cambodia), the Civil Codes of the respective protectorates applied.

When a male French citizen married a Chinese female, the female party kept her nationality. However, the female party could acquire French nationality by express demand and completing the requisite formalities if she so desired.[168] According to the 1930 *Décret*, when a Chinese male married a French female citizen, the female party could lose her citizenship automatically upon marriage if the law of her husband's nationality necessarily required her to acquire her husband's nationality. Chinese law did not require the wife to acquire Chinese nationality, but gave the wife the option of acquiring the same by making a declaration of her intention.[169] Therefore, in marriages between Chinese nationals and French citizens, the wife's volition (subject to the requisite formalities) determined her nationality after marriage.

More common than marriages between French male citizens and Chinese nationals were marriages between Chinese male nationals and French subjects.[170] When a Chinese male married a French subject, the female party automatically lost her French nationality, thus taking on the nationality of the husband.[171] However, upon dissolution of such a marriage, the female party could regain her French nationality if she had been living in Indochina, or had obtained permission to permanently return. If a French subject married a female Chinese national, the female party acquired French nationality upon marriage.[172] However, unlike the situation involving a Chinese male and a female French subject, a Chinese female who had acquired French nationality by her marriage to a French subject kept such nationality upon dissolution of the marriage.

The position in the protectorates was different between Tonkin/Annam and Cambodia. In Tonkin and Annam, if a male Chinese national married a French *protégée*,[173] the nationality of the female party upon marriage was governed by the Civil Codes of Tonkin and Annam.[174] Under these Codes, upon marriage to a foreigner, the *protégée* lost her original nationality (that is, Annamite or Tonkinese, as the case may be), unless the laws of the husband's country did not confer the husband's nationality on her. In such cases, the *protégée* would retain her original nationality. As discussed above, Chinese law did not automatically confer Chinese nationality upon foreigners marrying Chinese nationals, but they were given the choice of acquiring Chinese nationality. For practical purposes, if the wife did not elect to acquire Chinese nationality and if the couple remained in Tonkin or Annam, it would seem more favourable to construe the law so that the wife retained her original nationality. Legally, however, this remained an unclear area of law. Where a female Chinese national married a French *protégé*, the wife retained her Chinese nationality even after marriage.[175]

Marriages between Chinese and Cambodians often took place in Cambodia and were governed by the Cambodia Civil Code.[176] Accordingly, if a Cambodian female married a male Chinese national, she retained her nationality. However, if a Chinese female married a Cambodian male, the wife became a Cambodian national by virtue of marriage.

Immigration and Freedom of Movement

In the light of their various commercial activities, one basic right that was important to the Chinese was the right of movement within Indochina. After the Nanking Convention negotiations, the Chinese became the subject of a special régime regulating their right of movement,[177] which was, in a number of aspects, more favourable than the regular régime applicable to foreigners. The rules governing the entry and exit of Chinese non-immigrants[178] were almost as onerous and complex as before the signing of the Convention. A Chinese person visiting Indochina had to produce a passport that was delivered by the Chinese authorities to a French consulate in China. The local authorities in Indochina would then deliver to the Chinese visitor the necessary papers to allow access to Indochina.[179] However, the new regulations did not displace the existing system of temporary and permanent passes established in favour of residents of the frontier areas[180] or the privileges accorded to the crew and passengers of ships calling into port, and fishermen fishing on the Indochina coasts.[181]

The situation in respect of immigrants improved after the signing of the Convention. The 1935 *Arrêté* made provision for power being delegated to the local heads of administration to dispense with passports for certain immigrants and to determine the categories of immigrants who would benefit.[182] To take this step further, in 1936, the Governor-General of Indochina declared that certain categories[183] of Chinese nationals immigrating to Indochina would not be forced to produce a passport, although they would have to undergo certain formalities to ascertain their destination, identity, health, good conduct, and financial situation.[184] However, in addition to these relaxed conditions, Chinese wishing to travel within Indochina still had to deal with the issue of identity cards.

After the signing of the Convention, not all Chinese were obliged to carry the identity card. Only men between the ages of 18 and 60 had to carry the identity card,[185] which was granted to the Chinese at a lower rate than for other foreigners. All other Chinese only needed to hold a pass (*laissez-passer*) which was renewable each year. The internal check-point system was also modified so that Chinese immigrants no longer needed to apply for special permits to cross into another part of the Indochinese Union, but only had to present their five-year identity card, or *laissez-passer*, to obtain a pass valid for thirty days. For Chinese non-immigrants, they could travel throughout Indochina freely upon presentation of their regular passport.[186] Exceptions to the obligation to present a passport included passengers on ships calling into port,[187] Chinese crews,[188] fishermen,[189] and persons living in the frontier regions.[190]

The Congrégations

While the main principle embodied in the Nanking Convention was that the Chinese were to be accorded the same treatment as other nationals, the parties agreed that there was to be no derogation of the existing privileges that the Chinese enjoyed in Indochina. It was in the light of such principles that the parties considered the nature of the *congrégations*. The Chinese side did not wish to abolish the organization, but the French ultimately wanted to legally assimilate the Chinese as ordinary foreigners, rather than differentiating them as a particular group of foreigners. Finally, the parties agreed to keep the *congrégations*. The *congrégations* became subject to the 1935 *Décret* that regulated the elections for chief and sub-chief, their tenure, and other related matters.[191] The *congrégations* were recognized as possessing civil personality, but were limited in capacity and prohibited from owning buildings necessary for their function.[192] However, the juridical nature of the *congrégation* was not clear, for if the congrégation constituted a moral person under public colonial law (*personne morale du droit public colonial*), it came under the protection of the administration. However, if it constituted a moral person under indigenous law, it would be subject to local rules and customs only. The courts recognized the former solution,[193] albeit with much criticism.

Employment

The Nanking Convention had the effect of formalizing the privileged position of the Chinese *vis-à-vis* other foreigners rather than creating any new rights in respect of employment. Generally, the Chinese were free to undertake any occupation except those not open to foreigners, such as public servants and diplomatic positions. The privileges that were enumerated in the Convention included the right to fish in the waters of Indochina,[194] the right to run schools to teach the Chinese language,[195] the right to work as a printer, and the right to run hotels.[196]

Special Taxes

The greatest bone of contention to the Chinese was the imposition of special taxes on Chinese persons. Therefore, at the outset of the negotiations, the Chinese demanded the abolition of these taxes.[197] However, from the French perspective, the demand to abolish taxes was incompatible with the retention of all the Chinese privileges. In the end, the special taxes were retained, as were the special privileges. To make the compromise seem more palatable to the Chinese, the taxes were changed from being known as "registration tax" and "head tax" to "personal tax levied on foreigners entitled to a privileged status" and " fixed tax" respectively.

Representation

One of the more symbolic gestures achieved by the Nanking Convention was the setting up of Chinese consulates. Although the French were formally opposed to providing for a consular office in the Convention, in the face of Chinese demands for the opening of three consulates, the French conceded to two being set up in Saigon and Hanoi or Haiphong.[198] The Chinese wanted to set up a consulate in all three places, but this was refused. As a compromise, the Chinese set up a visa office in Haiphong, which was a *de facto* vice-consulate. The consular staff had to be Chinese and was not allowed to engage in commerce or industry. The powers of the consulates were limited to matters such as delivering passports, registering the births and deaths of Chinese nationals, and celebrating marriages between Chinese nationals. Notably, the Chinese consulates did not have any special powers in relation to the death of Chinese nationals, and could not intervene in the resulting succession matters.[199]

Private Rights

The privilege of being able to own land in the protectorates continued to be enjoyed by the Chinese as a traditional exception to the rule against ownership by foreigners.[200] Since such rights derived from custom, indigenous law governed the ownership of land by the Chinese in the protectorates. This was in spite of the fact that, after the signing of the Nanking Convention, the Chinese became subject to French laws as they moved from being assimilated foreigners to foreigners entitled to a privileged status.[201]

CONCLUSION

As the Nanking Convention showed, the French system of administration and legislation was not entirely successful in assimilating the Chinese into the indigenous population, or controlling Chinese activities. At the same time, however, the Chinese never proved to be an imminent political threat to French authority. In many ways, against the backdrop of the relations between China and France, the relationship between the Chinese and the French authorities in Indochina was mutually beneficial despite the contradictions between French ideals and actual administration. The commercial activities of the Chinese contributed significantly to French revenue, and bridged the vacuum between the lack of local knowledge in respect of commercial transactions, and the inability of the French and Europeans to understand the indigenous culture. However, this did nothing to improve the relations between the Chinese and the local population. Centuries of underlying tensions, exacerbated by the French occupation, manifested in the communist treatment of the Chinese in Vietnam, which once more reflected the contradictory relationship between the Chinese and the indigenous people.[202]

Notes

1 Victor Purcell, *The Chinese in Southeast Asia* (London: Oxford University Press, 1965), pp. 200–7.

[2] Alexander Barton Woodside, *Vietnam and the Chinese Model: A Comparative Study of Nguyen and Ch'ing Civil Government in the First Half of the Nineteenth Century* (Cambridge, Massachusetts: Harvard University Press, 1971).

[3] Ibid., p. 60.

[4] Nguyen Ngoc Huy, Ta Van Tai, and Tran Van Liem, *The Lê Code: Law in Traditional Vietnam: A Comparative Sino-Vietnamese Legal Study with Historical-Juridical Analysis and Annotation* (Ohio: Ohio University Press, 1987), pp. 4–7; and Luong Nhi Ky, *The Chinese in Vietnam: A Study of Vietnamese-Chinese Relations with Special Attention to the Period 1862–1961* (Michigan: University Microfilms International, 1979), pp. 109–17.

[5] Woodside, op. cit., pp. 60–111.

[6] Cf. Khac Vien Nguyen, *Vietnam: A Long History* (Hanoi: Foreign Language Publishing House, 1987), pp.52–90.

[7] Purcell, op. cit., pp. 6–7.

[8] Ramses Amer, *The Ethnic Chinese in Vietnam and Sino-Chinese Relations* (Kuala Lumpur: Forum, 1991), p. 8.

[9] Decision of the 12th year of the reign of Gia-long, 1813.

[10] "Notice sur la Situation des Chinois en Indochine", *Revue Indo-Chinoise* 12, no. 11 (November 1909): 1063, 1067.

[11] Decision of the 13th year of the reign of Gia-long, 1814.

[12] Maw-Kuey Tsai, *Les Chinois au Sud-Vietnam* (Paris: Bibliothèque Nationale, 1968), pp. 29–31.

[13] Decision of the 13th year of the reign of Gia-long, 1814.

[14] Decision of the 11th year of the reign of Tu-Duc, 1858.

[15] "Notice sur la Situation des Chinois en Indochine", *Revue Indo-Chinoise* 12, no. 11 (November 1909): 1063, 1068.

[16] Ibid., p. 1069.

[17] Ibid., p. 1066.

[18] The extent of Chinese influence on Vietnamese Indochinese society has been a subject of dispute among a number of scholars. See, for example, William J. Duiker, *China and Vietnam: The Roots of Conflict* (California: Institute of East Asian Studies, University of California, Berkeley, 1986), pp. 4–5.

[19] Ibid., p. 1.

[20] For a brief account of France's entry into Indochina, see Luong Nhi Ky, op. cit., pp. 114–6.

[21] William J. Duiker, *The Rise of Nationalism in Vietnam, 1900–1914* (London: Cornell University Press, 1976), p. 107.

[22] "Notice sur la Situation des Chinois en Indochine", *Revue Indo-Chinoise* 12, no. 11 (November 1909): 1063, 1069.

[23] For the unofficial attitudes of the French towards the Chinese, see Purcell, op. cit., pp. 204–5.

[24] Stephen H. Roberts, *The History of French Colonial Policy 1870–1925* (London: Frank Cass & Co. Ltd., 1963), p. 21. Part of this anti-colonial sentiment was

due to the view that colonies were costly and a drain on the colonizing country. See Thomas E. Ennis, *French Policy and Developments in Indochina* (New York: Russell & Russell, 1936), pp. 68–69.

25 For example, the tenets of Voltaire and Rousseau.

26 The prevailing belief in the 1870s and 1880s was that colonialization was a drain on the country's economic resources. See Pierre Gourou, *Les Paysans du Delta Tonkinois* (Paris: Mouton, 1936).

27 Roberts, op. cit., pp. 13–20.

28 This was a result of the industrialization in France and its subsequent need for markets. Ibid., p. 15.

29 Ibid., p. 23.

30 For a discussion of French theories of colonial relationships, see ibid., pp. 64–75.

31 Ibid., p. 27–28.

32 Ibid., p. 28.

33 Ennis, op. cit., pp. 52–72.

34 Roberts, op. cit., p. 430.

35 See below.

36 *Presidential Arrêté*, 23 August 1871; *Arrêté* of the Governor-General of Tonkin, 20 December 1888.

37 Franco-Japanese Treaty, 14 October 1854.

38 Ibid., pp. 167–79.

39 Purcell, op. cit., p. 191.

40 *Arrêté*, 5 December 1892, Article 2. France and China entered into a commercial convention on 20 June 1895.

41 *Réglement pour l'execution d'une police mixte sur la frontière sino-annamite* [Regulations for the Creation of a Mixed Police Force on the Sino-Annamite Border], Articles 12–17.

42 *Arrêté*, 11 August 1902, Articles 1–2.

43 *Arrêté*, 15 May 1890, modified by *Arrêté*, 28 November, and *Arrêté*, 11 August 1902.

44 *Arrêté*, 11 August 1902, Article 3.

45 *Arrêté*, 27 December 1892.

46 *Arrêté*, 15 May 1890.

47 *Arrêté*, 15 November 1900.

48 *Arrêté*, 23 November 1895.

49 *Arrêté*, 27 December 1886, *Arrêté*, 5 August 1901, modified by *Arrêté*, 6 December 1907.

50 *Arrêté*, 31 January 1891.

51 See the following discussion of the use of the *bang* system by the French.

52 *Arrêté*, 16 October 1906; and *Arrêté*, 16 August 1907.

53 See below.

54 *Arrêté*, 16 October 1906.

[55] *Arrêté*, 16 October 1906.

[56] *Ordonnance*, 31 December 1891. This Ordinance also governed the contravention of immigration regulations.

[57] See below.

[58] *Arrêté*, 16 October 1906, Article 28.

[59] See below.

[60] *Arrêté*, 3 May 1897.

[61] See above.

[62] Virginia Thompson, *French Indo-China* (London: George Allen & Unwin Ltd, 1937), p. 170.

[63] See ibid., and Jean Thibaut, "Le Mouvement Révolutionnaire Chinois au Tonkin en 1907", *Revue Indo-Chinoise* (August 1909): 803 generally.

[64] Ibid., p. 167.

[65] M. B. Hooker, *A Concise Legal History of Southeast Asia* (Oxford: Clarendon Press, 1978), p. 154.

[66] Treaty of Hué, 6 June 1884.

[67] *Décret*, 27 January 1886.

[68] Hooker, op. cit., p. 172.

[69] *Arrêté*, 27 December 1886, Article 4.

[70] "Notice sur la Situation des Chinois en Indochine", *Revue Indo-Chinoise* 12, no. 11 (November 1909): 1063, 1089.

[71] Thompson, op. cit., p. 170.

[72] However, if the chief or the sub-chief was absent and failed to administer his *congrégation* for six months consecutively, he would lose this privilege. If he was absent for a further three months, re-elections would be called: *Arrêté*, 27 December 1886, Article 14.

[73] *Arrêté*, 5 August 1901.

[74] *Arrêté*, 27 December 1886, Articles 11 and 15.

[75] *Arrêté*, 27 December 1886, Article 16.

[76] *Arrêté*, 4 May 1889; *Arrêté*, 25 July 1895.

[77] *Arrêté*, 9 September 1895.

[78] A. E. Hückel, "Notice sur la Situation Administrative des Asiatiques Étrangers en Indo-Chine", *Revue Indo-Chinoise* 1, no. 89–90 (15–30 September 1908): 289, 291.

[79] First Chamber of the Court of Appeal of Hanoi, 26 July 1935.

[80] Hooker, op. cit., p. 168.

[81] In 1909, there were about 5,000 Chinese in Annam, as opposed to more than 100,000 in Cochinchina, and 22,000 in Tonkin. See "Notice sur la Situation des Chinois en Indochine", *Revue Indo-Chinoise* 12, no. 11 (November 1909): 1063, 1069–1070.

[82] The recognized *congrégations* were those of Guangzhou (Canton), Chaozhou (Chiuchow), Hainan, and Fujian (Fukien).

[83] *Arrêté*, 9 September 1895.

[84] Cochinchina was officially given the status of a colony by Article 18 of the *Sénatus-Consulte*, 3 May 1854. It was ceded to France by the treaties of 5 June 1862 and 5 March 1874. Hooker, op. cit., p. 154.

[85] *Arrêté*, 21 December 1864.

[86] *Arrêté*, 23 August 1871, which subjected the Chinese to the régime established by the *Décret* of 25 July 1864. However, in 1880, the French Penal Code was extended to apply to the local population and Asian foreigners such as the Chinese. Hooker, op. cit., p. 158.

[87] *Arrêté*, 16 October 1906.

[88] *Arrêté*, 12 January 1907.

[89] See discussion above.

[90] Second Chamber of the Court of Appeal of Saigon, 13 December 1934 (unpublished).

[91] The *congrégations* recognized in Cambodia were those of Guangzhou (Canton), Fujian (Fukien), Chaozhou (Chiuchou), Hainan and Kejia (Hakka). Royal Ordinance, 31 December 1891.

[92] "Notice sur la Situation des Chinois en Indochine", *Revue Indo-Chinoise* 12, no. 11 (November 1909): 1063, 1091.

[93] June 1885.

[94] *Arrêté*, 8 July 1908 (Tonkin); *Arrêté*, 21 November 1878 (Cochinchina); *Arrêté*, 15 January 1890 (Cambodia).

[95] *Arrêté*, 3 June 1903 (Tonkin). Foreigners (including Chinese) in Cochinchina were not prohibited from this area (*Arrêté*, 7 April 1904), while in Cambodia, Asian foreigners were only prohibited from long-term systematic exploitation of forest resources (this privilege was reserved for French subjects. Article 32, *Arrêté*, 17 October 1905).

[96] *Décret*, 25 February 1897 (Tonkin); and *Arrêté*, 27 June 1896 (Tonkin and Annam).

[97] See "Notice sur la Situation des Chinois en Indochine", *Revue Indo-Chinoise* 12, no. 11 (November 1909): 1063, 1073–75 for a breakdown of the Chinese population in Saigon and Cholon by occupation.

[98] Victor Purcell, *The Chinese in Southeast Asia* (London: Oxford University Press, 1965), pp. 193–94; Luong Nhi Ky, op. cit., pp. 83–84.

[99] Purcell, op. cit., pp. 195–97; Luong Nhi Ky, op. cit., pp. 85–93.

[100] For possible reasons why this was so, see Étienne Dennery, *Asia's Teeming Millions [Foules d'Asie]* (London, 1931), p. 131.

[101] A. E. Hückel, "Notice sur la Situation Administrative des Asiatiques Étrangers en Indo-Chine", *Revue Indo-Chinoise* 1, no. 89–90 (15–30 September 1908): 289, 294.

[102] *Arrêté*, 15 December 1893; *Circulaire*, 23 December 1893.

[103] *Arrêté*, 1 June 1897.

[104] These were Quang-yen, Tuyen-quang, Yen-bay, Lao-kay, Cao-bang, Lang-son, Mon-cay, Thai-nguyen and Van-bu: *Arrêté*, 12 December 1885, 27 December

1886, 19 February 1889, 1 October 1899, 6 June 1892, 14 April 1893, 1 June 1897, and 18 November 1892.

105 *Arrêté*, 12 December 1885, 27 December 1886, 19 February 1889, 1 October 1890, 6 June 1892, 14 April 1893, 1 June 1897, and 18 November 1902.

106 *Arrêté*, 6 June 1892, and 20 May 1902.

107 Article 4, *Arrêté*, 24 June 1889.

108 *Arrêté*, 9 February 1897; *Décret*, 21 May 1897; *Arrêté*, 12 January 1907; and *Arrêté*, 16 August 1907. Note that there was a system of flat-rate and progressive personal taxes in Saigon and Cholon: "Notice sur la Situation des Chinois en Indochine", *Revue Indo-Chinoise* 12, no. 11 (November 1909): 1063, 1085.

109 *Arrêté*, 16 August 1907.

110 *Ordonnance royale*, 31 December 1891.

111 *Arrêté*, 3 May 1897, applied by *Ordannance royale*, 12 February 1898.

112 A. E. Hückel, "Notice sur la Situation Administrative des Asiatiques Étrangers en Indo-Chine", *Revue Indo-Chinoise* 1, no. 89–90 (15–30 September 1908): 289, 296; "Notice sur la Situation des Chinois en Indochine", *Revue Indo-Chinoise* 12, no. 11 (November 1909): 1063, 1077.

113 25 April 1886, supplemented on 23 June 1887 (by an exchange of letters); 26 June 1887 (convention of Beijing [Peking]), and 20 June 1895 (complementary convention).

114 *Arrêté*, 31 December 1891.

115 The Chinese agreed to indefinitely postpone the appointment of a consul under the 1886 convention until the two governments were of the opinion that circumstances permitted such appointment. See exchange of letters, 23 June 1887. See also A. E. Hückel "Notice sur la Situation Administrative des Asiatiques Étrangers en Indo-Chine", *Revue Indo-Chinoise* 1, no, 89–90 (15–30 September 1908): 289, 296.

116 *Décret*, 11 July 1908.

117 *Arrêté*, 21 September 1896, 21 September 1899.

118 *Arrêté*, 4 February 1886, modified by *Arrêté*, 2 August 1892.

119 *Arrêté*, 4 February 1886, modified by *Arrêté*, 2 August 1892.

120 *Arrêté*, 21 April 1890.

121 *Arrêté*, 31 March 1892 and 17 December 1894.

122 *Arrêté*, 23 August 1904.

123 *Décret*, 8 January 1877.

124 *Décret*, 29 April 1881.

125 *Arrêté*, 20 October 1879.

126 *Arrêté*, 14 November 1901.

127 *Arrêté*, 27 July 1904.

128 This includes international instruments as well as domestic legislation.

129 25 April 1886.

130 See Marcel Caratini, "La Preuve de la Propriété et des Droits Réels Immobiliers en Pays Annamites, *La Revue Indochinoise Juridique et Économique* 11 (1939): 543, 561.

[131] June 1885.
[132] Advice from the consultative committee of the legal department of the general government of Indochina, 20 September 1921.
[133] By a treaty between Spain and Annam dated 5 June 1862, Spain was able to demand for its nationals treatment equivalent to that accorded to the Chinese. However, whether the Spanish legally had real property rights equal to those of the Chinese is questionable: see Court of Appeal, Hanoi (1st Chamber), 1 May 1936.
[134] Treaty of 15 March 1874, Articles 9 and 12.
[135] Treaty of 6 June 1884.
[136] Edicts (*Du*) of the Emperor of Annam, 1 October 1888, 27 September 1897.
[137] Court of Appeal, Hanoi (1st Chamber), 1 May 1936. Since the treaty of 25 April 1886 was not domestically promulgated in Indochina, nations that had signed most-favoured-nation agreements with France were not able to take advantage of the concessions to the Chinese that were formalized by the 1886 treaty. The non-promulgation of this treaty had no effect on the Chinese, as their real property rights were pre-existing and were founded on customary recognition of the same.
[138] *Décret*, 25 July 1864, confirmed in *Décret*, 17 May 1895.
[139] *Décret*, 25 July 1864; *Décret*, 17 May 1895.
[140] *Décret*, 25 May 1881; *Décret*, 17 May 1895.
[141] The indigenous tribunals were officially superceded by the French tribunals in accordance with the *Décret* of 25 May 1881. However, this was not carried out immediately, as in districts other than Saigon, crimes committed by indigenous people or Asian foreigners were heard by indigenous tribunals until French tribunals were set up (*Arrêté*, 7 November 1881, M. Le Myre de Vilers).
[142] *Décret*, 27 February 1892.
[143] *Décret*, 6 May 1898.
[144] *Arrêté*, 30 December 1888.
[145] *Décret*, 1 December 1902.
[146] 1st Chamber of the Court of Appeal of Hanoi, 20 November 1936.
[147] Article 1, *Décret*, 1 December 1902.
[148] *Décret*, 17 February 1890, promulgated in Tonkin on 7 April 1901.
[149] 29 June 1925.
[150] For a detailed discussion of the negotiations between France and China, see Georges Levasseur, "Les Répercussions des Accords de Nankin sur les Problèmes de Droit International Privé en Indochine", *La Revue Indochinoise Juridique et Économique* 1 (1937): 57, 65–75.
[151] The final agreement consisted of the text of the Convention itself (11 articles), four Annexes (consisting of letters exchanged between the representatives of both parties), and a protocol.
[152] 19 July 1935.

153 The French government made it officially known to the Chinese government that the Convention would not be ratified until two issues had been addressed: the ransacking of the French consulate in Longtcheou and the abolition of internal customs duties (*likin*).

154 As of December 1936, these provinces were Guangdong, Yunnan, Guizhou, Jiangxi, Sichuan, Hunan, Hubei, Jiangsu, Anhui, Gansu, Shenxi, Henan, Fujian, and Zhejiang.

155 These were Manchuria (which was occupied by the Japanese), Outer Mongolia (in the hands of the communists), and Tibet.

156 While this was not initially clear in the text of the Convention itself, it was clarified in the exchange of letters annexed thereto (*échange de letters*, no. 2).

157 This *Arrêté* laid down the classification of European/*assimilés* (to whom French law applied) and Asian foreigners (to whom indigenous law applied).

158 This was confirmed in a letter from the French negotiator to the Chinese negotiator, dated 16 May 1930.

159 By this stage, there were five types of foreigners in Indochina: (1) French protégés, (2) residents of Guangzhouwan (ceded to France by China for 99 years by a convention dated 16 November 1899), (3) foreigners who had assimilated with the indigenous population, (4) foreigners with privileged status and (5) other foreigners.

160 Official statistics taken in 1936 indicated 62,000 *métis* in Cochinchina and 11,000 in Tonkin. The numbers for the other areas were uncertain.

161 *Décret*, 24 August 1933.

162 However, the applicability of the 1933 *Décret* in Cambodia in relation to the nationality of a *métis* was upheld. See the decision of 26 May 1934 of the Court of Saigon.

163 *Ordonnance* 66, 5 June 1934 (Cambodia); *Du*, no. 78, 16 October 1936 (Annam and Tonkin).

164 Article 5.

165 Article 21.

166 See *Arrêté*, 16 October 1906.

167 *Décret*, 3 October 1883.

168 Article 13, *Décret*, 4 December 1930.

169 Georges Levasseur, op. cit., pp. 83, 111.

170 Indigenous persons living in areas under direct French rule (Cochinchina, Hanoi, Haiphong and Tourane).

171 Article 19 of the Civil Code of Cochinchina, 1804.

172 Article 12 of the Civil Code of Cochinchina, 1804.

173 Indigenous (and assimilated) persons living in the protectorates.

174 Article 15 of both Codes.

175 Article 16 of both Codes.

176 As amended by the *Ordonnance Royale* of 5 June 1934.

[177] *Arrêté*, 6 December 1935. Notably, the Chinese were not subsumed under the circulation regulations pertaining to French and European nationals, again highlighting their unique status.

[178] Any foreigner staying for more than one month was considered to be an immigrant. *Arrêté*, 6 December 1935, Articles 19 and 26.

[179] Article 58, *Arrêté*, 6 December 1935.

[180] Article 4, *Arrêté*, 6 December 1935.

[181] Article 20, *Arrêté*, 6 December 1935.

[182] Article 27. This provision was put into effect by the Governor of Cochinchina on 3 February 1936, and by the Résident Superieur of Cambodia on 14 February 1936.

[183] This included foremen, industrial workers, agricultural workers, and domestic helpers.

[184] *Arrêté*, 10 October 1936.

[185] Article 32, *Arrêté*, 6 December 1935.

[186] Article 21, *Arrêté*, 6 December 1935.

[187] Article 22, *Arrêté*, 6 December 1935.

[188] Article 24, *Arrêté*, 6 December 1935.

[189] Article 23, *Arrêté*, 6 December 1935.

[190] Article 25, *Arrêté*, 6 December 1935.

[191] Articles 4–11, *Arrêté*, 6 December 1935.

[192] Such as meeting halls, schools, hospitals, and cemeteries. Article 2, *Arrêté*, 6 December 1935.

[193] *Court of Saigon*, 27 February 1886; *Saigon*, 20 October 1923; *Saigon*, 8 June 1933; *Saigon*, 10 August 1933; *Saigon*, 13 December 1934.

[194] This was not a privilege exclusive to the Chinese, as all foreigners could fish in Indochina waters. *Arrêté*, 5 December 1935.

[195] *Arrêté*, 27 January 1925; *Décret*, 13 August 1930; *Arrêté*, 7 July 1932 and 28 November 1933. The retention of Chinese language schools was a strong factor that prevented the Chinese from assimilating into the indigenous population. See Purcell, op. cit., pp. 37 and 568.

[196] This occupation was generally closed to foreigners for political reasons. *Décret*, 31 August 1933.

[197] See Georges Levasseur, "La Situation des Chinois en Indochine", *La Revue Indochinoise Juridique et Économique* 3 (1937): 96, 133.

[198] Article 3, Convention, 16 May 1930.

[199] Georges Levasseur, "La Situation des Chinois en Indochine", pp. 96, 124.

[200] See the above discussion on property rights.

[201] Georges Levasseur, "La Situation des Chinois en Indochine", pp. 96, 145.

[202] See Lewis Matthew Stern, *Vietnamese Communist Policy Toward the Overseas Chinese, 1920–82* (Ann Arbor: University Microfilms International, 1984); Luong Nhi Ky, op. cit., pp. 151–97; and Ramses Amer, op. cit., pp. 25–130.

References

Articles

"Les Sectes Chinoises". *Revue Indo-Chinoise* 5, no. 118 (21 January 1901): 66.

"Notice sur la Situation des Chinois en Indochine". *Revue Indo-Chinoise* 12, no. 11 (November 1909): 1063.

Camerlynck, G. H. "Cour d'Appel de Hanoi (1ére Chambre) 1er Mai 1936". *La Revue Indochinoise Juridique et Économique* 1 (1937): 172.

Caratini, Marcel. "La Preuve de la Propriété et des Droits Réels Immobiliers en Pays Annamites. *Revue Indochinoise Juridique et Économique* 11 (1937): 543.

d'Enjoy, P. "Associations, Congrégations et Sociétés Secrétes Chinoises", *Revue Indo-Chinoise* 1, no. 55 (15 April 1907): 440.

Giret, E. "Chinois Chez Eux", *Revue Indo-Chinoise* (17 September 1900), p. 897.

Hückel, A. E. "Notice sur la Situation Juridique et Administrative des Étrangers Européens et Assimilés en Indo-Chine". *Revue Indo-Chinoise* 1 no. 81 (15 May 1908): 637; *Revue Indo-Chinoise* 1, no. 82 (30 May 1908): 735.

————. "Notice sur la Situation Administrative des Asiatiques Étrangers en Indo-Chine". *Revue Indo-Chinoise* 1, no. 89–90 (15–30 September 1908): 289; and *Revue Indo-Chinoise* 1, no. 91–92 (5–30 October 1908): 567.

Levasseur, Georges. "Contribution a l'Établissment d'une Bibliographie du Droit Indochinoise". *La Revue Indochinoise Juridique et Économique* 9 (1939): 139.

————. "Les Répercussions des Accords de Nankin sur les Problèmes de Droit International Privé en Indochine". *La Revue Indochinoise Juridique et Économique* 1 (1937): 57; and *Revue Indochinoise Juridique et Économique* 2 (1937): 83.

————. "La Situation des Chinois en Indochine". *La Revue Indochinoise Juridique et Économique* 3 (1937): 96.

————. "Les Conflits de Lois et de Jurisidictions Intéressant les Chinois en Indochine". *La Revue Indochinoise Juridique et Économique* 4 (1937): 42.

————. "Réglementation générale du travail en Indochine" (Publication du Gouvernment général); and IDEO H. Hanoi 1937". *La Revue Indochinoise Juridique et Économique* (1938), p. 176.

Thibaut, Jean. "Le Mouvement Révolutionnaire Chinois au Tonkin en 1907". *Revue Indo-Chinoise* (August 1909), p. 803.

Books

Amer, Ramses. *The Ethnic Chinese in Vietnam and Sino-Chinese Relations*. Kuala Lumpur: Forum, 1991.

Chang, Pao-min. *Beijing, Hanoi and the Overseas Chinese*. Berkeley: Institute of East Asian Studies, University of California, Berkeley, 1982.

Duiker, William J. *China and Vietnam: The Roots of Conflict*. California: Institute of East Asian Studies, University of California, Berkeley, 1986.

Duiker, William J. *The Rise of Nationalism in Vietnam, 1900–1914*. London: Cornell University Press, 1976.

Ennis, Thomas E. *French Policy and Developments in Indochina*. New York: Russell & Russell, 1936.

Hill, R. D. *Index Indochinensis: An English and French Index to Revue Indochinoise, Extrême-Asie, Extrême-Asie- Revue Indochinoise and La Revue Indochinoise Juridique et Économique*. Hong Kong: University of Hong Kong Press, 1983.

Holmgren, Jennifer. *Chinese Colonization of Northern Vietnam: Administrative Geography and Political Development in the Tongkin Delta, First to Sixth Centuries A.D.* Oriental monograph series, no. 27. Canberra: Australian National University, Faculty of Asian Studies, 1980.

Hooker, M. B. *A Concise Legal History of Southeast Asia*. Oxford: Clarendon Press, 1978.

Luong, Nhi Ky. *The Chinese in Vietnam: A Study of Vietnamese-Chinese Relations With Special Attention to the Period 1862–1961*. Michigan: University Microfilms International, 1979.

Lafarque, Jean Andre. *L'Immigration Chinoise en Indochine*. Paris: H. Jouve, 1909.

Marsot, Alain G. *The Chinese Community in Vietnam Under the French*. New York: The Edwin Mellen Press, 1993.

Nguyen Ngoc Huy, Ta Van Tai and Tran Van Lien. *The Lê Code: Law in Traditional Vietnam: A Comparative Sino-Vietnamese Legal Study with Historical-Juridical Analysis and Annotation*. Ohio: Ohio University Press, 1987.

Nguyen The-Anh. *Bibliographie Critique sur les Relations entre le Viet-nam et l'Occident*. Paris: GP Maisonneuve & Larose, 1967.

Nguyen Van Nghi. *Étude Économique sur la Cochine Française et l'Infiltration Chinoise*. Montpellier: Firmin et Montane, 1978.

Norindr, Panivong. *Phantasmatic Indochina: French Colonial Ideology in Architecture, Film, and Literature*. Durham: Duke University Press, 1996.

Purcell, Victor. *The Chinese in Southeast Asia*. London: Oxford University Press, 1965.

Roberts, Stephen H. *The History of French Colonial Policy 1870–1925*. London: Frank Cass & Co. Ltd., 1963.

Stern, Lewis Matthew. *Vietnamese Communist Policy Toward the Overseas Chinese, 1920–82*. Ann Arbor: University Microfilms International, 1984.

Thompson, Virginia. *French Indo-China*. London: George Allen & Unwin Ltd, 1937.

Tsai, Maw-Kuey. *Les Chinois au Sud-Vietnam*. Paris: Bibliothèque Nationale, 1968.

Woodside, Alexander Barton. *Vietnam and the Chinese Model: A Comparative Study of Nguyen and Ch'ing Civil Government in the First Half of the Nineteenth Century*. Cambridge, Massachusetts: Harvard University Press, 1971.

3

LAW AND MEMORY, *DE JURE* TO *DE FACTO*

Confucianization and Its Implications for Family and Property in Vietnam

Esta Ungar

Given that the Vietnamese legal texts, written in classical Chinese,[1] the court language, embodied Confucian legal principles and not necessarily Vietnamese social practice, it is no wonder that European travellers in nineteenth-century Vietnam were struck by cultural resemblances between Vietnam and China. French colonial scholars, like their British[2] and Dutch counterparts, translated classical legal texts which embodied ideals of the élite culture, and inevitably these were used by administrators as the basis for colonial law. The distinction between black letter law and social practice, however, appears to have been lost on colonial legal commentators, with unfortunate results for women in particular. Indeed, French practice enshrined in Vietnamese law the precepts of the last reigning dynasty,[3] notable for its strict adherence to the Chinese Qing legal model.[4] After independence, aspects of French colonial law, based on the Confucian model, became part of Vietnamese administrative law, especially with regard to family, property, and inheritance. This legal evolution moved further with the Marriage Law of 1986, and Land Laws of 1988 and 1993 which, in their implementing regulations, followed customary law.[5] Thus, in the space of four centuries, Confucian law, originally an instrument of government, has become social practice. In the process, the memory of pre-Confucian forms of ordering family and property has been attenuated or erased from the collective consciousness.

Prior to state attempts to Confucianize Vietnamese society, family and property relations maintained a certain equity between males and females and between older and younger brothers and sisters. As a result, however, of the combined forces of Confucian government with colonial law and their attendant social effects, patrilinial and patriarchal social organization supplanted the earlier model. By the end of the twentieth century, for example, critical aspects of customary law applied to land use, and inheritance included the provision that land is held by the head of household, normally defined as the oldest direct descendant on the paternal side of the family. Following current law, only one person can be designated head of household; and following custom, that person is the eldest in the patrilineal line of descent. Why? Because Confucian custom decrees it. The irony is that Confucian-inspired custom is a relatively recent phenomenon in historical terms when compared with the notion of a Vietnamese ethnic and cultural consciousness which itself had found political expression many centuries earlier.[6]

The Vietnamese state in the fifteenth century adopted Confucian law for the prime purpose of centralizing the state and creating a system with greater revenue control over the population. The government in its laws and decrees, enforced by rigid punishments, seized on the Confucian-structured family and household as a social, religious, and economic[7] unit. When Confucian strictures were first introduced, this process did not go unchallenged. At that time, many aspects of family and communal life were very resistant to the new system. In fact, the first Confucianized law code[8] itself, the main substantive laws of which were first enacted in the fifteenth century, became a testament to this contest. In spite of the attempt by the state to introduce Confucian practice in this code, the text itself is remarkable for its retention of the decidedly non-Confucian customs of bilateral kinship and inheritance[9], which were not weakened appreciably until the publication of the nineteenth-century code of the Nguyen dynasty. Beyond that, the Hong-duc code and its sources record a number of contemporary social practices which were meant to be supplanted by the new Confucian prescriptions. Thus, the fifteenth-century regulations, decrees, and historical records, together with the formal Lê Code, provide a compelling case of the power of the state to suppress existing social practices through the use of law.[10] Confucianized legal texts and decrees offer a compelling way to enter the world of popular resistance to the new rules of social conduct and organization introduced in the fifteenth century. At the same time, the "Confucianization" of law becomes a tale of how law and its implementation may function to corrupt or erase social memory. In the case of Vietnam, the erasure of social memory has occurred to such a degree that Confucian notions of gender and property relations have been naturalized, and earlier practices at variance with the present ones have been lost to view.

The implications of this loss of social memory are significant. When gender and property rights, more equitable than present custom allows, are brought up for discussion, they tend to founder on the notion that Confucian norms are the bedrock of Vietnamese culture and therefore demand respect. If present reality admitted the possibility of non-Confucian practice, then more equitable arrangements in marriage and property would find easier social justification.

This chapter investigates what legal texts of various kinds have to tell us about social practice. Reading these texts "against the grain" illuminates the dynamics of cultural resistance and suppression in the "Confucian revolution" of law, forcefully imposed in fifteenth-century Vietnam. The chapter first outlines the underlying principles of Confucian social organization, then turns to fundamental principles of Chinese and Confucianized Vietnamese law codes. This leads to the core of this study: the gap which opens up between Confucianized law and contrary social practices as the link between court rites and village custom is severed;[11] the transformation of Confucian values, by the twentieth century, from *de jure* to *de facto* as the basis for implementing laws and regulations relating to family and property; and finally, the loss and partial recovery of collective memory and its implications. This process will be examined specifically through laws and customs relating to mourning, sexuality, funerary rites, marriage, residence, procreation, and property and their combined effect in altering the structure of the family.

The Underlying Principles of Confucian Law as They Relate to Social Organization

The underlying principles of Confucian ideology, as exemplified in law, concern the imperative, in an administrative sense, to maintain a stable farming population. This population was to be organized in families, whose households were set up to be religious and social, as well as economic units. The organizing principle of the administrative household unit was the family, structured as a stable patriarchal unit. In the Confucian system, another critical factor in defining the household unit, and keeping it fixed in one geographical location, was a series of religious practices based on ancestor-worship. Confucian ancestor-worship was itself based primarily on patrilineality, that is, on a family unit — a family unit predicated on an ancestral line continuing through the father's side to his sons and grandsons, with the eldest son being foremost in each generation. Ancestral rites were to be paid to the ancestors whose remains were meant to be buried in the soil of their native place and, in the case of farmers, on their own land. Confucian ancestral rites thus formed another and very powerful reason for the descendants' family to remain in the same place — so that they could properly perform the rites to the ancestors buried on ancestral land.

The worship of ancestors had its counterpart in the structure of the living family where those closest to the ancestors received the highest status. Thus, the aged, in particular the male aged, were to be given the highest respect among the family members. The veneration of age, coupled with the centrality of worship of the paternal ancestors, led to the privileging of age over youth, of death rituals over birth rituals,[12] and of those whose reproductive powers were in decline over those with the full power of fertility.

Within the family itself, the structure followed these principles: males in each generation were superior in status to females and age took precedence within the generations as well as between them. Thus, the eldest son had precedence over the next eldest, and so on, and the same went for the daughters. In the Chinese Confucian system, a man's marriage partner must be chosen from outside his village. A woman was raised from birth to accept that her true family would be the line into which she married, and her natal family was merely a temporary home until then. For her status to improve in her husband's family, she would have to produce a male heir. This son would inherit the family's land which would be divided out equally among all the sons only. The eldest son would be granted an additional share as it was his responsibility to care for his aged parents.

Fundamental Principles of Traditional Chinese and Confucianized Vietnamese Legal Codes

The classic Chinese legal code from which all succeeding ones drew their inspiration was the eighth-century code of the Tang dynasty. The Tang code was not only the basis of all subsequent Chinese dynastic codes, it was also the lodestone for all architects of government in the East Asian region who sought to imitate the structures and centralizing power of the Chinese state. The core provisions of the Tang code enshrine the Confucian values of obedience and filial piety to the state and its mirror, the family. Thus, of the ten heinous crimes enumerated at the beginning of the code, six deal with instituting and policing order within the family, and the family as a reflection of the state. The ten heinous crimes[13] as listed in the Tang code are:

1. plotting rebellion
2. plotting great sedition
3. plotting treason
4. contumacy
5. depravity
6. great irreverence
7. lack of filial piety
8. discord
9. unrighteousness
10. incest

In the Lê Code, they are the "Ten Heinous Crimes" (Le):[14]

1. plotting high treason (v. the sovereign)
2. plotting grave insubordination (acts v. imperial ancestral temples…)
3. plotting treason (v. the country; serving the enemy)
4. wicked insubordination: beating and plotting to kill one's grandparents, parents or killing of these relatives: father's brother or wife of father's brother, father's sister, elder brother or elder sister, maternal grandparents, husband, husband's grandparents, or husband's parents.
5. inhumanity: killing three persons in a family not condemned to death, killing and dismembering any person; breeding venomous animals; putting on a curse by witchcraft.
6. *lése-majesté* — stealing articles of worship from imperial temples, etc.
7. lack of filial piety: denouncing, cursing … one's grandparents or parents, disobeying one's parents or grandparents; failing to provide for them sufficiently; getting married, participating in musical or theatrical entertainments, or wearing clothes other than mourning garb during the period of mourning for one's parents [25 months]; knowing the death of one's grandparents or parents … yet concealing … news [of it] and not publicly showing grief; falsely alleging death of grandparent or parent.
8. discord: plotting to kill or sell any relative of the … [fifth] or closer degree of mourning; beating or denouncing one's husband or a senior relative of the … [third] or closer degree of mourning, or a senior relative of higher generation than oneself … of the … [fourth degree] of mourning.

9. disloyalty: killing the official in active service who heads the office or administrative area under whose jurisdiction one works or lives; students killing their current teacher; clerks or runners killing the official heading their service; wives, knowing of the death of their husband, concealing such news and not publicly showing grief or, during the period of mourning participating in musical or theatrical entertainments, wearing clothes other than the mourning garb, or getting married.
10. incest (*ni luan*):[15] having sexual relations with any relative of the ... [fourth] or closer degree of mourning, or with a secondary wife of one's grandfather or father. Both the principal and his or her consenting partner shall be punished... .

In terms of the way the crimes were regulated, crimes 1–5, 8 and 10 were treated similarly.[16] Under the seventh crime, the Vietnamese code of the Lê (unlike that of the nineteenth-century Nguyen dynasty in Vietnam) permitted children to maintain households and hold property distinct from their parents. In contrast, the Tang code held such action to be a crime.[17] Another important difference, according to Nguyên Ngoc Huy and Ta Van Tai, was the fact that Vietnamese judges had greater discretion in handing down penalties than did their Chinese counterparts.[18]

One can see from this overview of the key principles of the Chinese dynastic codes and their Vietnamese manifestations, that Confucian principles lay at the very heart of their legal codes. These took as their dictum that "the family was the root of the state" and embodied the five relationships: ruler-minister, parent-child, elder-younger brother, teacher-student, friend-friend with the weight of obligation clearly on the subservient. Age is given precedence to youth by means of direct injunctions on filial piety as expressed in the five relationships and in the funerary and mourning regulations. In the process of enforcing these relationships, the state restructured social relations to make the family the key agency of social control.[19] Since social concerns are inextricably bound up with government and livelihood, the properly ordered, Confucianized family in Lê Vietnam was equally "regarded ... as an indispensable instrument of political control and economic management".[20]

Confucian Crossroads: Community, Family and State in Fifteenth-Century Vietnam

Restructuring social relationships is at the best of times an exercise fraught with tension. In the fifteenth century, as the Vietnamese nation emerged from twenty years of guerilla warfare (1407–27) with its hugely powerful neighbour, Ming China, a triumphant but battered leadership sought ways to strengthen the state. Defining moments in this effort occurred up to 1460. Then from 1460 to 1497, a ruler arose who combined a commitment to Confucian ethics and scholarship with a ruthless determination to centralize the state. To that end, the king, Le Thanh-tong, launched a powerful assault on non-Confucian practices in order to impose a strict Confucian model, particularly on the social élite. So effective in the long term was this effort at social engineering that the only programme comparable to it was the attempt to introduce socialism in the twentieth century to revolutionize society and production. Up to now, Confucianization has had a far more profound influence than socialism in transforming society.

The Vietnamese will often look back on the injustices in their lives, which are really a product of Confucianization, and assume that they are the natural order of things, ordained by their culture which goes back such a long way. Borrowed Confucian norms seem to have been transmuted into society's cultural core. In this loss of social memory, law functioned as a key instrument, obscuring the fact that:

> the coordination of individual and group memories, whose results may appear consensual, are in fact the product of intense contest, struggle, and in some instances, annihilation.[21]

Transit Points to Confucianization

An examination of legal sources for the Lê dynasty[22] reveals that while the battle to impose Confucian morality was well and truly joined in the first three decades of the dynasty, the period from 1460 to 1497 witnessed the severest enforcement of Confucian strictures, aimed at the élite and government officials. These restrictions weighed most heavily against sexual practices.[23] The ways in which the Lê Code, and its fifteenth-century antecedents, conformed to the Chinese Confucian model of family were very much shaped by the pre-existing structure of Vietnamese society. Thus, any investigation of Confucianization is necessarily a consideration of other long-enduring Vietnamese cultural practices. The section below describes a number of flashpoints in the first period of Confucianizing activity between 1427 and 1459 as mourning and fertility rites conflict.

Rituals performed at the ancestral temple of the royal founder became the first point of attack in the Confucian war of rites and customs that punctuate the history of the fifteenth century. In 1437, the official history reported that the king went to perform rites to the spirit of the dynastic founder and he travelled to the former king's birthplace in Thanh Hoa province where the ancestral temple was located. There, the king banned the singing of *cheo*[24] and the performing of lewd music (*nhac dam*).[25] *Cheo* (oar) music was used traditionally among the Vietnamese and ethnic minorities to accompany the soul of the deceased person on the passage to the next world. *Dam* music refers to music which the court began to outlaw for mourning rites because it was not solemn and respectful as was the Chinese ritual music which scholar-officials at court were attempting to substitute. Gradually, *dam* music became the music of the villages and divorced from the practices at court where it had been routinely performed until the Lê dynasty.

The next assault on ancient tradition came in 1448, when it led to the banning of a dance invoking a fertility custom so ancient that it is depicted on the bronze drums of Ngoc Lu[26] and others found in major archaeological sites in north central and northern Vietnam and some parts of southwest China. The official history recorded that in 1448 the emperor, the empress dowager, and all the princes came to the alternate capital at Lam Son, birthplace of the dynastic founder, in Thanh Hoa province.

> The people of Thanh Hoa watched the king arrive, boys and girls alternately led in singing the *li lien* [*ri ren*] at the arrival ground; according to the *li lien* custom (a group) half of boys and half of girls, intertwined hands and sang, or interlaced their [bodies at] feet and neck [in a rite] known as "*cam hoa ket hoa*" [pollinating the flower to close the flower],[27] a very disgraceful behaviour. The official … on the platform informed the Chief Minister … : "This licentious custom should not be profanely performed before the royal palanquin". Henceforth it was forbidden and ceased.[28]

The antiquity of this rite and its association with the people of Vietnam was so central that it was adopted by the Chinese courts as the name for Vietnam under Chinese rule: Chinese, *Jiao zhi* [*Chiao chih*], Vietnamese, *Giao chi.* The best explanation in Chinese records of the meaning of this name is in the *Li Zhi*, the Chinese *Classic of [Confucian] Rites*, and its Tang dynasty commentator.[29] His description echoes the dance described several centuries later in the passage above. The fertility rite represented by the *li lien* performance was so specific to Vietnamese culture that the name was not depicted with Chinese characters but, in an unusual departure for the official history, in *nom*, Vietnamese demotic characters.

The *li lien* dance also evoked the power of the bronze drums, which had been used in fertility rites, prayers for rain, and dances of war. The three levels of the drum depicted a cosmology comprising sky, earth and water. The drums themselves were the revered property of particular communities. As a signal of war, the sound of the drums was said to strike such fear into the hearts of the enemy that their hair would turn white. Other examples of the struggle between the culture associated with the bronze drums, and the newer Confucian norms occurred in the Thanh Hoa region where the Le founder and his followers were born. When drought struck and the political situation became unstable, the court used the ceremonies for the New Year to invoke the old customs, with officials dancing the "Binh Ngo" [Pacify the Ngo] martial dance which the dynastic founder had used in the titanic struggle against the Ming dynasty before 1427. An official at court who had the temerity to criticize this practice as contrary to the [Confucian] rites, was punished.[30] The reassertion of an older custom did not end there. In 1456, as the crisis of confidence deepened, the court returned to Thanh Hoa to reinvoke the spirit of the founder, and they did so in the manner of their ancestral home. Just before they arrived, the rains came. Once again, they invoked the music of their triumph over the Ming. Following older non-Confucian rites they slaughtered four buffaloes, beat the bronze drum, sang and danced the music and songs of war and allegiance to the court. Then they sacrificed buffaloes to the spirits of the brothers of Lê Loi, founder of the dynasty.[31] This was the last time a bronze drum was sounded at court as the incapacity of these military leaders to rule an entire state gave way to a new order at the government level.

Thorough Confucianization: Mourning and Marriage Rites

Given the chaotic history of the preceding two decades, it appears, on the one hand, unsurprising that the new ruler would seek an effective strategy to bring unruly courtiers under control. Yet, on the other, the route this king chose to enforce order appears extreme in terms of his laws, decrees, and regulations. At the same time, forty years of Confucian-inspired social discipline centralized the state to a greater degree than before and brought the court more strongly under the control of the ruler. The greatest legacy of the Hong-duc (Overflowing Virtue) era, however, was not any bureaucratic structure that would survive its founder's passing, but rather, the socialization and Confucianization of the family. Over the centuries, these changes permeated down to the society at large in ways still very much apparent today. How the foundation was set for this revolutionary change is the subject of the following section.

The unremitting campaign to inculcate proper mourning rites among the élite was the primary focus of the state's intensive programme of Confucianization. By 1470, the throne issued a decree authorizing punishments of death or exile for those who violated the mourning period and were thus unfilial to parents or spouses, particularly of the male line.

> Children must mourn parents, wives must mourn husbands following the system of three years mourning and nothing else, and not act contrary to the rites. Children must mourn parents and wives and concubines must mourn husbands. If wives or concubines get pregnant during the mourning period, they will be punished with exile. [A wife in mourning for her husband, who commits incestuous acts] or before the end of the mourning period puts off mourning clothes to wear ordinary dress, as well as those women who are encouraged to take another husband, together with the man who marries that woman, will be sentenced to death.
>
> If during the mourning period they go out and join celebrations and do not avoid them, they will be sentenced to exile …
>
> Also for the Man people [ethnic minority peoples] who have sexual relations ('incest') with wives or concubines of elder or younger brothers who have died, together with the officials who have taken bribes and concealed the act, will all be executed.[32]

This decree is echoed in the Lê Code under the ten heinous crimes. The *Hong-duc Thien-chinh* reiterates the importance of following the mourning rites for five generations. It then goes into great detail on the degree of punishment to be accorded to each type of infraction.[33] Not only do these regulations police sexuality by their complex restrictions and heavy punishments, but the injunctions against music strike at the existing non-Confucian funerary practices. Music is also mentioned in the ten heinous crimes and in this case refers to *cheo* entertainments which the court prohibited at the imperial temple at the beginning of the dynasty. The universal way to honour a person's passing up to this time was to have a wake filled with music and entertainment as a way to guide the spirit of the departed across the water to the next world. This custom was not only common to the Vietnamese but to local ethnic minority groups as well as among the Zhuang in southwest China.[34]

After the three years' mourning period, descendants were required to perform rites on the anniversary of the death of an ancestor. For not following these ceremonies and being unfilial to one's ancestors,

> Prominent or ordinary, official or peasant (in accordance with the law), there is no difference. According to the law the guilty party will have 60 strokes of the cane and lose their portion of the family inheritance.[35]

Even after the mourning period, marriage between close relatives was prohibited. Thus, levirate (marrying the widow of a deceased brother) was banned[36] and the penalty was strangulation,[37] although this was a common practice among Vietnamese and neighbouring ethnic minorities prior to this time. Once again, Confucian presciptions were introducing practices which were at odds with the prevailing mores. In 1499, the court handed down an edict prohibiting "all people, from princes down to the common people, from marrying women of the Cham race".[38] By this time, the dynasty had pushed its borders further south, encroaching on the Cham kingdom, whose people did, and still do, carry on inheritance of land and lineage through the mother's line. It was obviously feared that such marriages would undermine the Confucian principle of the male as head of the household.[39]

Marriage and Residence

Marriage was another critical area where Confucian norms were set against the pre-existing system. Article 100 of the *Hong duc thien chinh* decreed that the male's family must follow the proper marriage rites and not past customs:

> At the day of meeting the bride and accompanying her [to the groom's house] the girl must go to live at her husband's house and not follow the old customs, which force the boy to live at his wife's house for three years before the girl is allowed to go to her husband's house.[40]

The law went on to say that this was the custom of the Qin dynasty, was not to be followed, and would be punished according to the law.[41] In fact, this was a custom (*gui re* — "sending the bridegroom") of the Vietnamese and of several ethnic minorities (including the Zhuang in south China). Folk poems of the early twentieth century still made reference to it. One song about the hard work of the son-in-law goes like this:

> … I dream of the work I've given during the two years I've lived at your home …
> In the ninth month the rain and the wind [buffet me],
> Lifting the buckets of water, my arms and legs are breaking.[42]

This practice continues to be common to this day among various Tay, Nung, Thai,[43] and Zhuang groups. The period of time specified is between one and three years. It is also practised in other parts of mainland Southeast Asia.[44] Another aspect of this interim period between engagement and formal marriage was the relative freedom of young people.[45] Formal marriage was not even necessary in law. According to Nguyen Ngoc Huy and Ta Van Tai, "no legal text specifically stated that due to lack of any of the above ceremonies, a marriage would be considered null and void".[46] They also reported that under the preceding Tran dynasty, a couple who were too poor to hire a match-maker and to pay the marriage gift could "by themselves marry each other".[47] At the same time, the Hong-duc ruler issued decrees which became part of the Lê Code, such as the one in 1469 which checked on the marital status of officials who were in line for appointment or promotion. Those without the appropriate papers showing that their own marriage ceremonies conformed to the Confucian rites were required to report this and correct the situation. Anyone falsely claiming to have done this would be punished with tattooing.[48] The edict in the Lê Code on this matter states:

> Whoever, instead of bringing adequate gifts to the home of a girl's parents [or relatives] ... to celebrate a wedding ceremony cohabits unlawfully with the girl, shall be demoted one grade and must pay the girl's parents reparation commensurate with the social standing of her family. (...) The girl in question shall receive fifty strokes of the light stick.[49]

The material in this article as well as that above on marriage and mourning show quite clearly the intention of the state to institute a patrilineal and patriarchal system of marriage and family, one which was quite distinct from prevailing social practices. Many supplementary edicts prohibiting the breaking of engagements and similar rules[50] attempted to rigidify the practices surrounding marriage and bring them more and more within the purview of the Confucianizing state.

In lesser ways also, the state issued rules and admonitions to promote filial piety, obedience to authority, and the separation of the sexes. The *Hong duc Thien Chinh* (which, despite its name, contains laws from the early part of the dynasty as well as after 1497), harking back to ancient Chinese admonitions from the Confucian classics, calls for young persons to show politeness on meeting teachers, or be punished for disrespect; children should respect parents by following rules for the whole mourning period.

> Girls and boys should not sit on the same mat, should not bathe together on the same side of the river, and should not hold hands.[51]

All these offences would be punished.[52] Older children who were "trouble-makers", or unfilial were to be treated severely.[53] A number of edicts banned *cheo* and "profane music" (*dam nhac*). Such entertainment was forbidden at court and in all the royal palaces. An imperial decree of 1465 prohibited persons singing *cheo* songs to scoff at parents or officials.[54]

> Among the common people boys must learn rites and obligations [*le nghia,* including politeness]. They cannot sing *ca dao* [popular song form] about love affairs (*trang gio*) out on the street and criticize well-meaning persons; girls should stay within the gates ... not speak loudly

> [and follow the Confucian Chinese prescription on the behaviour of young women].[55]

Why was this music so offensive to the Confucian ear? Not only was it subversive of the Confucian mourning rites with their solemnity and patriarchal ordering of ceremonies, it was also bawdy, sexy, ribald, poked fun at authority, and could spread unwelcome political messages. In fact, the picture one draws of Vietnamese village life from the practices that these laws prohibit, to the folk carvings and woodblock prints, songs, proverbs and verses, as well as collections on folk customs is of a very lively, humorous people who liked to sing and drink, dance and enjoy the fruits of sexual pleasure. Thus, on the one hand, Vietnamese life pulsed with the customs of the countryside and, on the other, a new royal house determined to use force as well as moral suasion to bring at least the élite to heel.

Both the preoccupations and punishments of the Hong-duc ruler targeted popular customs in order to effect a complete reformation of the court and the official class. Any examination of the laws and decrees of the late fifteenth century brings forth striking evidence of the ruler's concern to police and control sexual offences to Confucian morals, and the heavy use of punishments to enforce the authority of the state in this project. In 1467, seven years into the Confucianizing offensive, the official history reported 323 executions for violations of the new laws.[56]

> Under Le Thanh Tong, the tendency toward severe penalties for sex offences grew even stronger and it is noteworthy that the Vietnamese seemed to be more Confucianist than the Chinese in this respect.[57]

Other articles indicate once again the particularly punitive attitude towards sexual offences and the escalating definition of sexual activities, which were being criminalized. Thus, Article 402, exclusive to the Lê Code stated:[58]

> Whoever entices a virgin girl shall be charged with fornication and shall pay her parents reparation commensurate with the parents' social position. The girl shall not be prosecuted. Any intermediary shall be condemned to penal servitude or exile.[59]

In Article 403, it states:

> Rape shall be punished by exile or death, the reparation to be paid by the offender shall be one degree higher than that for fornication .... If death results, the offender's property shall be seized and handed over to the victim's family.[60]

Article 406,[61] setting out the punishments for incest (defined to include not only blood relatives but also all those within the five degrees of mourning), followed the rest of the Lê Code which "uniformly imposed decapitation on all the cases of incest mentioned".[62] A regulation in the *Hong-duc thien chinh* forbade sexual relations between a student and the wife of his teacher, a contravention of one of the five sacrosanct social relationships. In the case cited, the student guilty of this act was condemned to death; the teacher's wife was beaten with "50 strokes of the light cane" and her property was transferred to her husband's name.[63]

Property and Inheritance[64]

Other features of the Lê laws, which might be expected to further the goal of Confucianization, were those pertaining to family property and inheritance. Unlike the laws regulating moral conduct and social space, however, laws relating to property continued to follow pre-existing social practice. Property rights were reaffirmed for all children equally, and the recognition of separate property held on the maternal side. In this area, Vietnamese law of the Lê diverged from Chinese law of the Ming and Qing as well as from nineteenth century Nguyen dynastic and French colonial law (which supported the latter overall).[65] For a brief discussion on property, the annotations to the Lê Code by Nguyen Ngoc Huy and Ta Van Tai provide an excellent introduction. Here they note (in reference to Article 375, "First addition to the chapter on property"):

> In summary, these regulations gave the wife property rights equal to those of the husband, with only this slight difference, due to custom: the usufruct of the widow ceased upon her remarriage while the same right of the widower only expired at his death.[66]

Again, in Article 377, with regard to the disposition of property after the death of a husband and where the children are still minors, they note:

> ... article 377 demonstrates that under the Le *the widow with children preserved, even after remarriage, her administrative powers over the family estate.* [*sic*] ... this is another basic difference between the Le Code on the one hand and the Chinese and Nguyen Codes on the other.[67]

While not disrupting earlier inheritance practices, the government set down the principle of *huong hoa* (incense and fire) land to be passed on by the family to support rituals and ceremonies to the ancestors. The "remainder of the estate would be *divided among the children equally without distinction as to sex* [*sic*]". Article 388 was explicit about this in using the terms "brothers and sisters".[68] The law was firm on the equal division of the inheritance among all the children of the same mother. Secondary wives and female serfs, however, were left with smaller portions,[69] and "children of extramarital unions were not given any inheritance rights".[70]

Although the Lê followed local practice with regard to the disposition of family property because of the deep commitment to it among the population, the gradual spread of the Confucian family system had by the nineteenth century further undermined the social position of women. As a result, the nineteenth-century Nguyen dynasty did not perceive the need, unlike the Lê, to reaffirm the status of women and their more equal claims to property earlier. This change was detrimental to their status, as has been said, and it carried through to the French administration and later to the Vietnamese administration, as will be mentioned below.

De Jure to *De Facto*: Law and Society in the Nineteenth and Twentieth Centuries

The overthrow of the Lê and the accession of a new dynasty in the early nineteenth century left the new government with the problem of unifying a fractious state with far more territory to control than before. To meet the challenge, it turned to the same strategy as the Lê in the fifteenth century, and intensified the Confucianization of the law code and regulations of the dynasty.[71] Once again, this had a detrimental effect on the position of women, on gender relationships, and on society at large. While not the subject of this chapter, the changes to the Nguyen code in general deprived women and children (particularly female children) of property rights in marriage, concubinage and widowhood, for example.[72] The acquiescence of the population to this stronger iteration of the code indicates that the Confucianized regulations imposed on society in the fifteenth century had apparently become the *de facto* situation of the late nineteenth century.

Western visitors and French scholars in Vietnam from the nineteenth century tended to confirm this picture. In their case, the assumption prevailed that the Vietnam they encountered was a part of the "timeless Orient". French scholars, reading the classical Chinese-language court texts, accepted the representation in official records that Vietnam was thoroughly Confucianized in the fifteenth century. A host of travellers during this period described the country as "little China", "smaller dragon", and so on. These writers saw confirmation of their view on the Confucianization of Vietnam in Vietnamese literature and culture. Vietnamese books on folk literature and poetry, and their translations into Western languages, recorded a litany of songs on the woman's lot as a long-suffering yet loyal wife, mother, and daughter-in-law.[73] Vietnamese scholars called foreigners' attention to Vietnamese classics like

Kim Van Kieu and the *Plaint of the Warrior's Wife*, so well known to the Vietnamese reading public, and as time went on, to foreign translations.[74] Students in Western universities to this day often assume without question the image of the downtrodden women of Vietnam or China, oppressed by the unremitting weight of tradition.[75]

Yet the literary sources used in the study of women and the family actually contain a number of competing voices. The Confucian discourse, however, often seems to drown the others out. The works mentioned above and many others like them, provide (like many of the edicts, laws and decrees of the fifteenth century) a continuous counterpoint to the sombre Confucian melody by evoking another world where girls and boys exchanged songs of love, husbands went to work for the families of their wives, and peasant couples celebrated their work together in the paddy fields. A class divide begins to open up as well. Some wives of Confucian scholars criticize lazy husbands who let their wives do all the work in the fields. Other women aspire to marry a scholar in the hope of having an easier life. Anthologies of classical poetry all include the witty and elegant verse of the famous eighteenth-century poetess Ho Xuan Huong. Not for her the pallid verses of a borrowed literary genre.

> Snail
>
> Father and mother joined to breed a snail.
> I grovel night and day among foul weeds.
> Sir, if you love me, take my breastpiece off.
> Don't wiggle, please, your finger in my hole![76]

All these examples serve to underscore the critical point that Vietnamese society comprised, and comprises, a complicated pattern of cultural influences, with non-Confucian and Confucian custom existing side by side. Nowhere is this more apparent than in records of village customs which even in the nineteenth and twentieth centuries invoke far more ancient cultural practices.

In 1875, the renowned Vietnamese Catholic educator, Petrus Truong Vinh Ky, made a journey to northern Vietnam and wrote in the conventional Sino-Vietnamese genre a record of his travels. In it are descriptions of music, dance and contests echoing ancient fertility rites — exactly the sort of practice that the late fifteenth century Lê ruler strove so valiantly to eradicate. Here is part of Truong Vinh Ky's account of village ceremonies in the province of Hanoi (the region outside the city itself):

> During the eighth month it is the custom of people to hold a banquet in the communal house of the village, to make sacrifice to the spirits, and to pray for peace .... On these occasions, it is their custom to listen to performances given by singing girls, ... watch [various] contests ...

> They also participate in eel-catching competitions, and a game called "statue carving". Prizes are offered for the winners of all these competitions.
>
> The competitors in the eel catching contest are a boy and a girl who embrace one another, each placing one arm about the other's shoulders. They then thrust their free arms into the neck of a deep jar in which an eel has been released. The first one to catch the eel wins the prize.
>
> In the statue carving or sculpting contest a beautiful and seductive singing girl wearing a thin diaphanous silk dress and shiny taffeta trousers sits on a platform erected in a pond or lake. The young men who are the competitors in the game put on loincloths made from paper, go out to the platform, and pretend to sculpt the girl sitting there. When a competitor is unable to restrain his passion any longer his penis rises into an erection and burst through the paper loincloth. This bursting of the loincloth eliminates him from the contest. Whenever it happens the competitor dives head first into the water to hide his shame.[77]

Even in the present day, a number of villages in Vinh Phu province have festivals celebrating the New Year with ceremonial objects in the form of genitalia.[78] The game of "grabbing eels" described above in 1875 is again recorded here.

> The game of "grabbing eels" was also common in Vinh Phu and Ha Bac provinces during the New Year. In one variant in Vinh Phu province, "each team of a young man and a woman, observed the following rule: while trying to catch the eel in the jar, neither the young man nor the woman could look into the jar, and the young man had to keep one hand on the young woman's breasts. At the same time, a committee of judges closely watched, along with fellow villagers who called out and teased them. [The author goes on to say that this ancient custom symbolised sexual relations and abundant fertility].[79]

In a village in Ha Bac province, "the game of jostling" is still practised. "During the Spring Festival, men and women jostle against each other".[80] The game takes place as part of the New Year ceremonies "at the temple where the female god Linh Son My Nuong is worshipped".[81] The game is played again at the end of the festival.

> The closing day of the festival ends as the lights of the communal house go out and young men and women are free to express their love for each other. Those couples that become husband and wife only pay half a *cheo* (fee) and girls who become pregnant on this evening are not fined or condemned by others.[82]

A number of other festivals in these provinces allowed sexual relations without penalty as part of the ceremonies to renew the earth and bring abundance.

> In Quang Lam Commune, Ha Bac Province, young men and women sang songs expressing their love for each other between the 5th and 12th days of the third lunar month. …
>
> On these days, they would sit close together, arms around each other's shoulders, singing songs. … After the festival, couples that sang to each other could marry if they wanted.[83]

The last custom has echoes of the ancient dance of intertwining arms and legs, the practice that was of concern to early fifteenth-century Confucian scholars. The music mentioned in all these examples refers to the types of "profane music" to which the Le enforcers of the Confucian rites took such exception.

To sum up, while some villages maintained folk customs, which gave greater importance to youth, fertility and sexuality, in the cities the Confucian ethic fostered a more puritanical attitude. This tendancy continued throughout the socialist period until after 1986.[84] Since that time, the economic and social climate under the *renovation* policy, which introduced aspects of a market economy and fostered wide economic and cultural contacts beyond the socialist world, has generated a new openness and sense of inquiry into aspects of Vietnamese cultural identity. Yet the question remains why, given the legal history outlined above, Confucian social practices are assumed by legal and government specialists, and certainly by the older generations (anyone over forty) to be the basis of customary law. As such, these customary practices become the reference point for implementing regulations where the law itself, on land and marriage, for example, is ambiguous.

History, Law and Memory

What has happened to collective memory of the non-Confucian past, so clearly illustrated throughout this discussion? Why until recently has the voice of Confucian discourse drowned out that of other customary practices? Historians working in the area of history and memory,[85] have begun to consider such issues on a theoretical level. Thelen, writing about memory and American history, offers one answer:

> The struggle for possession and interpretation of memory is rooted in the conflict and interplay among social, political, and cultural interests and values in the present.[86]

Today as the social climate in Vietnam (and not only in Vietnam but also around the world) grows more open, the interests of groups that have been subordinated for a long time are now coming to the fore. These include the interests of women and youth. The discourse in which new social concerns are being raised, however, is not a legal one but arises out of the need to consider issues of health and the prevention of disease, for example, in the context of changing social relations. In 1989, when I was doing research in Vietnam, an article appeared in the state newspaper which generated comment because it addressed "social evils" in the guise of prostitution. It was a rare event at a time when the socialist policy of reporting still encouraged coverage of positive rather than negative stories to show society in the best possible light.

A decade later, interest in the sociology of sexuality[87] is developing with applications in the research and prevention of sexually transmitted diseases (STDs). There is a resurgence of interest in local customs of a non-Confucian kind, as evidence cited above reveals. The fact that publications are appearing which describe "non-Confucian" social influences in a climate of somewhat greater personal and social space (at least in urban areas) reveals efforts at a reassessment of social identity and, perhaps, a reclaiming of parts of the social heritage that had been suppressed earlier.

Law and Memory

If social and economic changes are leading to public acknowledgement in social sciences and literature of a Vietnamese society with a non-Confucian heritage similar to mainland Southeast Asian and Thai-speaking groups, what has been the situation in the area of law? Rather than reflecting these changes in issues of marriage and land, for example, the law in many ways appears to be functioning as the conservator of Confucian values. It maintains a silence in a number of key areas, leaving it to the communes to sort out the anomalies on a case-by-case basis.[88] In law, the impact of Confucianization remains omnipresent today both in the cities and in the countryside. For example, women who marry expect to live with their husbands' family, especially if they marry eldest sons. Daughters in the city (particularly in the over-thirty age group[89]) will complain that they take more responsibility in the care of their parents than their brothers do, and yet when the parents pass on, the eldest sons will still inherit the house and they are left with no position at all. At the same time, the Marriage and Family Law 1986 states that "children have equal duties and rights in the family" which commentators interpret to mean that "girls have equal rights with boys to inherit from their parents".[90]

In terms of land law, in the countryside, the person designated as the official head of the household with the authorization to keep the papers on the family's land allotment, or for credit purposes, is the oldest living relative on the male side. In a case from the early 1990s, for example, a 53-year-old woman was a widow and the main support of her husband's elderly mother and her young adult (and unmarried) children (two sons and a daughter). Her mother-in-law was, as a matter of course, designated the head of the household; the daughter-in-law who was the designated principal labourer complained that she had all the responsibility and no authority over the property (house) or land. Her elderly mother-in-law was still in charge.[91] When officials are asked about situations such as these, they often agree that it would have been best in the regulations to require both the husband and wife's signatures on land-use certificates (LUC).[92] When the question is pursued, the reply generally given is that while the state has its sphere of authority, the commune possesses the authority of custom. The fact that these village customs may be more the product of nineteenth-century revision of an older and more equitable code has up to now been lost to collective memory.

The importation of a Western legal framework in the area of family and property law leads to other contradictions as well. The family law is based on the Western example (which is itself predicated on the nuclear family). It speaks in terms of equal rights for spouses, simultaneously with the duties of the children to care for their parents. Thus, it makes no allowances for the existence of minor wives and their children, for example.[93] At the same time, the state (which recently amended the law to recognize the legitimacy of single mothers, in June 2000), in its land and property laws makes no statements in law to encompass social realities which fall outside the constraints of the legal framework of the Marriage Law and Land Law.

While women complain about these injustices in their lives, and officials often agree that these practices are unjust, the common conclusion is that it is "our culture" and "our customs". This makes it very difficult for law-makers, especially women law-makers, for instance, to argue for greater equality in property holding and inheritance.

One would hope that the trend towards a reclamation of the past that is evident in some areas will spread to law and lend weight to the arguments of those who are working to re-legitimize the status of women and children in law, particularly in relation to issues of family and property.

Appendix

Glossary of Chinese and *nom* (Vietnamese demotic) characters

cheo [music]

優

Dai Viet Su Ky Toan Thu,

大越史記全書

Hong-duc Thien Chinh Thu

洪德善政

Le Tac, *An Nam Chi Luoc*

黎崱，安南志略

Liji, Shisan jing zhushu buzheng

禮記，十三經注疏

Quoc Trieu Hinh Luat

國朝刑律

li lien (ri ren)

哩嗹

Notes

[1] Continued by the French colonial administration, following former Imperial Court practice.

[2] See, for example , the practice of British colonial courts as described by Thomas Metcalf, *Ideologies of the Raj* (Cambridge, 1994).

[3] The Nguyen dynasty, 1802–1945.

[4] A. B. Woodside, *Vietnam and the Chinese Model* (Cambridge: Harvard University Press, 1971).

[5] See Esta S. Ungar, "Gender and Real Property in Vietnamese Law and Practice: Commune, Household and Individual", in *Asian Law Through Australian Eyes*, edited by Veronica Taylor (Sydney: LBC Information Services, 1997), pp. 286ff.

[6] Cf. K. W. Taylor, *The Birth of Vietnam* (Berkeley, 1983); and O. W. Wolters, *History, Culture and Region in Southeast Asian Perspectives* (Ithaca: Cornell Southeast Asia Programme Publications, 1999).

[7] With the household unit being the lowest level in the chain of social organization, while the commune or village remained the lowest level administrative unit.

[8] The Lê Code, popularly known as the Hong-duc Code (after the fourth ruler), was based in the main on the edicts, decrees, and laws promulgated from 1434 to 1497 in the first century of the dynasty. See the *Hong Duc Thien Chinh* [Book of Good Government of the Hong-duc period] (Saigon: Nam-ha An-quan, 1959) (Chinese and Vietnamese text) which contains a number of decrees dating from the fifteenth century of the Lê dynasty. Another indispensable source is the section on the fifteenth-century Lê dynasty in the official dynastic compilation of the history of the Vietnamese dynasties: *Dai Viet Su Ky Toan Thu*, collated edition (Chinese script), by Ch'en Ching-ho (Tokyo: Tokyo Daigaku, Toyo Bunka Kenkyujo Fuzoku Toyogaku Buken Senta, Showa 59–61 [1984–1986] (hereafter cited as *CCH*); and romanized Vietnamese edition, *Dai Viet Su Ky Toan Thu* (Hanoi: Khoa Hoa Xa Hai, 1972), vol. 3 (hereafter cited as *DVSK*). The formal *Quoc trieu Hinh Luat* [Penal Code of the Reigning Dynasty] (or *Le Trieu Hinh Luat* [Penal Code of the Le dynasty]) whose existing editions were compiled later in the dynasty, was the product of these and similar sources, no longer or only partially extant, like the *Thien Nam du ha tap* (1487). For a detailed discussion of the sources and editions of the Lê Code, an indispensable source is the magisterial translation and commentary: *The Lê Code: Law in Traditional Vietnam: A Comparative Sino-Vietnamese Legal Study with Historical-Juridical Analysis and Annotations*, translated and annotated by Nguyen Ngoc Huy and Ta Van Tai, with Tran Van Liem (London: Ohio University Press, 1987), 3 vols. On editions and sources of the code, see vol. 1, pp. 19–29. For extensive notes on the legal and historical commentary, see vol. 2, subtitled "Legal and Historical Annotations on the Le Code" (Accompanied by comparisons with other traditional Chinese and Vietnamese codes). For further comparison of Vietnamese and Chinese law, especially for the seventeenth and eighteenth centuries, see the excellent study by Yu Insun, *Law and Society in Seventeenth and Eighteenth Century Vietnam* (Seoul: Asiatic Research Center, Korea University, 1990), first published in 1978.

[9] Prof. Dinh Gia Khanh stated categorically that the inclusion of bilateral kinship and inheritance in the Hong-duc Code was due to the fact that this custom was too strongly held for the state to overturn it. This differs from the interpretation sometimes given that its inclusion may be construed as a sign of the court's respect for local custom. Interview with the author, Hanoi, July 1989.

[10] For a European comparison, see the role of the church courts in moral regulation, in Martin Ingram, *Church Courts, Sex and Marriage in England, 1570–1640* (Cambridge: Cambridge University Press, 1987).

[11] See Dinh Gia Khanh and Chu Xuan Dien, *Van hoc dan gian* [Folk literature] (Hanoi: Dai hoc va trung hoc chuyen nghiep, 1972), v. 1, p. 246 regarding the new separation in the fifteenth century between court and common folk with respect to rites and music.

[12] The classic Chinese literary depiction of these principles occurs in Ba Jin's epic novel of the 1930s, *The Family*, where the climactic tension between youth and age erupts in the scene where the eldest son's wife is forced from the paternal family compound, outside the city walls, across a bridge, locked into a room in a strange house, there to give birth without disturbing the spirit of the clan patriarch whose body lies in state in the ancestral hall of the compound. As she gives birth, her husband pounds frantically on the door of the birthing room, stopped by custom from contact with the polluting female act of birthing. Ba Jin (Pa Chin), *The Family*, translated by Stanley Shapiro, 3rd ed. (Beijing: Foreign Languages Publishing House, 1978), pp. 255–69.

[13] *The Tang Code*, translated, with an introduction by Wallace Johnson (Princeton: Princeton University Press, 1979), p. 17.

[14] Nguyen Ngoc Huy, Ta Van Tai, with Tran Van Liem, *The Le Code: Law in Traditional Vietnam: A Comparative Sino-Vietnamese Legal Study with Historical-Juridical Analysis and Annotations* (Ohio: Ohio University Press, 1987), vol. 2, pp. 21–22.

[15] As in the Tang and all later Chinese imperial codes, the term *nei luan* (civil war) is applied to "incest" as well, thus underscoring the sacrosanct nature of the Confucian family as the microcosm of the state.

[16] Nguyen Ngoc Huy et al., *The Le Code*, vol. 2, p. 21.

[17] Ibid., p. 21.

[18] Ibid., p. 20.

[19] M. Foucault, *The History of Sexuality* (London: Penguin, 1978), vol. 1, p. 120.

[20] To apply Foucault not to the "conventional" bourgeois family emerging in early nineteenth-century Europe but to Confucianization of the family in Asia, see Michel Foucault, *Sexuality*, vol. 1, translated by Robert Hurley (London: Penguin, 1990), p. 122.

[21] John R. Gillis, ed., "Memory and Identity: The History of a Relationship" in *Commemorations: The Politics of National Identity* (Princeton: 1994), p. 5.

[22] Le dynasty (1427–1788).

[23] Nguyen Ngoc Huy et al., *The Le Code*, vol. 2, pp. 234, 237, 265, and discussion below.

[24] For a reading of the Sino-Vietnamese character *uu* as *phuong cheo*, see Thieu-Chuu, *Han-Viet Tu-dien* [Chinese-Vietnamese Dictionary], (Saigon: Khai Tri, 1942), p. 36.

[25] *DVSK*, vol. 3, p. 116; and CCH edition, p. 595. Duong Dinh Khue wrote that in 1437 the Lê ruler banned the *dam* music used in the courts of the earlier dynasties back in the tenth century. In this style of court music, the dancers '"wore loincloths and bared their chests to dance … sang *cheo* music …". See Dinh Gia Khanh, op. cit., p. 246.

[26] For an illustration, see Vien Khao Co, *Hung vuong dung nuoc* [Hung Kings found the nation] (Hanoi: Khoa hoc xa hoi, 1970), vol. 4, p. 169. The Viet Muong people who live in the hills northwest of Hanoi retained the use of bronze drums in their ceremonies, and their customs (like those of the Tay, Nung, and Thai mentioned below) are similar in a number of respects to the non-Confucian customs of the ethnic Vietnamese.

[27] This is preserved in a children's game "*cai hoa cai nu*". For information on this passage, on the *li lien* dance as the vestige of a powerful fertility rite, and its connection with the ancient power and magic, as well as its depiction on the bronze drums, I am indebted to Professor Le Van Lan, Institute of Historical Research, Hanoi, June 1989.

[28] *DVSK*, vol. 3, p. 139; and CCH edition, p. 613.

[29] *Liji, Shisan jing zhushu* 12 (Taibei: Shijie shuju, n.d.): 15b–16a. The commentary explains that the Chinese called the Vietnamese territory "Jiao Zhi" because of the rite of females and males intertwining their necks and ankles in the dance (as depicted on the bronze drums). I am grateful to Professor David Holm, Institute of Asian Languages and Societies, Melbourne University, for furnishing me with this information and reference, July 2000.

[30] *DVSK*, vol. 3, p. 150; and CCH edition, pp. 620–21.

[31] *DVSK*, vol. 3, p. 164; and CCH edition, p. 631. The annotator of the Hanoi edition suggests that the music and dance mentioned here are preserved in some form in the dance of the village of Xuan-pha near the founder's birthplace in Thanh Hoa (p. 164, note 140).

[32] *DVSK*, vol. 3, p. 227. It is important to point out that his provision refers to the ethnic minorities as well, many of whom followed practices which gave greater status to women and the woman's familial line, a practice completely contradicting the Confucian Chinese model. (On the ethnic minorities and their perpetuation of customs which were followed by the ethnic Vietnamese until the fifteenth century and after, see below.)

[33] *Hong-duc Thien Chinh Thu* [Book of Good Government of the Hong-duc period], translated by Nguyen Si Giac, preface by Vu Van Mau (Saigon: Nam-ha An-quan, 1959), Article 128, pp. 59–60 (hereafter cited as *HDTC*).

[34] For information on the Zhuang, I am grateful for a discussion with Prof. David Holm, Melbourne, July 2000.

[35] *HDTC*, Article 301, p. 137.

[36] Nguyen Ngoc Huy et al., vol. 1 (*Lê Code*), Article 323, p. 186.

[37] Nguyen Ngoc Huy et al., vol. 2, p. 181, Article 324.
[38] Ibid., p. 185 (commentary on Article 334).
[39] Ibid., p. 185 (commentary on Article 334).
[40] *HDTC*, Article 100, pp. 46–47; Nguyen Ngoc Huy et al. cite the *Du Ha Tap* for an edict of 1470 fixing the marriage ceremonies. See vol. 2, p. 177; also on the edict of 1478, see the *DVSK*'s description of the ceremonies to be held for marriage, vol. 3, p. 263.
[41] *HDTC*, Article 100.
[42] Duong Dinh Khue, "La littérature populaire vietnamienne" (Saigon, 1967), p. 90; in Vietnamese, "Cong anh lam re da hai nam rong ... Thang chin mua bui gio may, Cat lay gau nuoc chan tay rung roi".
[43] Do Thuy Binh, *Hon Nhan va Gia Dinh cac dan toc Tay, Nung va Thai o Viet Nam* [Marriage and Family among the Tay, Nung and Thai peoples in Vietnam], (Hanoi: Khoa Hoc Xa Hoi, 1994), p. 194 and p. 197. In Thuan Chau and the Dien Bien valley, the period of time between the marriage ceremony and entry into the husband's house lasts from one to three years. "The male must do every kind of work in the [female's] family, the most difficult and heaviest tasks". (p. 197).
[44] "The most common pattern of post-marital residence is one that leads a husband to settle with his wife's family, at least for a short period following marriage. The rural peoples of northeastern Thailand, Laos, and northern Thailand almost invariably follow this pattern, whereas in Cambodia and Burma, the pattern is followed by a majority, but not all of the people. Charles F. Keyes, *The Golden Peninsula: Culture and Adaptation in Mainland Southeast Asia* (London: Collier Macmillan, 1977), p. 133.
[45] According to Do Thuy Binh writing in the 1990s, among the Tay and the Nung peoples, after a woman has formally taken a husband, "she is still relatively free ... and still has the freedom to sing 'alternating chants' with other male friends .... Only when she is about to give birth to her first child, will the bride definitely move in with her husband's household". Do Thuy Binh, op. cit., p. 195.
[46] Nguyen Ngoc Huy et al., vol. 2, p. 177.
[47] Ibid.
[48] Ibid., vol. 2, p. 177; and *DVSK* (1469), vol. 3, p. 226.
[49] Nguyen Ngoc Huy et al., vol. 1 (Article 314), pp. 184–85.
[50] *HDTC*, no. 278, p. 125 (and related laws in this section).
[51] *HDTC*, "Admonitions", nos. 95–99, p. 45.
[52] *HDTC*, p. 45.
[53] *HDTC*, no. 269, pp. 115–16.
[54] Dinh Gia Khanh and Chu Xuan Dien, *Van hoc dan gian* [Folk literature] (Hanoi: Dai hoc va trung hoc chuyen nghiep, 1972), 2 vols. (hereafter cited as *DGK*), vol. 1, p. 246; and *DVSK*, vol. 3, p. 194.
[55] *HDTC*, no. 117, p. 55.

[56] *DVSK*, vol. 3, p. 221.

[57] Nguyen Ngoc Huy et al., vol. 2, p. 233. In addition to the examples given above, the annotators of the Lê Code cited many others; for example, in the same passage, referring to the Lê Code, Article 401: "Thus, unmarried people who had sexual relations, even as a prelude to their marriage or after marriage but before the complete delivery of the wedding gifts, were punished (Decree no. 1, 6, 7 of 1489 reported in *DHT*, pp. 33b–34a, and *HDTC*, par. 288): the man with penal servitude (as a paddy-farming soldier), the woman with 50 strokes of the light stick. Even if they merely talked together alone at night, penal servitude would be imposed (Decree 10 of the 1489, in *DHT*, p. 34a). (Probably, the penal servitude applied only to the man, and the woman would also receive 50 strokes of the light stick).

[58] Ibid., vol. 2, p. 234.

[59] Ibid., vol. 1 (*Lê Code*), p. 207.

[60] Ibid., vol. 1, p. 207.

[61] Ibid., pp. 207–8.

[62] Ibid., vol. 2, p. 235. The commentators point out that this was a more severe punishment than the Tang code, which punished a number of cases with exile to only 2,000 *li*.

[63] Ibid., vol. 2, p. 181; and *HDTC*, no. 286, pp. 128–29.

[64] For an extensive discussion of property and inheritance from a specialist historian's point of view, see the fine chapter by Insun Yu, *Law and Society in Seventeenth and Eighteenth Century Vietnam* (Seoul: Asiatic Research Centre, Korea University, 1990), pp. 89–104.

[65] Nguyen Ngoc Huy et al. give an example of the French dilemma, citing "what Robert Lingat … called an eighty-year struggle within the French judicial system between the Chinese conception of the family and the genuinely Vietnamese conception". See vol. 2, pp. 209–10. On the French tilt towards the Chinese practice, see Nguyen Phu Duc, *La Veuve en Droit Vietnamien* [The Widow in Vietnamese Law] (Saigon: Ministere de l'Education Nationale, 1964).

[66] Nguyen Ngoc Huy et al., vol. 2, p. 208.

[67] Ibid., p. 210.

[68] Ibid., p. 225.

[69] Ibid., p. 225. The authors also point out a difference under the Nguyen dynasty, which followed the Chinese model "stipulating equal parts for all kinds of sons" and "omitted the daughters completely". See vol. 2, p. 225.

[70] Ibid., vol. 2, p. 225.

[71] Cf. A. B. Woodside, *Vietnam and the Confucian Model* (Cambridge: Harvard University Press, 1971).

[72] Cf. Nguyen Phu Duc, *La Veuve en Droit Vietnamien* [The Widow in Vietnamese Law] (Saigon: Ministere de l'Education Nationale, 1964).

[73] Huynh Sanh Thong, ed. and trans., *The Heritage of Vietnamese Poetry* (New Haven: Yale University Press, 1979). For biographical information, see Nguyen Khac Vien, et al., *Anthologie de la litterature vietnamienne*, with

introduction and notes by Nguyen Khac Vien and Huu Ngoc, translated by Le Van Chat, et al. (Hanoi: Foreign Languages Publishing House, 1973), vol. 2; P. Grace, et al., eds., *Vietnamese Women in Society and Revolution: The French Colonial Period*, with translations by Nguyen Hoi Chan and Ngo Vinh Long (Cambridge, MA: Vietnam Resource Center, 1974); and Ngo Vinh Long, ed. and trans., *Before the Revolution: Vietnamese Peasants under the French* (Cambridge, MA: MIT Press, 1973).

[74] These classic works of poetry, with all their beauty and skill, thematically reaffirm the official culture with the sacrifice of their heroines in conformity to Confucian virtues.

[75] I come across this image regularly in student essays for my classes in the History Department at the University of Western Australia.

[76] Huynh Sanh Thong, op. cit., p. 99; for biographical information see, Nguyen Khac Vien, op. cit., vol. 2, p. 170.

[77] P. J. B. Truong Vinh Ky, *Voyage to Tonking in the Year At-hoi* (1876), translated and edited by P. J. Honey (London: School of Oriental and African Studies, University of London, 1982), pp. 90–91.

[78] Bui Xuan My, cited in Khuat Thu Hong, *Study on Sexuality in Vietnam: The Known and Unknown Issues*, Regional Working Papers, no. 11 (Hanoi: Population Council, 1998), p. 12.

[79] Ibid., p. 12.

[80] Ibid., p. 12.

[81] Ibid.

[82] Ibid., p. 13.

[83] Ibid.

[84] Ibid., pp. 22–34.

[85] A sub-set of historical studies that has grown up since the 1980s out of the work of historians of peasant society, of European medieval history, of the Holocaust, of commemorations and cultural "nation-making" in the nineteenth and twentieth centuries.

[86] David Thelan, "Memory and American History", *Journal of American History* 75, no. 4, (1989): 1127.

[87] A pioneering work in this field is by Khuat Thu Hong, *Study on Sexuality in Vietnam: The Known and Unknown Issues*, Regional Working Papers, no. 11 (Hanoi: Population Council, 1998). See also for a brief discussion of this trend towards openness and a reassessment of aspects of cultural identity.

[88] Ungar, op. cit., pp. 290–91.

[89] Younger people in the cities (the twenty-somethings) are beginning to question these customs, however.

[90] Ungar, op. cit., pp. 288–94.

[91] Case study from fieldwork in Ha Tay, March 1993, carried out in conjunction with the Centre for Women's Research, as part of the SRV-UNDP Feasibility Study on Vietnam Land Management System (VIE/91/004).

[92] Ungar, op. cit., pp. 292–94. This would allow rural wives, for example, whose husbands are often away in the city working and are out of touch for months at a time, to qualify for credit against the certificate for the use of the family. Under the situation as it stands, only the designated head of household (normally the husband) can authorize any actions regarding the LUC.

[93] Ungar, op. cit., pp. 291–92; Le Thi, "Thuc trang gia dinh Viet Nam va vai tro cua nguoi phu nu trong gia dinh" [The real situtation of the Vietnamese family and the role of women in the family], In Centre for Women's Research Vietnam Social Sciences Committee, *Nguoi phu nu va gia dinh Viet Nam hien nay* [Women and the family in Vietnam today] (Hanoi: Social Sciences, 1991), p. 16; and Mai Huy Bich, "A Distinctive Feature of the Meaning of Reproduction in Confucian Family Tradition in the Red River Delta", in *Sociological Studies on the Vietnamese Family*, edited by Tuong Lai (Hanoi: Social Sciences Publishing House, 1991), pp. 54–56.

References

Anthologie de la littérature vietnamienne, with Introduction and Notes by Nguyen Khac Vien and Huu Ngoc, translated by Le Van Chat, et al., vol. 2. Hanoi: Foreign Languages Publishing House, 1973.

Ba Jin (Pa Chin). *The Family*, translated by Stanley Shapiro, 3rd edition. Beijing: Foreign Languages Publishing House, 1978.

Ch'en Ching-ho, ed. *Dai Viet Su Ky Toan Thu*, collated edition [Chinese script]. Tokyo: Tokyo Daigaku, Toyo Bunka Kenkyujo Fuzoku Toyogaku Buken Senta, Showa 59–61 (1984–1986). 3 vols.

Dai Viet Su Ky Toan Thu, vol. 3. Hanoi: Khoa hoc xa hoi, 1972.

Dinh Gia Khanh and Chu Xuan Dien. *Van hoc dan gian* [Folk literature]. Hanoi: Dai hoc va trung hoc chuyen nghiep, 1972. 2 vols.

Do Thai Dong. "Modifications of the Traditional Family in the South of Vietnam". In *Sociological Studies on the Vietnamese Family*, edited by Tuong Lai, pp. 69–83. Hanoi: Social Sciences Publishing House, 1991.

Do Thuy Binh. *Hon Nhan va Gia Dinh cac dan toc Tay, Nung va Thai o Viet Nam* [Marriage and Family among the Tay, Nung, and Thai Peoples of Vietnam]. Hanoi: Khoa Hoc Xa Hoi, 1994.

Duong Dinh Khue. "*La litterature populaire vietnamienne*" [Vietnamese folk literature]". Saigon, 1967.

Foucault, Michel. *Discipline and Punish: The Birth of the Prison*. New York: Vintage Books, 1977.

————. *The History of Sexuality*, vol. 1: *Introduction*, translated by Robert Hurley. London: Penguin, 1990.

Gillis, John R., ed. "Memory and Identity: The History of a Relationship". In *Commemorations: The Politics of National Identity*. Princeton: Princeton University Press, 1994.

Hong-duc Thien Chinh Thu [Book of Good Government of the Hong-duc period], translated by Nguyen Si Giac, preface by Vu Van Mau. Saigon: Nam-ha An-quan, 1959. (Copy of original Chinese character text with romanised Vietnamese translation).

Huynh Sanh Thong, ed. and trans. *The Heritage of Vietnamese Poetry*. New Haven: Yale University Press, 1979.

Keyes, Charles F. *The Golden Peninsula: Culture and Adaptation in Mainland Southeast Asia*. London: Collier Macmillan, 1977.

Khuat Thu Hong. *Study on Sexuality in Vietnam: The Known and Unknown Issues*. Regional Working Papers, no. 11. Hanoi: Population Council, 1998.

Nguyen Ngoc Huy and Ta Van Tai, with Tran Van Liem. *The Le Code: Law in Traditional Vietnam: A Comparative Sino-Vietnamese Legal Study with Historical-Juridical Analysis and Annotations*. London: Ohio University Press, 1987. 3 vols.

Le Tac. *An Nam Chi Luoc*, translated and edited by Ch'en Ching-ho [Tran Kinh Hoa]. Hue: University of Hue, 1961. (Chinese script with romanised Vietnamese translation and annotations.)

Le Thi. "Thuc trang gia dinh Viet Nam va vai tro cua nguoi phu nu trong gia dinh" [The real situation of the Vietnamese family and the role of women in the family]. In Centre for Women's Research, Vietnam Social Sciences Committee, *Nguoi phu nu va gia dinh Viet Nam hien nay* [Women and the family in Vietnam today]. Hanoi: Social Sciences, 1991.

Le Trieu Hinh Luat [Law Code of the Reigning (Le) Dynasty], translated by Nguyen Si Giac, with preface by Vu Van Mau. Saigon: Truong Luat-khoa dai-hoc [Faculty of the Law School], 1961. (Includes facsimile of Chinese character woodblock text.)

Liji, Shisan jing zhushu buzheng. Taibei: Shijei shuju, n.d.

Mai Huy Bich. "A Distinctive Feature of the Meaning of Reproduction in Confucian Family Tradition in the Red River Delta". In *Sociological Studies on the Vietnamese Family*, edited by Tuong Lai, pp. 49–56. Hanoi: Social Sciences Publishing House, 1991.

Ngo Vinh Long, ed. and trans. *Before the Revolution: Vietnamese Peasants under the French*. Cambridge, MA: MIT Press, 1973.

Nguyen Phu Duc. *La Veuve en Droit Vietnamien* [The Widow in Vietnamese Law]. Saigon: Ministere de l'Education Nationale, 1964.

Nguyen Thi Dinh (trans. Nguyen Tu Huyen). "La loi sur le mariage et la famille et l'emancipation de la femme" [The law on marriage and the family and the emancipation of woman]. *Bulletin de droit* (Hanoi, 1987), p. 1.

Nguyen Tu Chi. "Preliminary Notes on the Family of the Viet". *Sociological Studies on the Vietnamese Family*, edited by Tuong Lai, pp. 57–67. Hanoi: Social Sciences Publishing House, 1991.

Nguyen Van Huyen and Hoang Vinh. *Nhung trong dong Dong Son da phat trien o Viet-Nam*. Hanoi: Vien Bao Tang lich su Vietnam, 1975.

"La nouvelle loi sur le mariage et la famille" [The new law on marriage and the family]. *Bulletin de droit* [Law Review], special edition (Hanoi, 1987), p. 1.

P. J. B. Truong Vinh Ky. *Voyage to Tonking in the Year At-hoi (1876)*, translated and edited by P. J. Honey. London: School of Oriental and African Studies, University of London, 1982.

Quoc Trieu Hinh Luat [Law Code of the Reigning (Le) Dynasty], translated by Cao Nai Quang. Saigon: Truong Luat-khoa dai-hoc [Faculty of the Law School], 1956. (Includes facsimile of Chinese character woodblock text.)

The Tang Code, translated with an Introduction by Wallace Johnson. Princeton: Princeton University Press, 1979.

Thelan, David. "Memory and American history". *Journal of American History* 75, no. 4 (1989): 1117–29.

Tuong Lai, ed. *Sociological Studies on the Vietnamese Family*. Hanoi: Social Sciences Publishing House, 1991.

P. Grace, et al., eds., with translation by Nguyen Hoi Chan and Ngo Vinh Long. *Vietnamese Women in Society and Revolution: The French Colonial Period*. Cambridge, MA: Vietnam Resource Center, 1974.

Ungar, Esta. "Gender and Real Property in Vietnamese Law and Practice: Commune, Household and Individual". In *Asian Law Through Australian Eyes*, edited by Veronica Taylor, pp. 281–96. Sydney: LBC Information Services, 1997.

Vien khao co hoc. *Hung vuong dung nuoc* [The Hung kings found the nation], vol. 4. Hanoi: Khoa hoc xa hoi, 1970.

Woodside, A. B. *Vietnam and the Confucian Model*. Cambridge: Harvard University Press, 1971.

Yu, Insun. "Bilateral social pattern and the status of women in traditional Vietnam". *Southeast Asia Research* 7, no. 2 (1999): 215–31.

————. *Law and society in seventeenth and eighteenth century Vietnam*. Seoul: Asiatic Research Center, Korea University, 1990.

4

ENGLISH LAW AND THE INVENTION OF CHINESE PERSONAL LAW IN SINGAPORE AND MALAYSIA

M. B. Hooker

Personal law is a unique phenomenon and is found only in the ex-British possessions which had English (common) law as the general law for the population. It may be defined as rules (a) applicable only to persons of a specified race or religion (b) formulated in English law terminology (c) derived from indigenous manners or customs (d) but subject to English law standards of justice, equity, and good conscience. Well-known examples include the various African customary laws, the Anglo-Muslim laws of India, Pakistan, and Malaysia, the native laws of Sabah and Sarawak, Burmese Buddhist law, the Malay *adat* (customary) law and, the subject of this chapter, Chinese personal law.[1]

Personal laws are sometimes called "hybrid" laws, and so they are in the sense that they are the offspring of quite different parents. However, they are more than just that. From the earliest days of their being, which we conventionally date from 1781[2] in Calcutta, they have taken on a life of their own. In some instances, for example, Burmese Buddhist law, they are a pure invention of the nineteenth century English judicial mind. By "invention", I mean no denigration; on the contrary, this law, like all personal laws, can be seen as a true multicultural creation, the worth of which has stood the test of time. This is true also for such major systems as the Anglo-Muslim and Anglo-Hindu laws. Purists can and do criticize the complex rules developed over the past 200 years on the grounds of serious judicial error in understanding the classical texts of Islam and Hinduism. This is a perfectly legitimate complaint. However, the mistakes of 200 years ago live on and the whole corpus actually works quite well; it has a social as well as a judicial utility. The source of a personal law, whether it is by mistake or invention, does not really matter; it is the process of its growth and development which is important. The law reports contain rich material for what is now called "cross-cultural" studies but it remains under-used by historians and social scientists. One example is given in this chapter.

The Chinese personal laws of Singapore, Malaysia, and Burma have been described elsewhere.[3] They are alive and well in 1999 in Malaysia and Singapore although their position in Burma is not known. Why are they still alive and well and what is their strength? One answer to this question lies in their intellectual heritage and this will be demonstrated by an analysis of one of the most famous judicial decisions among all personal laws. This is the case of the *Estate of Choo Eng Choon decd.*,[4] commonly cited as the "Six Widows Case", decided in 1908. While this decision was made ninety years ago, it is not just a matter of academic legal history. That decision set the intellectual paradigm for all subsequent judgements in Chinese personal laws. As we examine the judgement we will see the English-educated judge(s) trying to understand a foreign culture and to fit it into the technical demands of the existing laws at that time. This intellectual effort, of course, continues today for all the personal laws of the ex-British colonies. The colonial legacy is a fact of legal life as well of contemporary history.

The best introduction to the facts and the decision is to read the headnote, which is reproduced here. The reader should note that this was a split decision, with one judge dissenting from the majority view. Two judges recognized the offspring of polygamous unions as entitled to succeed to a deceased's estate, while one voted against. All the judgements are technically competent and as we study each one, the reasons for the different answers will become apparent.

> A Chinese British-born subject domiciled in Singapore died intestate. During his life-time at various dates he had contracted unions with both "principal wives" and "inferior wives", and had had issue by them. One of his "inferior wives", was married [to him] after she had borne him a son. On Appeal from LAW Ag. C. J.:
>
> *Held* by the Court of Appeal. (HYNDMAN-JONES C. J., and BRADDELL J. *dissentiente* SERCOMBE SMITH, J.).

The Chinese are polygamous. The Courts of the Straits Settlements will recognize polygamous unions for the purposes of succession and legitimacy among native inhabitants whose religion permits polygamy; this, either by Charter of 1855, or *ex comitate.*

In any case it has been the well-established practice of the Courts here to do so; following *In the goods of Lao Leong An,* and *In the goods of Ing Ah Mit,* this Court ought not now to reverse those decisions, and the practices based thereon.

The widows whether "principal" or "inferior" are entitled to divide equally amongst them the one-third share which the Statute of Distributions gives to the "widow".

A child legitimised *per subsequens matrimonium* according to Chinese Law is entitled to share in the two-thirds share which the Statute of Distributions gives to the "children".

While the Court will pay every respect to the evidence of expert witnesses, they cannot be permitted to decide for the Court. The Court must weigh their evidence and decide for itself, nor [sic] hesitating to disagree with experts, if necessary.

Per SERCOMBE SMITH J.:
Unions contracted by Chinese British-born subjects domiciled within the Straits Settlements are governed by the English Common Law, and a marriage to be valid at Common Law must be celebrated in the presence of an episcopally ordained clergy man. Unless a Chinese British-born subject so domiciled is married according to Common Law his marriage is held to be invalid and the issue illegitimate.

Further, the Chinese are polygamous; the Courts here cannot recognize polygamy. Polygamous unions are therefore invalid and the issue illegitimate.

Held per LAW Ag. C. J., on motions to vary the Registrar's certificate:
The word "widow" is a word in itself capable only of a quite limited construction and cannot include persons who are not "lawful widows", following *Quaih Kee Hoch v. Wee Geoh Neo.*

Previous decisions are binding on a Court of co-ordinate jurisdiction unless there are very strong reasons to the contrary.

These proceedings began in November 1907 before an exceptionally strong Bench and with the participation of leading Straits Counsel.[5] This is a point to be borne in mind. The quality of a judgement depends on the quality of judges and the arguments put forward by Counsel. One of the reasons for this judgement having lasted so long is the quite exceptional competence of the lawyers taking part, including the judge at the first instance (Law Ag. C. J.) and on appeal (Hyndman-Jones C. J. and Braddell J.[6]) as well as such notable barristers as R. G. Van Someren and E. R. Koek, both of whom are referred to by the judges in the course of the proceedings.

This is an appropriate place to briefly consider one aspect of the common law adversarial system, the relationship between the judge or judges and counsel. The job of counsel is "to assist the Court". What this means in practice is that counsel would advance propositions with which "the judge is forced to come to terms, openly and explicitly."[7] For this reason, exchanges between the judge and counsel are especially important in understanding how a decision is arrived at. Unfortunately, the general run of law reports do not give the exchanges although, as in the present case, parts of the counsel's presentation and cross-examination of witnesses are sometimes given. In other words, as Professor Zander points out,[8] our understanding of the court's decision is less than complete. Included are some of the passages, especially on evidence, to which we now turn.

The first is a passage between Mr Montague Harris, Counsel for one of the widows, who tried to persuade Law Ag. C. J. that as the British Courts in India had recognized that Jews were polygamous, British Courts generally had recognized polygamous marriages. The judge refused to be drawn by this, saying (at p.141):

> [Law Ag C. J. But surely Jews in England are not polygamous?] No; they are not by custom but there is nothing to prevent it in their laws. In Saigon and Singapore Chinese are polygamous, how can it be said then that the Chinese are not a polygamous race. The customs of native races are never interfered with by the British Government. If there were any case when the Courts had not recognised the validity of second marriages amongst the Chinese it is curious *Mr Registrar VELGE is unaware of it, and also Mr Van Someren, two gentlemen who have more experience of these Courts in point of time than any others in the Colony.* (emphasis added)

The reference to the reputation of local counsel is notable. A further passage, this time from the Supreme Court, is equally interesting as examples of judicial intervention (report at pp. 170–73):

> *Hon. E. C. Ellis* (with him *R. G. Van Someren*) for the appellant.
> In this Appeal there are two questions: (1) Does polygamy exist in China? (2) If so, will the courts here recognize it in the case of a British-born subject domiciled in Singapore?
>
> [Hyndman-Jones C. J. — Is there not this further question "assuming the Courts have been wrong in the past, can we now upset such a current of authority?"]
> *Ellis* — I am prepared to argue there is no such current of authority but even if there were, I shall argue that your Lordship should not hesitate to upset it.

> [Hyndman-Jones C. J. — Then I will call your attention to the case of …

Mr Ellis then went on to deal with Straits precedent (see below) and Statute. Concerning the latter, we have the following exchanges on the Mohameden Marriage Ordinance (1880). Mr Ellis proposed that the Ordinance "was passed not to remove doubts about Muslim law but about the way the Courts had interpreted and adopted it".

> [BRADDELL J. — Was not that Ordinance passed for purposes of codification? There is nothing in the preamble to show it was passed to remove doubts such as you suggest.]
>
> *Ellis* — I think not. Parts III, VI and V only confirm what the Courts had previously done, and therefore if the Courts were correct, that was so much waste. Parts I and II do not make any startling alterations.
>
> There has been no such legislation in the case of the Chinese. Why? Because either polygamy does not exist in China or the legislature deemed it was a custom to which its sanction should not be given. Mohamedan polygamy had long ago been known to exist, and the Court decisions as to Chinese go back as far as its decisions as to Mohamedans. Yet the Legislature has not intervened as regards Chinese though Judicial decisions regarding them are in *pari materia* with those affecting Mohamedans
>
> [Hyndman-Jones C. J. — would it not have been more necessary for the legislature to intervene in the case of Chinese to negative decisions if they were wrong?]
>
> *Ellis* — I prefer to look at it from the other point of view. Non-legislation for Chinese was due to the assumption that polygamy did not exist among them and therefore there was no need to validate an alleged custom not recognized as existing at all.
>
> He then referred to affidavits of *Suen Sze Ting*, *Tao Ping Ling*, and *Wong Kim Fah*, and of *Lao Chong Yow in Rex v. Sim Boon Lip*. These show that concubinage, not polygamy, is recognized by the law of China. A concubine should not be called a secondary wife. A ceremony for taking a concubine exists but is not always performed.
>
> [SERCOMBE SMITH J. — If secondary wives go through a ceremony does it indicate polygamy and not concubinage?]
>
> *Ellis* — There are no degrees of concubinage; they have no rights whatever in the household. As to *Staunton*'s translation of the Chinese Penal Code, it is not exact.
>
> [SERCOMBE SMITH J. — No; see what he says himself at pxxxi of the preface].

The headings seem not to be in the original text. The expression "secondary wife" is *Staunton's* preference, cf. Note at p. III. Again I find "wives" is used. I understand there is no Chinese plural.

[SERCOMBE SMITH J. — There is a way of denoting the plural, sometimes by a special word and also by inflection.

The note at p. iii of *Staunton* gives the keynote to his translation of the Chinese character as "inferior or secondary wife" rather than as "concubine".]

[BRADDELL J. — Were any Chinese dictionaries referred to in the lower Court?] None. *Staunton* merely preferred the term "inferior wife" to "concubine".

[SERCOMBE SMITH J. — But there is a word for concubine. It is composed of the characters "crime" and "woman".]

In these extracts we can see the judges being invited down various paths but objecting and suggesting different routes.

ORAL SOURCES AS TO CHINESE CUSTOM

The court took oral evidence from five sources: two Consuls-General of China, two prominent Chinese merchants and the Supreme Court's Chinese interpreter. This spread of sources is interesting because it demonstrates the wide definition of "expert" then in vogue in the Straits Settlements. In particular, the recourse to two prominent merchants was carried over from the nineteenth century tradition of appealing to notable members of the Straits Chinese community, dating obviously from the period of the "Kapitan China" in early Straits Chinese history.[9] On the other hand, recourse to the Consuls-General represented a new trend which indicated the importance with which the Imperial Government attached to the affairs of the Chinese outside China. Equally important, it shows that the colonial court was willing to take seriously the competence of imperial officers as expert witnesses in its judicial administration. The Court's own Chinese interpreter was an obvious choice because it was with him that the court felt most at home; after all, he knew the procedure and he was able to formulate his evidence in terms he knew the court would understand. These comments need to be borne in mind in the description which follows.

1. First, the Acting Consul-General, Mr Suen Tze Ting. He described himself as the former holder of the office of Judicial Assistant to the Prefect of

Canton. He relied on this as his main qualification, stating further that only persons of official position "... are learned in the law ... I have studied the law of China and read Chinese law books". His evidence can be summarized as follows. A Chinese man may have only one lawful wife who gains her status and honour (that is, official honour) through her husband. A Chinese man may take a "concubine" who attains official honour through her sons but "not through the father of her children who is not her husband but her lord and master". She may be purchased with money without any ceremony. The evidence then set out the essentials of a marriage at Chinese law; these included the "three marriage documents, six stages of ceremony, the go-between, and the escorting of the bride from her house in procession". The authority cited was the *Ta Tsing Leau Li.*

There was no cross-examination on this affidavit, which is significant because all the other oral evidence was questioned. What was its fate in the judgements? It is mentioned only briefly and even then, it is lumped together with the evidence of the second Consul appointed to Singapore in October 1907.

2. The Chinese Consul-General, Mr To Ping Ling. His evidence was brief: Chinese law permits only one wife, the others are concubines. The law reports say that he was examined by Mr Van Someren but gives no details.

The evidence of the two Consuls was assessed twice, in the lower courts and on appeal. As to the former, Law Ag. C. J. thought that the Consul's evidence was "asked to prove too much" (judgement at p.146), by which he meant that while the evidence purported to define "marriage" for the Chinese, this was not the same as an "ordinary marriage in Christendom" — the "marriages" were "... two different things". The definition of marriage in China was not the same as the definition in France or Italy or Britain. In short, because of what we would now call cultural difference, the evidence of the Consuls-General was "unhelpful".

The same judge then went on to question the relevance of the evidence for conditions in the Straits Settlements. His point was that, whatever the position in China, these women whom the Consuls would dismiss as concubines actually had a legal "status" (emphasis in the original) in the Straits (judgement at pp. 151–52). In other words, the evidence of the laws of China could not be decisive in the Straits. In any case, "it was not sufficiently set out for us to be able to form a definite opinion on the matter".

In the appeal, two views of the evidence were taken. The first was that accounts of the laws and customs of the Chinese in *China written by English scholars/observers* can be read to show that the Consul's evidence was at best partial and, generally, debateable at best. Hyndman-Jones C. J. went through the Consul's evidence (pp.186–87) and found contradictions. Essentially, his view was that the oral evidence from these sources was unsafe in the light of contemporary scholarship. Secondly, he raised the important and difficult issue of the status of the expert evidence given to the court. He says (at p.135)

> However great the respect we may entertain for the views of these gentlemen, we cannot allow them to decide this question for us.

We turn now to other oral evidence offered.

3. From two prominent Chinese merchants.
   The evidence of both (one Hakka, one Kheh) consisted entirely of describing the prescribed ceremonies to constitute a marriage where the woman was the principal wife ("*C'hi*"), not a secondary wife ("*Ch'ieh*"). Both affidavits went into elaborate detail as to proposal, exchange of papers, gifts, worship of the gods and ancestors, dressing of the bride, the acceptance of the bride into the husband's family and giving of wedding feasts for family and guests. The whole, as described, was an elaborate affair involving contractual premises, and intention given in public to marry. There was no doubt that there was a change of status in the woman's legal position (see judgement at pp.125ff).

The interesting feature is that none of the judges referred to this mass of evidence. On the other hand, the two Chinese merchants were subject to very elaborate cross-examination by all counsels on points of ceremonial detail. For example, Mr Wong Kim Fah was cross-examined at length and some of his answers include:

> Been to Chinese school in Muntok up to 13 or 14 years of age — went into business after that — I have read when required — have not done any reading — I don't know Dutch or English — I can write Chinese fairly well — and read it but not quite well — I have lived in China — went there when 17 and returned when 18 — only twice I have been in China — I lived in a big town in the prefecture of Kwee Chew — I am a Hakka — never lived in Saigon — I knew *Choo Eng Choon* but not very intimately — I did not know any of his wives — Invited to a wedding at his house twice but did not attend — both invitations in one month — I have never investigated the question of the number of human relationships — The marriage *document is the most important*

> point in a legal marriage — A woman who lives with a man and is not properly married is a "*Chip*" — A Chinaman can have only one wife and she is called a "*Ch'i*". I have one wife and another woman — I have three children, a son and three daughters by the other woman — She is a "*Chip*" — I do not regard her as a wife — She is living in the same house — If a man went through the same ceremonies with two women one would be considered a "*Ch'i*" and the other a "*Chip*" — The "*Chip*" would not get a share of his property — her children would — All the children except the eldest share alike — but the eldest gets more — one share more than the others — Amongst rich people there are five ceremonies or six called "*Koh Niang San*", "*Koh Chew Li*", "*Siong Tean*" (*Cheoh Tow*), "*Niang Chin*", "*Sam Chew*", "*Chip Nee Cheow*" — They are performed in the order given but not on the same day — on different days. Among poor people the whole thing is done in one day. Some of the ceremonies are left out. I should say the following ceremonies would constitute a good marriage — the "*Siong Tean*" (*Cheoh Tow*) and the joint worship of ancestors without any further ceremony.

The whole point of this detail was clearly to impress on the judges the essential nature of ceremony[10] because it is this which distinguishes the different status of wives. The evidence from both the affidavit and arising out of the cross-examination *took for granted the fact* of polygamy in Straits Chinese custom. The point appears to have been accepted without argument by the court as to this evidence (see below on textbooks).

4. From the Supreme Court Chief Chinese Interpreter
   The evidence here laid less stress on ceremony than the previous affidavits. In the opinion of the interpreter, the essential elements were the worship of the gods and the ancestral tablets. These constituted the formal marriage. An additional ceremony was optional and was at the discretion of the parties involved. More elaborate ceremonials were common among the wealthy. There was some cross-examination (p. 33) but only to clarify what the interpreter meant by "joss" and "ancestral tablets".

A final comment on the oral evidence: it was assumed throughout that the Chinese are polygamous but the judges were not prepared to accept this on its own as decisive. We turn now to the next source.

BOOKS AS EVIDENCE OF CHINESE CUSTOM

Traditionally, textbooks have never been highly regarded as authority in common law.[11] However, this has never been the case in Britain's eastern possessions. From India right through to China, there has been a consistent and widespread recourse to law books on all the major legal systems from at least the late eighteenth century. Books on the "laws of China" have been freely cited in the earliest Straits Settlements cases, and in this case were intensively argued about.

The issue was the place of scholarship in the common law courts. It must be remembered that it was not until the mid-nineteenth century that courses in English law were accepted as university subjects. Before that time, law was learnt through an apprentice system, "on the job" as it were, and was thus a matter of learning a technique or a vocation. It was not part of a "liberal" (code for "intellectual") education. This is a view which, even in the mid-twentieth century in some places, still had its adherents with quite important subjects (for example, commercial law) being taught in universities by part-time lecturers who were full-time practitioners. The whole tone of teaching was essentially anti-intellectual, and the word "academic" is still commonly used to mean "of no practical relevance". It is pejorative. A rational explanation of this has been given by Mr Justice Megarry in commenting on the authority of his own textbook, actually cited to him in court:[12]

> The process of authorship is entirely different from that of judicial decision. The author, no doubt, has the benefit of a broad and comprehensive study of his chosen subject as a whole, together with a lengthy period of gestation, and intermittent opportunities for reconsideration. But he is exposed to the perils of yielding to preconceptions, and he lacks the advantage of that impact and sharpening of focus which the detailed facts of a particular case bring to a judge. Above all, he has to form his ideas without the aid of the purifying ordeal of skilled argument on the specific facts of a contested case. Argued law is tough law. ... I would therefore give credit to the words of any reputable author in book or article as expressing tenable and arguable ideas, as fertilisers of thought, and as conveniently expressing the fruits of research in print, often in apt and persuasive language. But I would do no more than that; and in particular I would expose those views to the testing and refining process of argument. Today, as of old, by good disputing shall the law be well known.

This was written in 1968 but it is still quite applicable to 1908. We take four authors who appear prominently in the "Six Widows" litigation.

(a) Sir George Staunton: his *Ta Tsing Leau Li* (or *Lee*) was published[13] in 1810 and, amazingly, remained the only English version[14] of a Chinese law text until Professor Johnson published his *T'ang Code* in 1979.[15] Staunton's sub-title is *The Penal Laws of China.* It can best be described as a partial translation together with some rationalization of the content. It retained a high status for later scholarly reference.[16] At the time of the "Six Widows" litigation, it certainly had an importance as the basic reference text and was referred to by all parties in the case.

The first important reference is in Law Ag. C. J. in whose judgement we read the following (p.142):

> The law is given showing the failing sons or legal representatives of sons by the "principal wife" (as *Staunton* calls her) the several sons or their representatives, according to seniority of the other "wives" (as he calls them), are entitled to succeed to hereditary rank and titles. Then at p. 84 the law is given showing that if the "first wife" (as *Staunton* calls her) has completed her fiftieth year and has no children living, it is allowed to appoint her eldest son by the other "wives" (as *Staunton* calls them) to the inheritance. ...
>
> On the page just referred to is given s. 103 of the Code, having "Regard to rank and priority among wives" (as *Staunton* calls them), and he points out in the footnote to the section, that he prefers to speak of "inferior wives" ...

I am not here concerned with the content of this passage but with the judicial comments in parenthesis ("as Staunton calls her, calls them"). What is being signalled here is a judicial caution as to the status of a well-known scholarship. Indeed, Law Ag. C. J., in a passage immediately preceding those just cited, drew attention to the generally recognized high status of Staunton's translation. Staunton was an FRS (Fellow of the Royal Society) and "... a real master of Chinese literature", but this did not determine the issue for the Acting Chief Justice.

The same issue was taken by Hyndman-Jones C. J. on appeal. He referred to "appropriate books and treatises written by various learned persons" (judgement at p.181), and then, with reference to Staunton, went on to say:

> Staunton's translation is admittedly not a literal translation of the original; he has endeavoured, as he says, "to draw the middle line" between the unfaithfulness of a "free" and the ungracefulness and almost ungrammatical obscurity of a "close version," and he has ventured "to embody in words these ideas which, though forming an integral part of the sense of the text, yet were left by a sort of ellipsis to be understood by implication and reference".
>
> While accepting his translation generally, it is important to remember these facts.

The judge here is using Staunton's own words to put the expert evidence, of however high a quality of scholarship, into a common law perspective. A little later (judgement at p. 184) he refers to him as a "learned author" with whom other "learned authors differ". In short, the "real master of Chinese literature" has now become just one of a number — perhaps not even a *primus inter pares*! That this is not mere suggestion on my part is borne out by a direct judicial questioning of Staunton's competence. Hyndman-Jones, for example, says with reference to Staunton's translation, "… I have been unable to find any reference to the subject …". I have no idea what the judge's qualifications were but it is clear that he was reading Staunton's translation and picking up inconsistencies within it. He then goes on (at p. 188):

> The interpreters tell us that the eleven paragraphs into which *Staunton* has divided the section appear in the original as five paragraphs; and that the paragraph to which I have referred is part of the two paragraphs immediately preceding it, which themselves are part of each other. These paragraphs therefore, of which *Staunton* has made three, really stand by themselves as one paragraph, and it is arguable that the words used by *Staunton*, viz., "in all the foregoing cases" are limited …

However, at least Hyndman-Jones was prepared to consider the evidence from the printed books. On the other hand, Sercombe-Smith J., the dissenting judge in this case, was not prepared to go even this far. At p. 197 of the judgement, he says that a text such as Staunton's cannot be taken as evidence of a foreign law because it does not fall within the requirement of the then (1893) Evidence Ordinance. While it is true that the Ordinance is rather restrictive, this seems to be going a little too far. It is certainly against the existing trend in earlier Straits and Indian cases where such material was freely admitted.

The second comment made by Sercombe-Smith J. is more to the point here. He doubts "the accuracy of Staunton's translation in which I myself have detected inaccuracies" (pp. 197–98 of the judgement). What he actually means is a published criticism of Staunton by George Jamieson, a noted authority on Chinese law (see below) who said (*on another matter*) "… Staunton seems to have misunderstood the drift of this …". In short, Sercombe-Smith is citing another writer but selectively to prove his own opinion. It is a classic case of selection, and in any "academic" or intellectual sense quite unacceptable.

(b) James Dyer Ball (referred to as Dyer Ball in the judgement) wrote *Things Chinese*[17] and his career was as a Chinese interpreter in the Supreme Court of Hong Kong. He is first cited by Law Ag. C. J. in part confirmation of Staunton and in part contradiction to him as to secondary wives or concubines. He uses the terms interchangeably. A much longer passage taken from his *Things Chinese* appears to Hyndman-Jones C. J. to mean (judgement at p.184):

> If *Dyer Ball* therefore is to be trusted it comes to this that the Chinese are monogamous, but that concubinage is a recognized institution, the dominant reason for the institution being that it is an all-important matter with the Chinese that a man should beget a son to offer sacrifices for him on his decease and to worship at his tomb; and the concubine is regarded, failing the wife, as the means by which this great essential may be attained. But is *Dyer Ball* to be trusted? I do not mean to imply that he has knowingly misrepresented the position; but it is possible that in dealing with such a variety of subjects as he has done in his very valuable treatise, he may have fallen into inaccuracies with regard to some of them.

The Chief Justice then goes on to cite other authorities, including Staunton, to the contrary (judgement at pp. 186–87) and concludes that the evidence is "very contradictory". However, he clearly prefers Staunton and, though not explicit, this seems to be because Staunton is translating and commenting on a law "text". Ball, on the other hand, is generally describing manners and customs rather than being solely concerned with a text which is recognizably "of law". I think this is an important point because it illustrates a predisposition in the judiciary to take "law texts" more seriously than material which is not so obviously a "law text". The "variety of subjects" he treated in his book may well have militated against him.

(c) George Thompson Hare. The comments just made about Ball seem to be borne out by the respect paid to this author. He was Protector of Chinese[18] in the Straits Settlements and Federated Malay States (FMS) and wrote *Notes on the Family Law and Usages of the Chinese.*[19] He is first cited in the preliminary judgement of Law Ag. C. J. at great length and with total approval (judgement pp. 144–45). The following passage demonstrates why his evidence was so persuasive:

> At p. 6 he gives the ceremonials usually observed in taking a "concubine" (as he calls her) and points out, at p. 7, that if these ceremonies are not observed, she is not generally recognized as one of the family. On the same page he points out that the "secondary wives or concubines" (as he calls them) have a legal status, though it is different from that of a principal wife; he shows that apparently an official may take a secondary wife but she must not be an actress

> or a woman of light conversation, p. 8. At p. 9 Mr Hare says that in taking a concubine a man can please his own taste if he first gets permission from his parents and his first wife. At p. 10 he says there is no dishonour in being the son of a supplementary wife. At p. 11 he says the child of a recognized concubine, publicly received into the family, is legitimate. At p. 12 he says it is considered the moral duty of a man who has unlawfully begotten a child by a woman to marry her as a principal wife if he has none or to marry her as a concubine (as he calls it) if he already has a principal wife. At p. 13 he says that after the wife has passed her fiftieth year, if she has no son, the eldest son of any of the concubines is to be regarded as the father's eldest son.

There is much more in the same vein. It is clear that Hare is writing on the practices of the Straits Chinese and he is writing with the authority of his position as Protector of Chinese. In other words, he is more that just the writer of a known text. He is a practical civil servant whose duty is to carry out an administration. His book is really a "manual for administration", and thus is "official" in a way other texts are not. This relatively high degree of status was important to Law Ag. C. J. and obviously tended to convert Hare's work into something approaching an authority in common law terms.

On the other hand, at appeal level, in the judgement of Hyndman Jones C. J., Hare has less impact. He is cited respectfully enough (judgement at pp. 182–83) and there is no dissent from his views. However, the Chief Justice is much more selective in his citations. Furthermore, Hare's comment is treated as but one among others. They are equal to those of Staunton and Dyer Ball. There is no question of superiority or authority stemming from the official nature of Hare's work. A similar approach was taken by Mr Justice Braddell in a short comment (at p. 225).

Sir George Staunton, Dyer Ball, and George Hare are the main authors, but I should draw attention to one further source which is, as far as I am aware, unique in the annals of British colonial law in Southeast Asia. This is the reference to French colonial law in Indochina, specifically to Cochinchina. The citation from Law Ag. C. J. is as follows (judgement at p. 150):

> I might here point out that in French Cochin China under a special law, polygamy in the case of Chinese, amongst other Asiatics, appears to be recognized, and marriages of the first and second rank it appears are registered. I would refer to the *Precis de la Legislation civil Annamite* [*sic*], published in 1884 at the Government Printing Office in Saigon, Cf. Art. 2 p. 35, Art. 13 p. 12, and what is said on pp. 18 and 19 under

> the headings of "Conditions of Validity and of Nullity of Marriage", and of "Rights and Duties it creates"; see also *Droit Annamite Doctrine et Jurisprudence et Matiere civile indigene*, by the Vice-President of the Court of Appeal in Indochina published at Saigon in 1900. Compare what is said at p. 120 about it being lawful for an Annamite to have several wives at the same time, but only one of the first rank, and see what is said in the introduction as to the attention that has been paid by the Court to native custom.

While I have had some difficulty in finding all the sources cited,[20] I have no doubt that the influence of French practice was important in this judgement. This is rather strange. Evidence of a foreign *colonial law*, whilst accessible, is certainly not in the tradition of Chinese personal law precedent in the Straits and Malay States. Why was it brought forward? The answer seems to be that it concerned "Chinese", but if so why was not the contemporary Netherlands East Indies (NEI) policy on "Chinese" (Foreign Orientals) referred to as well? The answer may be simply that the English judges knew French, but they could not read Dutch. The fact remains, however, that the French reference was made. With the benefit of about ninety years of hindsight, we can see that the reference was inappropriate. The French colonial legal system had nothing in common with British colonial law and, in respect of the various Chinese minorities quite different approaches were adopted. For the French, it was the political status (*citoyen, asiatique assimilé, sujet*) which was the defining element. For the British, it was race and/or religion. A further complication in the French material was that, in Indochina, the so-called Annamite Laws, which applied to the Chinese as *assimilé* were in fact "Chinese", that is, taken from the Vietnamese version of the (1813) Hong-duc law. None of this was in the minds of the judges in the case we are studying.

A further reference to French material also occurs in the judgement. It is put forward by Sercombe Smith J. (the dissenting judge) referring to a pamphlet by one Pierre Hoang entitled "Le Mariage Chinois au point de vue legal", published in Shanghai by the Catholic Mission. The judge gives no date and, at the time of writing, I have not been able to trace it. The extract is short and merely says that a husband may have only one recognized wife and that a concubine, while not a slave, has only a humble position. If the master is not pleased with her, she can be returned, "… *son renvoi est sans importance*". Obviously, it is impossible to judge the material from this short extract but given its source — the Catholic Mission — and Sercombe Smith's tendency to *partial* or selective quotation, it must be treated with some caution.

This concludes our summary of books as evidence of Chinese law and custom. The main conclusions we can draw are:

1. that the authority of a text for the court depends on the form — recognizably "legal" — in which it is written,
2. the status of the author; those who are lawyers or in law in some way are taken more seriously, and
3. the predilection of the individual judge.

Selective citation to buttress a view *already held* is apparent from this reading of the judgement. One need not be surprised at this; the phenomenon of judges deciding an issue and only then looking for supporting evidence is not a new discovery.[21] Neither is it to say that the court is acting impulsively or capriciously. It is merely a recognition of the fact that new or unusual circumstances, times, and places require judicial initiative.[22] Society does not stand still but legislation is often in a state of stasis; in the case of the colonies, much of the English precedent based on English legislation at the time of our case (early twentieth century) was just not suitable for local conditions, and it is to this we now turn.

ENGLISH PRECEDENT AND THE "POLYGAMIST"

A statute states the law, it says what the law is on the subject of the statute. Of course, that is not the end of the matter; how do we know what a statute means in a particular case? The answer is that courts tell us through the interpretation of a statute. Over time, a statute gets its meaning through a line of precedents, the result of which might well surprise the original legislators. These are commonplace comments, but they are not always understood by those who have no legal training.

With this preliminary, we can now look at the Chinese polygamist in the Straits and Malay States — not the individual as such but his estate, its administration and distribution in respect of or to the *widow*. What is a *widow* in the case of the polygamist? The judges had to start from the definition of "widow" in English law and, therefore, "marriage". One cannot recognize the former without the latter. We have to remember that the whole focus of the discussion is inheritance — to qualify, one had to be the "legitimate" child of a formally recognized marriage.

The basic legislation around which all revolved was the Statute of Distributions (1640) which for long had remained the determinant for inheritance both in Britain and in the colonies. It was not repealed until 1925, seventeen years after the judgements in our case. It must be remembered that the judges in the "Six Widows" case would have been educated and brought up within the bounds of the Statute. In modern parlance, it was "deep background" in their thinking about marriage and the incidents of marriage. The Statute and the cases arising from it set the agenda for debate and decision. The facts of Chinese life and cultures were, therefore, not taken "straight" but filtered through nineteenth century judicial education. Even allowing for the vagaries of precedent, this remains historically true.

For the purposes of this chapter, the Statute provided that if a husband died without leaving a will, the widow took one-third and the children two-thirds of the estate between them. This rule proceeded from the realization that while marriage is a contract, it is also a special sort of contract in that the terms are already regulated and not set by the parties. It has been described as a *status*. The Statute did not contemplate polygamy (polygyny). This was not within the original meaning of status or contract of an English marriage. It was not until the consequences of imperial expansion came to trouble the courts (from the nineteenth century) that the question of status even arose. It is with this background that we now turn to the English precedent cited in the "Six Widows" case. There are four precedents which all the judges mentioned. In order of dates these are:

Warrender v. Warrender (1835)[23]

The issue was the jurisdiction of a Scots Court[24] to hear a suit to dissolve a marriage *contracted in England*. Because the husband's *domicile* was Scotland, and the conjugal residence was Scotland, the essentials of the marriage were thus to be regulated by the law of Scotland, including a suit to dissolve the marriage. In other words, the *formalities* of the contract were not decisive.

Brooke v. Brooke (1861)[25]

A marriage was celebrated in Denmark between a domiciled Englishman and his deceased wife's sister, also domiciled in England. The marriage was legal by Danish law, but illegal at that date (1850) by English law. The House of Lords found that the marriage was void because the law of the husband's domicile did not allow it. As the court put it:[26]

> But while the forms of entering into a contract of marriage are to be regulated by the *lex loci contractus*, the law of the country in which it is to be celebrated, the essentials of the marriage depend on the *lex domicilii*, the country in which the parties are domiciled at the time of the marriage, and in which the matrimonial residence is contemplated.

Hyde v. Hyde (1866)[27]

An Englishman, who had become a Mormon, married a Mormon lady in Utah according to Mormon rites. Children were born but he later left his wife and petitioned for divorce in England, after his wife had already entered into another marriage under Mormon rites. The petition was refused because the original marriage was potentially polygamous, and the laws of England are wholly inapplicable to polygamy. The parties to such marriages are not entitled to relief under the matrimonial law of England. The latter contemplates "… a voluntary union for life of one man and one woman to the exclusion of all others".[28]

Re: Bethell (1888)[29]

The deceased, domiciled in England, married a Bechuana lady in accordance with her tribal custom. The marriage was potentially polygamous. Just after his death, a child was born. Was the child legitimate, that is, was the marriage valid for the purposes of inheritance under an English will? The answer was no; a person with an English *domicile* lacks the capacity to contract a (potentially or actual) polygamous union.

These were the precedents[30] which the court in the "Six Widows" case had to reconcile with the realities of Chinese marriage in the Straits Settlements. Taken collectively, the English precedent was not in favour of the Chinese marriage, which was potentially polygamous, had an unfamiliar form of celebration, and took no account of domicile or intended matrimonial home. How then can it be avoided, given the fundamental nature of the precedent in common law?

The answer lies in the technique of distinguishing — that is, are there material differences between the facts of the earlier precedent and the present case to justify not following the former? Underlying this is the acknowledged fact that rules are made for a particular set of circumstances, but circumstances change. How far can change be accommodated and how quickly can accommodations be made? These questions are at the heart of common law, and over the years a complex set of precedents has been developed to deal with the issue. This is not the place to discuss those precedents.[31] Instead, we shall look at how the judges in the "Six Widows" case dealt with the cases outlined above.[32]

We take first Law Ag C. J. (judgement at pp. 153–54) who admitted that these cases, and others cited,[33] could be read to show that English law cannot recognize polygamous marriages for any purpose. However, he then went on to say "… this is not perhaps clear". He then began to distinguish the earlier precedent. First, the *Hyde* case. He distinguished this case because it was concerned with the dissolution of marriage. It was not, as in the "Six Widows" case before him, a question of succession or legitimacy. All that the *Hyde* case decided was that, because of the nature of their marriage, the parties could not apply for relief under the (then) matrimonial laws of England. In short, he distinguished the *Hyde* case from the "Six Widows" case because the facts and issues in both were dissimilar — on the one hand, dissolution, on the other, inheritance.

Secondly, he adopted the same approach in dealing with the *Warrender* case. This was also one on dissolution only. However, Law then went further and cited a passage from the *Warrender* case which he had already wished to distinguish, so as to support a contrary position — that is, that polygamy *as such* is no bar to recognition, however undefined this might be. The passage[34] is as follows:

> If indeed there go two things under one and the same name in different countries, if that which is called marriage is of a different nature in each, there may be room for holding we are to consider the thing to which the parties have bound themselves, according to its legal acceptance in the country where the obligation was contracted.

Finally, in respect of the *Bethell* case, the fact that Mr Bethell had an English domicile was crucial. It was of course crucial in the *Bethell* case itself, but it was emphasized in Law's judgement as a point of departure. He said, in effect, that the then existing conceptions of private international law were always subject to local (that is, non-English) circumstances and that the principles of private international law were not necessarily applicable in a colonial English court in the same way that they might be in England.

The first two points I have made on the *Hyde* and *Warrender* cases are obvious. The last in the *Bethell* case, however, is fundamental. Polygamous people do exist in the British colonies; they do not live in England and have no interest in or recourse to English law in England. That was the position in 1908. These, then, are the three grounds on which Mr Justice Law distinguished the English precedents.

We turn now to the appeal judgements in the "Six Widows" case and we take first Mr Justice Hyndman-Jones' argument (judgement at pp. 188–192). He referred to the *Bethell* case (p. 189), saying:

> ... [T]hat concubinage is not only tolerated by the law but recognized as a legal institution, *then concubinage ceases to be that which Western nations are accustomed to understand by that name and becomes polygamy* ...[35] [Emphasis in the original].

His reference to the *Bethell* case at this point was simply to show that the "circumstances of plurality of women" was a known fact in British colonies.

At this point, he introduced the *Hyde* case by citing a passage from the judgement of Lord Penzance, who said:[36]

> The Court does not profess to decide upon the rights of succession or legitimacy which it might be proper to accord to the issue of polygamous unions; nor upon the rights or obligations which people living under the sanction of such unions may have created for themselves. All that is intended to be decided is that as between each other they are not entitled to the remedies, the adjudication or relief of the matrimonial law of England.

This was exactly the same point made by Mr Justice Law at the lower level.

The Chief Justice then returned to the *Bethell* case (after references to Straits cases — see below) to distinguish it on a rather obvious ground. He said that Mr Justice Sterling, in the *Bethell* case, appeared to have misunderstood the reservation of Lord Penzance in the *Hyde* case. This was a judicial reservation allowing the later court to distinguish the earlier judgement. Hyndman-Jones did not go so far as to say that Sterling J. was wrong but intimated that this was so. To intimate but not to say it outright is quite powerful, because there is no real defence. Hyndman-Jones then went on to say "… so far as I know, *Bethell*'s case is the only case against …". He then went on:

> But the conditions obtaining in these Settlements are very different from conditions obtaining in England; and as the fact are, only a fraction of the population here is, or has ever been Christian; and the remainder is almost entirely composed of races among whom polygamy has been an established institution from the earliest times, and a goodly proportion of these races are British born subjects domiciled here, as was *Choo Eng Choon* whose cause we are now considering, …

This was distinguishing with a vengeance! His final comment came in a citation from the majority of the court in the later decision, *Re Goodman's Trusts*[37] on the Statute of Distributions. This says that the Statute is not a Statute for Englishmen only:

> … but applied universally to persons of all countries, races and "religions whatsoever", and operated in favour of a person legitimate by the law of another country though not legitimate by the law of England.

He concluded, therefore, that the Statute could be made to apply to unions such as the Chinese customary marriage — this was not "… *an altering of the Statute as an application of it to existing circumstance*" [emphasis supplied].

We now come to the dissenting judgement of Sercombe Smith J., who in his survey of the same (and some additional) cases, came to the contrary conclusion. As we have already seen, this judge was not disposed to accept the evidence of the Chinese law books cited earlier. As far as the precedent was concerned, he took a narrow view of marriage which he defined as "one celebrated in the presence of an episcopally ordained clergyman" (judgement at p. 195).[38] Following this, he cited, with approval, Lord Penzance's proposition in the *Hyde* case:

> It may be and probably is the case that the women there pass by some word or name which corresponds to our word 'wife'. But there is no magic in a name and if the relation existing there between men and women is not the relation which in Christendom we recognize and intend by the words 'husband' or 'wife', but another and altogether different relation, the use of a common term to express these two separate relations will not make them one and the same, though it may tend to confuse them to a superficial observer.

It was obvious that no attempt at distinguishing was being made. Instead, there was a rigid application of English principle with no concession to the realities of Straits life and Chinese custom. They were excluded by their distinct and different nature from the application of the Statute. The points of distinction raised by Justices Law and Hyndman-Jones were, however, not totally ignored. It will be recalled that one of the distinctions made by the two earlier judges was that the definitions in the *Hyde* case were for a "Christian" country. Sercombe Smith J. flatly rejected the latter proposition, saying "… This colony is not a non-Christian country …". Obviously, he was being serious but, given this, how could such a position be justified? The so-called "Christian" population of the Straits was never more that 2 per cent of the total. The problem appears to be that this judge was fixated with the "Christian" marriage as the only type of marriage which the Straits ("English") courts could consider. Furthermore, while he was prepared to admit a valid foreign marriage as a "marriage" (following the *Warrender* case) he was not prepared to admit a non-Christian marriage contracted within the jurisdiction (that is, the Straits).

The whole judgement of Sercombe Smith J. (pp. 204–07) is an object lesson in judicial obfuscation stemming from a refusal to move from a definition of marriage which had all to do with "Christianity" in England[39] and nothing to do with the facts of Chinese life in the Straits Settlements.

We come finally to the third judgement, that of Mr Justice Braddell. His judgement was short and quite different in tone and treatment of the case from all the other judgements. The reason was that, among all on the Bench, he was a "local", coming from a family with long connections in Straits law and government. To an extent not found in other judgements, he provided an internal view of Straits Chinese legal life. In his own judgement, he truly represented a "marriage of cultures", expressed judicially. He said:

> The question [validity of Chinese marriages] is one of the highest importance to the Chinese who form the bulk of the population of this colony, a great number of whom are natural born British subjects who are descendants of settlers in the Colony, and have been brought up in the religion, usages and customs of their parents.

His view was that the English cases showed no more than that because the marriages in issue were not "answerable to the Christian definition", and therefore the law of England had no relevance. The judgement in the *Warrender* case was thus confined to the "Christian" world. Technically speaking, it was confined to ascertaining the jurisdiction of the courts of Scotland. These were his distinctions with respect to the *Warrender* precedent.

So far as the *Hyde* case was concerned, Mr Justice Braddell followed exactly the position of Hyndman-Jones, that is, that the case concerned the jurisdiction of the matrimonial courts and might thus be distinguished. Where the "thing" (that is, marriage) to which the parties have bound themselves "… differs essentially and materially from that over which jurisdiction was given to the Matrimonial Court, then clearly it could not be recognized …" (judgement, p. 212).

He then considered, and distinguished the precedent in the *Bethell* case but on a new ground — the ground of intention to marry. He said (judgement at p. 216):

> And it is clear when the case is examined that it involved firstly the question whether there was an intention on the part of Bethell to contract marriage in the sense in which it is understood in Christendom, and it was clear on the evidence that he did not have that intention, and it could not be inferred from the ceremony which was gone through inasmuch as he could have been married in a church and had refused to be so married, and so there was no necessity for adopting the Baralong form of marriage if he intended to contract a monogamous one. Therefore, the contract he was engaging himself to could only be

> regarded as a marriage as understood by the Baralongs, i.e., a polygamous marriage.

Mr Justice Braddell then went on to ask whether a religion, permitting polygamy, would thus be without effect. He thought not, citing the case of a British subject who was a Muslim domiciled in England and died, leaving issue from polygamous unions. The issue must be legitimate, "unless polygamy has been put ... beyond the pale of the Comity of Nations" (judgement at p. 218). From this, and so far as the Statute of Distributions was concerned, he concluded (judgement at p. 222):

> I agree that if, in order to make the rules of distribution under the Statute applicable to such a case, it were necessary to alter the scheme of distribution provided for by the Statute, the Court would not be justified in doing that. But the Court is not asked, as it seems to me, to interfere with or alter the scheme of distribution itself, but merely to declare that in applying that scheme to the estate of a Chinese intestate who has left more than one widow it is right and equitable that the share which falls to the widow under the scheme shall be divided equally between his widows.
>
> The principle of distribution provided for by the Statute is equality of division, having regard to the degree of kinship of the persons to be benefited by it, the object of the Legislature being to provide a will for a person who has neglected to make one for himself and to provide for an equal distribution of his estate.
>
> It seems to me that our Courts have done no more than to adopt that principle and object in directing, in a case when the deceased has left more that one widow whom the Court ought to recognise as lawful widows, that they shall take equally between them the share which under the Statute is allotted to the widow. That is not in my opinion to alter the Statute but merely to bring in aid of the Statute the equitable jurisdiction of the Court in declaring how that share ought to be divided, having regard to the rights of the persons claiming as widows of the intestate.

THE STRAITS SETTLEMENTS PRECEDENT: LEGAL REALITY

The final material for this chapter is the Straits precedents on Chinese law and the issue of polygamy. It is in these precedents that the foregoing is considered and summed up, with reference to the facts of Chinese life. It is the *local* precedent and the *local* law which finally determines the issue.

The first reference, a simple one, is by Law Ag. C. J. who said that Chinese (polygamous) marriages had always been recognized. He cited three cases.[40] The interesting point here is that this page of the judgement (p. 149) comes just after his review of the evidence from Chinese books, to which he was favourably disposed and just before his review of the English cases to which he was not. At that stage, he did not go into an extended analysis. Clearly, however, he was setting a scene which he developed later. This occurred on p. 155 of the judgement. His short reference reinforced his approval of Staunton and Hare and provided a warning about the *Hyde* and *Bethell* method of reasoning.

We can see this dualism illustrated at the next stage where he referred to the special nature of the common law in its new locality, the Straits Settlements. English law was originally introduced in the Letters Patent, "Charter of Justice" in 1807, repeated in the Charter of 1826, and finally in the Charter of 1855. All the Charters remained, although reformed in legislation, until at least 1907. By that time, the precedent given under the Charters was well established and, in fact, continues to this day. The important provision was that the laws of England were the laws of general application to the whole population of the Straits except with respect to the "religions, manners and customs" of that population. The exception very quickly came to be narrowly defined. It meant family law and some parts of religion. The provision was a concession to local realities, and quite an extensive precedent has grown around it.[41]

At that point in the judgement (pp. 155–57) there was a technical discussion of Straits legislation and its relationship to the original and later Letters Patent, in particular, the 1855 Charter. This part of the judgement is not directly relevant here except for one aspect. This is the language used by Law Ag. C. J. Normally his English is a model of what clear, direct legal language should be. A proposition is stated, discussed, and a decision reached on it. The extracts from his judgements reproduced above demonstrate this. His judgements are a model of judicial clarity. However, this was not so in his judgement on pp.155–57. Granted that the topic he was discussing — the effect of contemporary legislation on the Letters Patent of 1855 — is technically complex. Having said that, however, a close reading of the three pages seems to show a deliberate attempt to obfuscate, to blind the reader (that is, other judges) with technicality. Why did this happen? The answer seems to be that he was determined to preserve the past Straits precedent (on Chinese polygamous marriages) from any attack by later legislation, even if the "attack" was inadvertent rather than purposeful. The continuance of this precedent depended on the Charter exception — "religions, manners and customs".

On the other hand, I may have over-dramatized the language issue. Law Ag. C. J. did cite an important Straits appeal[42] to the Privy Council, which in effect said that some at least of the later legislation did preserve or re-enact the provisions of the Charters. However, a simple citation of this case would have been sufficient and the question still remains, why he felt it necessary to go into a technical discussion. It may be, indeed seems to be, that he was making an emphasis on the ecclesiastical side of the Straits court's jurisdiction in the Charters. This is a jurisdiction which does not determine the distribution of property as such, but the determination of *who has the rights* in a distribution — in this case "lawful wives". In the ecclesiastical jurisdiction, it is one's status ("wife", "not-wife") which is primary and this remains the prior object of the jurisdiction, whether property is involved or not. By way of illustration, Law Ag. C. J. cited cases on Jewish law and Muslim law[43] to show that polygamy conferred a status recognized in the ecclesiastical jurisdiction and, thus, a status justifiable in terms of the Letters Patent. The intention was to show analogies in distinct systems — Jewish in England, and Muslim in the Straits. The argument was actually quite subtle, and we would now call it a "sub-text". The clearest statement on this, and also cited by Law Ag. C. J. is the following:[44]

> In this Colony so much of the law of England as was in existence when it was imported here, and as is of general (and not merely local) policy and adapted to the conditions and wants of the inhabitants is the law of the land, and further that law is subject in its application to the various alien races established here, to such modifications as are necessary to prevent it from operating unjustly and oppressively on them. Thus in questions of marriage and divorce, it would be impossible to apply our law to Mohamedans, Hindus and Buddhists without the most absurd and intolerable consequences and it is therefore held inapplicable to them. Now the statement of law just quoted, whether it depends on the Letters Patent or not, was approved of by the Privy Council.

From here, the judge proceeded to cite a number of cases to show (a) that polygamy was generally recognized as conferring both status and right to inheritance and (b) that this principle had been applied to Chinese marriages (judgement at pp. 160–61). The argument was purely from precedent in the sense of citation and one would think this was sufficient in 1908 — the "age of precedent". Let me explain this comment. The mid-nineteenth century to the early twentieth century was an age of judicial authoritarianism. That which had been done before was followed. Of course, there were exceptions to this, but, nevertheless, the proposition that the dead hand of precedent determined the law in England remained generally true. This was not the case in the Straits Settlements but the judges were themselves well aware of the weight of authority. Law Ag. C. J. took almost a page (p. 162 in the judgement) to review the doctrine of precedent. He cited five cases, all of the first importance, on the binding effect of (English) Court of Appeal judgements and the status of ratio from courts of co-ordinate jurisdiction. Basically, this was all he did; his comments seemed little more than a genuflection towards doctrine. The reason I say this is that in the passage immediately succeeding (cited below) he dismissed the doctrine in favour of the facts of Chinese marriage which he had to decide.

He said (judgement at pp. 162–63):

> I think there can be no doubt that great hardship will probably be inflicted, if we do not recognise Chinese marriages as polygamous. The result I think will be that in the eye of the law here the women merely declared concubines will have no legal rights at all to maintenance or any provision, that they may be turned adrift to starve and that their children may be regarded by the law as bastards. There are I think probably a good many persons in the Colony at the present time whom a decision that Chinese marriages cannot be recognised as polygamous, will render liable to be affected in the way I have indicated. I have already indicated some of the protection afforded by the Chinese law or custom to inferior wives or concubines, whichever they may be called; ...

In the final part of his judgement, Law Ag. C. J. considered the effect of English and local legislation on the distribution of estates. He avoided the unwanted (by him) passages in the English statutes by showing, quite rightly, that the two sets of legislation were not the same in their respective provisions — they were not in *pari materia*. This is perfectly acceptable. However, in the course of his argument he went back on what he had already said on precedent. On page 167 of the judgement, he cited a famous passage from the (English) Court of Chancery,[45] which absolutely contradicted his previous position. The passage was by Jessel M. R.:

> When a series of decisions of inferior Courts have put a construction on an Act of Parliament, and have thus made a law which men follow in their daily dealings, it has been held even by the House of Lords, that it is better to adhere to the course of the decisions than to reverse them, because of the mischief which would result from such a proceeding.

This is one of the best examples I know of a judge reversing his position in the same judgement on the same point of law to justify a position he wished to maintain. It can be criticized "in logic" but what about "in law", that is, are judgements supposed to be logical? Or is there a special "legal" logic? These are questions that are discussed in the conclusion to this chapter but they are indicated here to be kept in mind.

We look now at the appeal and study first the judgements of Hyndman-Jones C. J. The main feature of the judgement itself is that out of the thirteen pages of the judgement, eight are on the textbooks and only four are on Straits precedent. This is a striking imbalance of reference for a common law judge, especially at the level of appeal. The imbalance is even more obvious when we see that the Chief Justice cited only four Straits precedents (judgement at pp. 192–93) and, apart from superficial comment, adopted them entirely — to recognize the validity of Chinese polygamous marriage and the legitimacy of offspring for distribution under the Statute of Distributions. There is a minimal reference to English precedent (*Hyde*), dismissed as not relevant. Before speculating about the reason or motive for such a proceeding, we will study the other two judgments in appeal.

From Sercombe Smith J., we have already seen a notable reluctance to take the evidence of Chinese law books or texts as decisive or even informative. On the other hand, he cited the Straits precedent in detail. Each of the cases is subjected to a detailed analysis. The first is *Re: Lao Leong Ann*,[46] decided in 1867, in which two wives applied for letters of administration for the estate of their deceased (common) husband. Administration was granted to the first wife and the second wife was granted an equal share in the deceased's estate. Sercombe Smith J. read the decision only as authority that administration might be granted to the first wife. The judgement in *Lao* regarding the second wife was, he thought, *obiter* and not binding on later courts. Not only that, he thought that the judge in 1867 was mistaken as to "Chinese law", that is, the *laws of China* as then known. On this ground, he distinguished *Lao* as not binding on Straits courts where the issue was the status of a Chinese polygamous marriage. His point was that the only issue in *Lao* was the granting of letters of administration, and that decision was only authority for this issue. As far as they go, these propositions are true but they are a very selective reading of the *Lao* judgement. They ignore the fact that the judge in *Lao* was not concerned with the law of China as such, but with the estate of a deceased Chinese who was *domiciled* in the Straits. This puts a completely different complexion on the decision. It is the law of the domicile which determines status and capacity. The laws of China (or of Lichtenstein for that matter!) have no bearing on the matter. In short, Sercombe Smith J. had managed to narrow the precedent in *Lao* and from that narrowness proceeded to the laws of China which he also seems to have misunderstood.

His second case was *Re: Ing Ah Mit*,[47] which was also referred to in the other judgements. The whole point about *Ing* was that the then judge, in 1888, gave letters of administration to *two* widows jointly. This was an extension of the ratio in *Lao* where administration was granted to one wife, although the second wife did have claims on the inheritance. For Sercombe Smith J., however, the decision in *Ing* was both an unwarranted extension of *Lao* and betrayed a misunderstanding (again) of Chinese law, by which he meant the laws of China. This consistent reference to the "laws of China" has already been shown to be mistaken. Apart from that mistake, Sercombe Smith J. himself was immediately guilty of inconsistency. In support of his "laws of China" theory, he cited the well-known decision in the *R. v. Willans* case[48] where the Straits courts declined to recognize adoption as part of "Chinese law". He ignored the fact that this case (a) was concerned with Chinese law in the Straits, (b) that the issue was adoption and not the status of secondary marriage and (c) the precedent on the status of "adopted child" for the purpose of inheritance was conflicting[49] at the time, as it remained until very recently. Finally, the judge faced the great difficulty in that the cases cited were over fifty years old, and had been consistently followed. This did not deter him, and he cited extensively (judgement at pp. 201–2) to show that prior precedent can be overturned. One citation[50] will suffice and it should be compared to the passage by Jessell M. R. cited immediately above:

> I am sensible of the inconvenience of disturbing a course of practice which has continued unchallenged for a long time and which has been sanctioned by high legal authority. But if it is really founded upon erroneous construction of an Act of Parliament, there is no principle which precludes the House of Lords from correcting the error. To hold that the matter is not open to a decision contrary to the intention of the legislature, merely because it had happened, for some reason or other, to remain unchallenged for some length of time.

Truly, a battle of precedents! The remainder of Sercombe Smith J.'s judgement is concerned with English precedent and with Straits legislation. As to the latter, the interpretations proposed are, without exception, strained and demonstrate an almost wilful determination to avoid giving credence to Straits Chinese custom.

We come finally to the judgement of Braddell J. who, it will be recalled, placed great stress on the facts of Straits Chinese life. It was this stress on locality and localism which was the decisive feature of his judgement, and this was illustrated in his citations from Straits precedent. He began with Sir Peter Benson Maxwell's judgement in *R. v. Willans*[51] but his interest was not on the strict ratio as such but on the more general propositions put forward by that judge. For example, the passage:

> In this place where the law of England has been for the first time brought to bear upon races among whom polygamy has been established from the remotest antiquity, the Court has had to consider the question and has always held polygamous marriages valid. Whether the local judicature has erred in not coming to this decision I do not stop to consider. It is enough to say that if it is decided rightly it is not because our Charter demands an exceptionally indulgent treatment of the question, but simply because the principal which makes the validity of a marriage depend upon the religions of the parties, extends to polygamous marriages; while if the Court has been wrong it has erred in not adopting a principle foreign to and at variance with the law of England but in stretching beyond its legitimate limits a perfectly well established one.

The crux of the matter of principle for Braddell J. is the last two lines of this citation "… stretching beyond its legitimate limits …". He did not think so and cited *Lao*'s case and *Ing*'s case, both of which were specific instances of the general principle, and themselves formed part of an established precedent in Chinese personal law. The English precedent[52] which he considered (judgement at p. 215 ff) was incapable of disturbing this general principle.

Mr Justice Braddell then went on to actually expand Sir Benson Maxwell's comments of fifty years earlier. He based it on the phrase "… religions, manners and customs …" which, in respect of ecclesiastical jurisdiction (that is, family law in general) means (judgement at p. 219):

> In the case then when the Court is asked to exercise this power in favour of next-of-kin of an intestate who contracted a polygamous marriage according to the religious ceremonies of the parties, and has left two widows and issue by them, is the Court to say to them and their children, you are not the lawful widows and next-of-kin of the deceased because English law does not recognize the validity of polygamous marriages, with the result that the property of the deceased escheats to the Crown? It seems to me that to say this would be to ignore the express direction in the clause conferring the jurisdiction which requires it to be exercised "so far as the several religions, etc., will admit". The institution of marriage among the Chinese makes it lawful for the husband to cohabit with an inferior wife and beget children by her who are lawful children under the law governing the institution. That being so, may not the words in the Charter be regarded as authorising the Court to extend the principle which makes the validity of a marriage to depend upon the religions of the parties to polygamous marriages, in cases where such

> marriages may be lawfully contracted according to the religions of the parties to them? I am of the opinion that they may, and that our Courts have done the right thing in applying the principle ..."

He went on to demonstrate that the same principle was carried through in various ordinances, in particular the Courts Ordinance of 1878 ("... religions, manners and customs ... *as have hitherto been recognized by the court*"),[53] and the Civil Procedure Code of 1907 where a closely equivalent phrase occurs. Braddell's judgement is in fact the one from which later precedent stems. It comes midway between the initial creativity of the 1850s and the later elaborations of the 1930s–40s. For the later post-independence period, it has remained authoritative.

CONCLUSION: LEGAL LOGIC AND THE MARRIAGE OF CULTURES

The four judges in the "Six Widows" case each considered four sets of authority: oral evidence, textbooks on Chinese law, English precedent, and Straits precedent. The precedents, of course, included those on statutes and ordinances. There is a wide divergence of approach among the four judges to each set of materials. Judges Law and Hyndman-Jones both placed great emphasis on oral evidence and textbook evidence. This was almost totally lacking in Braddell who primarily emphasized Straits precedent. This last judge read that precedent in detail but while referring to English precedent treated it as rather secondary. Both Law and Hyndman-Jones, on the other hand, gave far greater weight to the English precedent. All three judges came to the same conclusion but the actual legal logic varied from one judgement to another because of the varying weight given to the assessment of the materials. The dissenting judge, Sercombe Smith J., concentrated overwhelmingly on the English precedent, was rather dismissive of Straits precedent and was deeply suspicious of the textbook evidence except insofar as it could be used to support the English citations.

These are fairly obvious generalities. What do they tell us about the logic of precedent in the early years of this century? There are a number of answers in the case of the Straits Settlements.

First, there is always a personal element in the creation of precedent. As Lord Radcliffe said in 1968, a judge is not a machine in making a decision. Nor is it just his knowledge, experience and power of reasoning which determine his view; it is more "... his experience of life and the structure of thought and belief that he has built upon it".[54] This is not a plea for some sort of judicial psychology; on the contrary, it demonstrates that judicial logic is not at all deductive logic and those who seek for the latter will always be disappointed. If one compares the passages from Sercombe Smith with those of Braddell, the point is easily seen. The former is sterility, the latter is alive and real with its references to "comity", "tender solicitude", "protection by the courts", and the like. While one must be careful not to overstate the personal element in judicial logic, it always has to be borne in mind because all the personal laws, including those of the Chinese, are creations of the judiciary.

The second point, which we can call the "marriage of cultures", follows from judicial creativity. Its essential feature is that the judiciary is activist by necessity. The classic formulation in common law — do judges *make* law or only *declare* it? — is not a real question as far as personal laws are concerned. They are made by the judicial activists. This is true for all the personal laws of the former British Empire. The result of activism is a hybridization of laws, the marriage of legal concepts from two or sometimes more cultures.[55]

While both these points are amply demonstrated in this chapter, a number of implications should be briefly mentioned. The first concerns languages. The judges in the "Six Widows" case faced the following language complexity: (a) oral evidence translated into English from at least two dialects (Teochow, Hokkien) and from Mandarin; (b) texts translated from Mandarin to English; (c) and a further translation of this evidence from English into "legal" English. This last is a particular sort of technical English, the function of which is to provide a standard set of referents within which "facts" can be subsumed with a high degree of certainty. The special terminology is also a first instance classifier dividing facts into relevant and non-relevant. In other words, it is immediately selective. The obvious examples here are "marriage", "wife", and "concubine".

The use of language, whether "ordinary", "correct" or otherwise, is regarded by the law as being susceptible to confinement and specialization within the orbit of the court. On the general question of the relation between languages and concepts of law, the formulation of concepts for whatever purpose is based upon features of language which may or may not be universal. It assumes the possibility of adequate characterization of the uses of language, a position which is denied by some authorities. The particular concepts which flow from these views of language are limited to those linguistic usages upon which they are based, and do not necessarily extend to data from outside that system. Therefore, any cross-cultural application is not possible except if it is shown that the foreign data support this particular view of language use.

Because plural law appears in the form of judgements (positive law), it would seem that the analyses used in the original municipal systems could be applied directly to this situation. The objection to this, however, is that in many cases the mixing of concepts from a number of obligation systems discloses a usage in which it is not possible to make any of the assumptions outlined above in respect of usage.

The language theory of English law assumes that, as a matter of fact, the usage established by a court can and will be translated into action in the application and enforcement of any judgement. This is a reasonable assumption in Anglo-American jurisprudence, not just because of the efficiency of the legal machinery but also because, on the question of use, the pronouncements of the court are more or less cognizable to the individual concerned. Neither of these features is necessarily present in the Straits or later Malaysian and Singapore circumstances. In particular, the mode of procedure was and is based on concepts which are wholly alien to the majority of the recipient population. This also results in considerable difficulty in ascertaining usage in a specific instance, extending also to the non-possibility of ascribing a particular (legal) consequence to any usage.

The implications of this description and also of the foregoing examination of lawyer's language may be summarized as follows:

1. There is a clear distinction between lawyer's usage and the concepts of law necessary in the analysis of particular topics in law or systems of positive law.
2. For an adequate description of how a personal law works at all levels, a reliance upon the concepts of some particular positive system is not sufficient. This is simply because, in the question of usage, the particular system does not of itself admit the relevance of usages outside its own boundaries.
3. Finally, and as a result of these points, it is necessary to develop a method of adequately representing the reality of two laws in interaction. This is primarily a question of language, of ascertaining upon what basis the verbal symbols of various interacting systems are built up. At a superficial level, this is merely a question of translating words and phrases from one language to another. But as any comparative lawyer will know, grasping a foreign reality, and this is what is implicit in personal law, is much more complex. The reason for this is not difficult to see; language is not just a medium for the transmission of ideas but is an important factor in the formation of ideas. Our concept of what the world is, is related to the language in which we express our experience because this experience is

organized and interpreted in terms of our language structure. This was stated by Edward Sapir, who said:[56]

> Language is a guide to 'social reality'. Though language is not ordinarily thought of as an essential interest to students of social science, it powerfully conditions all our thinking about social problems and processes. Human beings do not live in the objective world alone, nor alone in the world of social activity as ordinarily understood, but are very much at the mercy of the particular language which has become the medium of expression for their society. It is quite an illusion to imagine that one adjusts to reality essentially without the ? of language and that language is really an incidental means of solving specific problems of communication or reflection. The fact of the matter is that the 'real world' is to a large extent unconsciously built up on the language habits of the group. No two languages are ever sufficiently familiar to be considered as representing the same social reality. The worlds in which different societies live are distinct worlds, not merely the same world with different labels attached.

Although not all jurists accept this statement without qualification, a close interrelationship between language and culture is accepted. The importance of this is particularly marked in studies of comparative law and in personal laws. The oral evidence and the evidence from the Chinese texts in the "Six Widows" case demonstrate this.

The "facts" of Chinese culture, here in respect of marriage were, as we have seen, accommodated within the common law but only on the terms and conditions of that law. The important point is that it was not the whole of Chinese culture which was in issue. It was only those parts, defined by the dominant common law system (as "relevant"), which were acceptable. This did not extend to admitting a total fact complex, to sorting out a man's relationship with the objective world, his "being-in-the-world". Only *some* facts of nature and some facts of morality or culture were and are permitted to determine the grounds for dealings between individuals. In short, we have a distortion of Chinese norms which is the result of this selective application. In their new form, these rules have become divorced from their original context. The original world of which these were a part is ignored and, indeed, this is an important element in the definition of colonial law or, now, in states which recognize a legal pluralism.

Perhaps we can leave the final word with Braddell J. (judgement p. 129) for whom the comments just made might or might not have been relevant.

> ... it was recognized that the law of England would necessarily require to be administered with such modifications as to make them suitable to

the religions and customs of the inhabitants who were intended to be benefited by them. They were dictated from a regard for that constant policy of our rulers to administer our laws in our Colonies with a tender solicitude for the religious beliefs and established customs of the races living under the protection of our Flag, and I regard them as such as a charge to our Courts to exercise its jurisdiction with all due regard to the several religions, manners and customs of the inhabitants.

Notes

[1] For an outline, see M. B. Hooker, *Legal Pluralism* (Oxford:The Clarendon Press, 1975). For Malaysia, see M. B. Hooker, *Personal Laws of Malaysia* (Kuala Lumpur: OUP, 1976).

[2] Hastings' Bengal Regulation of 1781. See M. B. Hooker, "The East India Company and the Crown 1773–1858", *Malaya Law Review.*

[3] See M. B. Hooker, *The Personal Laws of Malaysia* 2, no. 1 (Kuala Lumpur: OUP, 1969): 1–37. "The Chinese 'Confucian' and the Chinese 'Buddhist' in British Burma", *Journal of Southeast Asian Studies* 21, no. 2 (1990): 384–401. "Chinese Customary Law in Contemporary Malaysia and Singapore", *Australian Journal of Asian Law* 1 (1999).

[4] (1911)12 SSLR 120

[5] Surprisingly, there is no history of the Straits Settlements Bench and Bar with an analysis of judgements. This is a real gap in the history of English law in the East, particularly given the originality of the precedent and its continuing importance in contemporary Malaysia and Singapore.

[6] See the entry in A. W. B. Simpson, ed., *Biographical Dictionary of the Common Law* (Butterworths, 1984).

[7] Cited in Michael Zander, *The Law Making Process*, 2nd edition (London: Weidenfeld and Nicholson, 1985), p. 333.

[8] Ibid., p. 334.

[9] For "Kapitan China", see Victor Purcell, *The Chinese in Southeast Asia* (Oxford University Press, 1948).

[10] For a current assessment of ceremony in contemporary Malaysia and Singapore, see Hooker, op. cit., note 1. It is now much less relied upon.

[11] See Michael Zander, op. cit., pp. 335ff.

[12] Cited by Professor Michael Zander, op. cit., pp. 339–40.

[13] In London by Strahan and Preston.

[14] There was, however, a French version by G. Auberet, *Code Annamite* (Paris: Imp. Imperiale, 1865), subtitled *A Code of Annamite Laws.* It was in fact a version of the Vietnamese Gia Long of 1813, itself Chinese Qing. See Ta Van Tai, "The Vietnamese Texts", in *The Laws of South-East Asia (Vol I): The Pre-Modern Texts,* edited by M. B. Hooker (Singapore: Butterworths, 1986), pp. 435–96.

15 Wallace Johnson, *The T'ang Code* (Princeton NJ: Princeton University Press, 1979).

16 See, for example, Sybille van der Sprenkel, *Legal Institutions of Manchu China* (London: Athlone Press s.v. Staunton, 1962).

17 Various editions. The 3rd edition of 1900 is cited, published by Kelly & Walsh, Hong Kong, and also the 4th edition.

18 For this office, see Victor Purcell, op. cit., note 9.

19 Published by authority of the Selangor Government Printing Office, 1904. He also selected and edited a *Textbook of Documentary Chinese* for use by government servants in the Straits and FMS. Published by the Government Printing Office, Singapore, 1894.

20 The *Droit Annamite* is by Durwell, published by Claude & Co in Saigon in 1901. The *Précis* is probably from Aubaret and/or Deloustal. For sources, see M. B. Hooker, *A Concise Legal History of South-East Asia* (Oxford: The Clarendon Press, 1978). A basic bibliography is in *La Revue Indochinoise-Juridique et Economique* 9 (1939): 139–75.

21 See, for example, any standard textbook on *Jurisprudence: s.v. "Legal Realism"*.

22 The best early examples are in *Moore's Indian Appeals*, where the issue was discussed in both financial and political terms.

23 (1835) 2Cl. & Fin. 488.

24 This is a separate jurisdiction in the United Kingdom.

25 (1861) 9 HL Cases, 193.

26 Ibid., p. 207. This passage must have been cited hundreds of times during the past century or so.

27 (1866) LR 1 P & D 130

28 Ibid., p. 133, also cited some hundreds of times (see below).

29 (1888) 38 Ch. D 220

30 Other precedents are also cited but space forbids any extended description.

31 See Zander, op. cit., note 7, pp. 234.

32 These cases may induce a sense of *déjà vu* in many readers. All are a hundred years old and still appear as important decisions in the English conflict of laws. My own first experience of them was as a student in the late 1950s.

33 *Brinkley v. Ag* (1890) L.R. 15 P & D 76; *Ardaseer v. Perozeboye* (1856) 10 MOO. P.C. 375

34 *Warrender v. Warrender* (1835) 2CL. & Fin at 532 per Lord Brougham.

35 Emphasis added.

36 (1881) 50 L.J. Ch 425.

37 This is taken from *R v. Millish* (1844) 10Cl & Fin 534.

38 On the vexed question of the Chinese Christian marrying polygamously under Chinese custom, see Hooker, op. cit., note 3 and the sources there cited.

39 *Re: Lao Leong Ann* (1897) 4Ky 128. *Re: Ing Ah Mit* (1888) 4Ky 380; and *Lim Chooi Hoon v. Chok Yoon Guan* (1893) 1 SSLR 72.

40 See M. B. Hooker, *Legal Pluralism* (Oxford: The Claredon Press, 1975).

41 For a review of the cases, see M. B. Hooker, op. cit., n. 1.

[42] *Yeap Cheah Neoh v. Ong Cheng Neoh* (1877), LR 6PC381.

[43] The cases are: *Lindo v. Belisario* (1795), I Hagg.Con 216 (Jewish); *Re: Chua Siang Long* (1843), Leic. 460 (Straits Settlements Muslim).

[44] From *Choa Choon Neo v. Spottiswoode* (1869) 1 Ky.216 at p. 221.

[45] *Ex Parte Willey* (1883), 23 Ch.D. 118 at p. 127.

[46] (1867) I Leic. 418.

[47] (1888) 4 Ky. 380.

[48] (1859) Leic. 66. (1859) 3 Ky. 16.

[49] See M. B. Hooker, *Personal Laws of Malaysia* (Kuala Lumpur: Oxford University Press, 1976), p. 136 for a brief note of the cases.

[50] Lord MacNaughton in *Hamilton v. Baker* (1898), 14 App. Cas. 209.

[51] (1858) 3 Ky. 16.

[52] That is, *Warrender, Hyde, Bethell* (see above).

[53] Emphasis in the original.

[54] Cited in Zander, op. cit.

[55] An example of a "triple law" can be found in the laws relating to the Malays in British Malaya. We have (a) English laws (b) Malay custom (*adat*), and (c) elements of Syariah, combined in various ways. Inheritance of customary land is the focus.

[56] Cited in J. C. Smith, "The Unique Nature of Concepts of Western Law", *Canadian Bar Review* 46 (1968): 191–225, especially p. 194.

5

THE INDONESIAN CHINESE

"Foreign Orientals", Netherlands Subjects, and Indonesian Citizens

Charles A. Coppel

The legal position of the ethnic Chinese in Indonesia has been a tangled web for more than a century. The ramifications persist to the present day. For example, in 1979–80 the Coordination Body for the Chinese Problem of the State Intelligence Coordination Body (BKMC-BAKIN or Badan Koordinasi Masalah Cina — Badan Koordinasi Intelijen Negara) published a voluminous compilation of legislation (including various regulations and decrees as well as Acts of Parliament) with reference to the Chinese in Indonesia (BAKIN 1979–80). Notwithstanding the declared determination of the government under President Abdurrachman Wahid to abolish all legislation which discriminated against the ethnic Chinese, most if not all of the legislative products set out in the three volumes of the BKMC-BAKIN publication remain technically in force.

Aspects of the historical background of the present situation might be thought to be well-known, but a closer inspection reveals that the story is more complex and contested than is usually assumed. This chapter first re-examines the history of the legal category "Foreign Orientals" and then relates the history of "foreign" Netherlands subjects to that of Indonesian citizens of "foreign" descent.

EUROPEANS, NATIVES, AND FOREIGN ORIENTALS

It is one of the lesser-known curiosities of legal history that the planned introduction by the Republic of China around 1930 of a new Civil Code for China was the direct cause of the recruitment of a group of 75 young Dutch law graduates for service in the Netherlands Indies judiciary. The reason for this was the belief in some official quarters that the Code, which was to include a new system of family law, might have the effect of automatically redefining the status of all Chinese in the Netherlands Indies, so that they were classified as "Europeans" rather than "Foreign Orientals". This would in turn require a massive increase in the number of European judges employed in the colony because criminal cases involving Chinese would thenceforth have to be heard by the *Raad van Justitie* (European Court of Justice) rather than the *Landraad* (Native Court).[1]

When I first started to study Indonesian history about thirty-five years ago, it was a commonplace observation that the colonial government had classified the population of the Netherlands Indies into three groups (*bevolkingsgroepen*), namely, Europeans, Natives (*Inlanders*), and Foreign Orientals (*Vreemde Oosterlingen*). You could read that in standard texts such as Wertheim's *Indonesian Society in Transition*, or Furnivall's *Netherlands India* (Wertheim 1959; Furnivall 1944).

What was not clear to me then (and I think many others were similarly ignorant) was just how recently it was that this fully-fledged threefold classification had come into existence. To take the same two books, Wertheim passes over this point in silence, and Furnivall, while mentioning that the Chinese "were placed under the same legal footing as natives" by the Constitutional Regulation (*Regeerings Reglement*) of 1854, does not make clear when the threefold classification came into being. The same is true of many comparative or historical studies of Indonesian law (for example, Hooker 1975; Hooker 1988). The treatment in such "big picture" works of a concept such as the category "Foreign Oriental" in Netherlands Indies law, is of necessity so abbreviated that we lose all the complexity and contestation that went with it; and are left with a kind of snapshot or even a stereotype.

Indonesian nationalists, like nationalists elsewhere, often use the catchphrase that colonialists built their empires on the principle of "divide and rule" (*divide et impera*). The tripartite racial classification in the Netherlands Indies is often cited in this context. Although this notion contains more than a grain of truth, it also obscures the uncomfortable truth that the colonialists were often divided among themselves about how best to rule their colonies. Not only did the British in India and the Dutch in Indonesia have quite different ideas about the way in which the different peoples under their rule should be treated by the law. The Dutch also differed among themselves about whether all "races" should be treated equally under the law; or whether they should each be treated in accordance with their own customs.

Article 109 of the Constitutional Regulation of 1854 made a basic legal separation between "lords and subjects", as Wertheim (1997b, p. 1) nicely puts it. On the one hand, there were those identified as "Europeans and those equated (*gelijkgestelde*) with Europeans". On the other hand, there were the Natives, and those equated (*gelijkgestelde*) with them. Those equated with the Natives were Chinese, Arabs, Japanese and other — "*what would later be called*" — Foreign Orientals (*Vreemde Oosterlingen*) (Fasseur 1992b, my emphasis).[2]

The more closely one examines it, the more complicated this concept of "equating" (*gelijkstelling*) becomes, however. The 1854 Constitutional Regulation conferred power on the government to make exceptions to the classification just referred to. Within a year, the government was to exercise that power by passing an ordinance which "applied to all Foreign Orientals in Java the European Civil and Commercial Code while leaving them under the customary law [*adat*] in other matters" (Furnivall 1944, p. 241). The exception was designed to protect European business interests against insolvent Chinese, not with raising the status of the Chinese as a group. Various other pieces of legislation muddied the waters further, as in the case of the Agrarian Law of 1870, which prohibited the sale or permanent transfer of land from "Natives" to Europeans or other "Foreigners" like the Chinese. The Chinese were also required to reside in designated districts (*wijken*) and were not permitted to travel from one part of the colony to another unless they obtained a government pass.

Despite these and other departures from the dualistic classification set out in 1854, at the end of the century the category of "Foreign Orientals" was still legally a subset of those equated to "Natives" rather than a third category intermediate to those of "Europeans" and "Natives". According to an 1890 Malay-language booklet on the legal position of the Chinese in the Netherlands Indies, written by J. E. Albrecht, a former President of the *Weeskamer*, Chinese comprised the majority of those equated (*di samaken*) with the natives (*anak negri*), together with Arabs, Indians (Chodja and Kling) and "other foreigners below the winds" (*orang asing di bawah angin*) and all Muslims and unbelievers (*kafir*) (Albrecht 1890, p. 3).

Determining those who were to be "equated" with the Europeans became a complicated business. In 1871, it became possible for individual Indonesians or other non-Europeans like the Chinese to be equated with Europeans by decree of the Governor-General published in the *Indisch Staatsblad.* Such people became known as *Staatsblad-Europeanen* or Government Gazette Europeans. Illegitimate children of a non-European mother could become European through acknowledgment by the father; and where a European man married a non-European woman, she and their children acquired European status. It has been estimated that more than one-third of the increase in the European population between 1881 and 1940 (excluding immigration) can be attributed to such sources, as opposed to births arising out of marriages between Europeans (Fasseur 1992b, p. 224, citing Marle 1951–52, p. 500).

By the end of the 1890s, another important group of those "equated" with Europeans suddenly appeared. The Netherlands Government implemented a treaty with Japan by legislating that all Japanese nationals in the Netherlands Indies (including ethnic Chinese originating from Formosa [Taiwan]) should be equated with Europeans. For the next half-century, there were to be Chinese agitating for the colonial government to "equate" all Chinese in the Indies with Europeans. Chinese found it particularly offensive that, say, a Japanese prostitute or fisherman charged with a criminal offence should have the right to be tried by a European court (*Raad van Justitie*), whereas they, no matter what their education or social standing, would have to be tried by a native court (*Landraad*). This was not simply a matter of social discrimination. Defendants tried by the European court were protected by the provisions of the European criminal code with respect to arbitrary arrest and jail conditions, and they faced a legally qualified tribunal, whereas trials in the native court were conducted under the *Indisch Reglement* where only the presiding chairman was legally qualified.

The discrepancy between its treatment of the Japanese and Chinese — which had been brought about by the Japanese victory over China in the 1894 Sino-Japanese war — was one for which the government was never able to find a ready and persuasive explanation other than that of political convenience. Lurking behind its refusal to equalize all Chinese with Europeans was the problem of what should then be done in the case of indigenous Indonesians. No matter what measures it took to mitigate the legal discrimination between the different races or population groups (and there were a number of these), there were serious political and budgetary difficulties which stood in the way of creating equality of the races before the law, as was the case in British India or the American Philippines.[3]

This 1899 "Japanese law" (*Japannerwet*) contributed to an amendment to Article 109 of the Constitutional Regulation, which was adopted by the Netherlands Parliament in 1906 but only came into effect in 1920. By admitting all Japanese to European status, regardless of their religion or connection with European society, the government had "robbed Article 109 of its foundations", according to one later commentator (Prins 1933, p. 679). A new rationale for equalization had to be found. This amended Article 109, with minor changes, was renumbered as Article 163 of the Indies Constitution of 1925, which replaced the former Constitutional Regulation. Fasseur (1994, p. 40) has pointed out that this amended legislation had three significant features:

> First, the principle of racial classification in the new article was made conditional ("If other legal provisions distinguish between Europeans, Natives and Foreign Orientals ..."). Second, the Foreign Orientals were classified as a separate group and no longer "equated" with Indonesians. Third, the definition of Europeans was enlarged. Henceforth, it covered not only Dutchmen and other persons originating from Europe (Japanese included) but everyone who *in his country of origin* was subjected to a family and marriage law "mainly" based on the same principles as had been adopted in Dutch law. This last addition opened the door for Turks, Siamese and other Asians whose governments had incorporated European principles of family law in their *national* legislation or did so at any time in the future.[4]

The amendments which made their way into Article 163 of the Indies Constitution thus not only introduced the threefold classification of population groups into the basic law but also in effect made family and marriage laws enshrining monogamy the test of Europeanness for this purpose. A projected change in the Chinese Civil Code in the late 1920s, under which Chinese family law was to be reformed, thus would have constitutional implications for the position of the Chinese in the Netherlands Indies — or at least so it was believed by some in the colonial administration.

Before discussing this, however, there are more complexities in the Netherlands Indies legal system to be addressed. Dualism had been a feature of the legal system in the Indies for a long time and it was apparent in Article 75 as well as Article 109 of the Constitutional Regulation of 1854.[5] Article 75 provided that jurisdiction, legislation, and legal procedures for Dutchmen and other "Europeans" must be based upon regulations and ordinances as much as possible in conformity with the laws and procedures in the Netherlands. "Natives", by contrast, were subjected to their own "religious laws, institutions and customs" in so far as they were "not in conflict with generally recognised principles of equity and justice" (unless they had accepted or were deemed to have accepted European law). The Chinese, who were equated with the Natives, were subject to the same provisions, although the colonial government could, and often did, declare that the Native population (or a part of it, such as the Chinese) was to be subject to particular provisions.

In the early years of this century, there were two contradictory trends in the development of law in the colony. On the one hand, there were those who wanted to abandon the pluralism in law and judicial administration and to develop instead a modern, unified legal system. In this camp could be found those who saw a need for legal certainty as well as those proponents of the so-called Ethical Policy who believed that the indigenous population could only be emancipated or elevated on the basis of Western law. Cees Fasseur quotes Ethicus C. Th. van Deventer, famous for his formulation of the notion of the Netherlands' "debt of honour" to the native population of Indonesia, as saying that "one must recognize that the natural development for Orientals in a colony administered by a Western power is that they, albeit slowly, will have to conform to Western law" (Fasseur 1992a, p. 249).[6] In opposition to them stood the champions of the newly discovered *adat* law (*adatrecht*) under the vigorous leadership of the young Leiden University professor of *adat* law of the Netherlands Indies, Cornelis van Vollenhoven.

The conflict between the two camps came to a head over a Bill which was introduced into the Dutch Parliament in 1904. The intent of the Bill was to apply European law to native society, unless "the different needs" of the indigenous people made it necessary to use *adat* law. Somewhat surprisingly, the Bill was amended by its opponents, after two years of debate, to such effect that its thrust was reversed. Article 75 of the revised Constitutional Regulation was now to have the effect that European law would only apply to natives if the needs of native society required it. According to Fasseur, the outcome of the long debates was a stalemate. The "movement for unification ... gradually lost its momentum and finally petered out" (Fasseur 1992a, p. 251). In his view, the only success for its proponents was the adoption of a unified penal code for the Netherlands Indies in 1918, in which the separate codes for Europeans and natives (which had differed little anyway) were amalgamated. However, their attempts to introduce a uniform code of criminal procedure for all groups of the population broke down in 1919.

In the case of the Chinese, however, there was another move towards *gelijkstelling* on a group basis in the late 1920s. Even before it took its place in the Indies Constitution in 1925, influential people in the colonial administration were arguing that Article 163, with its system of racial classification, should be repealed. This was the recommendation of the *Herzieningscommissie* (Revision Committee) set up by Governor-General Van Limburg Stirum at the end of 1918 (and which reported in 1920) and was chaired by the president of the Supreme Court (*Hooggerechtshof*) in Batavia, J. H. Carpentier Alting. It was also the view of another small committee within the Justice Department, chaired by W. Sonneveld, a member of the Council of the Indies (*Raad van Nederlandsch-Indië*), which rejected the partial solution of equating Chinese with Europeans in favour of revoking what was then still Article 109 of the Constitutional Regulation (as amended). This was also the view expressed in 1922 by the eminent lawyer and friend of the Indies Chinese, Mr. P. H. Fromberg. Governor-General Van Limburg Stirum adopted the proposals of the Sonneveld Committee in January 1921, but the conservative Minister of Colonies, S. de Graaff, refused to entertain them (Fasseur 1994, pp. 43–48; Wertheim 1997a, p. 9, citing Fromberg 1926, p. 793).

The contradictions of discrimination on the basis of race kept cropping up, next in the context of an electoral bill in the *Volksraad* (People's Council). This new law, applied first in 1925, discriminated, formally speaking, on the basis of nationality (although in practice on race) by distinguishing between "Netherlanders"; "indigenous" Netherlands subjects (non-Netherlanders); and "foreign" Netherlands subjects (non-Netherlanders). Its author, J. J. Schrieke, was then Government Deputy for General Affairs (Fasseur 1994, p. 49).[7]

The Chinese and others kept the issue alive in the major Dutch newspapers in the Indies and the Netherlands; in the Malay press in the Indies; and through speeches in the *Volksraad*, with demands for the "odious Article" to be repealed. However, although indigenous Indonesians had not objected to the Japanese or the Siamese being given European status, their numbers in the Indies were very small compared with the number of Chinese; and there were those like M. H. Thamrin who opposed the equalization of the Chinese if the consequence was that the indigenous Indonesians would be left behind.[8] The political implications of the latter, and the prohibitive cost of extending the European system of justice to the whole population, were to be recurrent themes in the debates of succeeding years.

In 1927, Schrieke produced another Bill (after three years in the making) in which "Netherlanders" and "Netherlands subjects, non-Netherlanders" ("indigenous" and "foreign") were differentiated. This was dismissed by the Director of the Batavia Department of Justice, D. Rutgers (Fasseur 1994, pp. 49–50; Wertheim 1997a, p. 9). Governor-General A. C. D. de Graeff then appointed a committee of three professors (J. H. A. Logemann, B. ter Haar, and R. D. Kollewijn) of the newly founded Batavia Faculty of Law (*Rechtshoogeschool*) to find a solution, and their 1927 report rejected Schrieke's proposal but also recommended the repeal of Article 163. Rather than the criterion of nationality favoured by Schrieke, they preferred to introduce a system in which the "social needs" of any group of the population should form the criteria for differential treatment under the law. The influence of the *adat* law school was clearly evident in this approach. Rutgers, apparently an advocate of full legal unification, was equally opposed to this proposal (Fasseur 1994, pp. 50–51; Wertheim 1997a, pp. 9–10).

The Council of the Netherlands Indies (*Raad van Nederlandsch-Indië*) opted for yet another course. It proposed that Article 163 should be repealed and Chinese (but not other Foreign Orientals) be merged with Europeans. This bundle of contradictory proposals was sent for decision to the Minister of Colonies in The Hague in late 1928 (Fasseur 1994, p. 51).

In the meantime, news had reached the Dutch Government from its embassy in Peking that the Government of the Republic of China was to introduce a system of European family law on 1 January 1930. This implied, as previously indicated, that the Chinese in the Indies would automatically achieve the status of Europeans unless Article 163 was to be further amended. The Netherlands Government thus faced the spectre of having the small ranks of the European population in the Indies swelled by the much larger number of Chinese, with the certain prospect of further demands for equality of status from indigenous Indonesians — and all as a consequence of a change of the family law in China (Fasseur 1994, p. 51; Wertheim 1997a, p. 10)!

On 23 February 1929, the deputy Director of Justice, Mr. H. J. Spit, proposed to the Governor-General through the Supreme Court that the budget allocation should be increased to take account of an extra fifty jurists to be recruited in the Netherlands to meet "the possibility ... that within the foreseeable future the Chinese will have to be treated on an equal footing with the Europeans, with all its consequences, among others with respect to jurisdiction ..." The Governor-General cabled his adoption of this proposal to the Minister for Colonies on 7 May 1929 (Wertheim 1997a, p. 11).

In July 1929, the Dutch envoy in Nanking, W. J. Oudendijk, reported back to The Hague that it was very likely that Western family law would not, in fact, be adopted by the Chinese people for many years to come but that the Chinese Government would do what it could to promulgate a new Civil Code within the year. Meanwhile, Governor-General de Graeff in Batavia expected that Western family law would come into effect on 1 January 1930, and he publicly broached the implications of this in his address to the *Volksraad* in August 1929. "If this plan is realised", he said, "all Chinese in this country will be subjected to the law valid for Europeans". If the native population wanted this extended to them, he said, the government would welcome it if it were possible, but it could not be introduced overnight. However, members of the *Volksraad* might well consider that this was a reform which should be implemented with all due haste, and the government would systematically pursue a general unified criminal procedure and the like (Wertheim 1997a, pp. 12–13).

By the end of 1929 it had become apparent to the colonial administration that the new Chinese family law would not, after all, come into effect by 1 January 1930, but it now announced that "As already promised, the Government would, at short notice, of its own accord, realise equalization of the Chinese with Europeans, substantially in the realm of criminal procedure". It acknowledged that it could not delay this (pending legal unification for all ethnic groups) without breaking its word. The plan to equalize the Chinese with Europeans first, and then to equalize all native Indonesians as soon as possible thereafter, was generally welcomed in the *Volksraad* (Wertheim 1997a, pp. 13–14).

So what went wrong? A shift seems to have occurred in the course of 1930. On the one hand, envoy Oudendijk wrote from China to the Ministry of Foreign Affairs in The Hague casting doubt on whether the new Chinese Civil Code would after all satisfy Western norms with respect to family and succession law. Illegitimate children who were brought up in their father's household would thereby enjoy the same status as his legitimate children. In his view, this constituted a legitimation of concubinage, and the supposedly monogamous intent of the legislation was likely to be received as advisory rather than mandatory (Wertheim 1997a, p. 17). Meanwhile, Professor Kollewijn published an article on "The Modern Chinese Codification" in the *Indisch Tijdschrift van het Recht* (Wertheim 1997a, pp. 17–18; Kollewijn 1930, pp. 323–40). In his opinion, the question of whether the new Chinese legislation accorded with Article 163 should be submitted for determination by the Supreme Court as a test case, preferably through a criminal prosecution by the Attorney-General. After the books of the new Chinese Civil Code concerning family law and succession had come into effect on 5 May 1931, Kollewijn wrote a further article entitled "The Modern Chinese Family Law", in which he concluded that although monogamy had been officially introduced and bigamy was punishable as a crime, the marriage law, for technical reasons, "could not possibly be called 'Western'" (Wertheim 1997a, p. 18; Kollewijn 1931, pp. 107–111).

Meanwhile, the wind had changed again in Batavia. From 17 October 1930, the *Raad van Indië* had taken a view opposing Schrieke (who was by now the Director of Justice). They wanted to put aside his proposal in support of equalization, and not to permit any formal declaration of equalization of the Chinese. They now adopted the idea of a general criminal procedure for *all* ethnic groups. This shift may well have been influenced, as Wertheim suggests, by the admission of two Indonesians (Koesoemo Joedo and Achmad Djajadiningrat) to the *Raad* that year (Wertheim 1997a, p. 19).

Despite continuing opposition by Schrieke, the *Raad*'s position gained support from another quarter. This was the report of the Vonk Commission, which formulated a draft emergency ordinance on the simplification of criminal procedure (which was published on behalf of the Netherlands Indies Government) but proposed that it should also apply, as a first step, to the Chinese pending the preparation of a unified criminal procedure for all ethnic groups. This, in turn, was challenged by Ter Haar (Professor of *adat* law) who warned of the dangers to the quality of the native criminal jurisdiction if a unified criminal procedure was introduced in the way proposed because of the number of judges required. The effect of an ordinance designed to simplify criminal procedure was therefore watered down in response to his representations so that it applied only to Europeans (Wertheim 1997a, pp. 19–20).

Ultimately, the government in The Hague in the person of the Minister for Colonies made a decision. Essentially, it seems to have been a decision to sit on its hands, as far as Article 163 was concerned. Kollewijn's argument that the effect of the Chinese law should be determined by the Supreme Court was adopted, but without taking any proceedings to elicit such a determination. The Minister, like Ter Haar, was opposed, on the grounds of its expense, to a two-stage process in which European criminal procedure would be extended to the Chinese, with the later institution of an improved *Landraad* (Wertheim 1997a, pp. 23–25).

For the rest of the colonial period, the government retreated from its promised aim of a unified criminal procedure. It spoke about aiming for *gelijkwaardigheid* ("equivalence") rather than *gelijkheid* ("equality") of jurisdiction for all ethnic groups. No more was heard of the views of the Chinese Government or of the effect of the new Chinese Civil Code on the operation of Article 163. Presumably, as Wertheim suggests, they were too busy trying to cope with the Japanese aggression in Manchuria. The Visman Commission, which was set up on the eve of the Japanese occupation of Indonesia to study political reforms, discovered that the notion of "equivalence" had no appeal to the Chinese, whatever its attractions to the indigenous Indonesian population (Wertheim 1997a, pp. 27–28; *Verslag* … 1942, pp. 60–61).

Thus it was that the well-known division of Netherlands Indies society into three population groups — Europeans, "Foreign Orientals" and "Natives" — remained in existence to the end of the colonial period. However, the recentness of its introduction and the continuous challenges to its existence in Article 163 of the Indies Constitution seem to have slipped from the collective memory of Indonesians and even of legal historians. The history of the divided views of the Dutch ruling élite on this subject might be thought to give a new meaning to the old saying "divide and rule".

Fasseur (1994, pp. 54–55) ended his excellent discussion of this subject with a misleading and unduly optimistic conclusion:

> And so the Dutch colonial state remained in fact a state without citizens. It was article 27 of the Constitution of the Indonesian Republic, proclaimed in August 1945, which definitely put an end to any form of racial classification before the law in declaring solemnly: "All citizens are equal before the law and before the administration".
>
> The breach between colonial Indonesia and the post-war Indonesian Republic is, at least in this respect, entirely obvious. We cannot speak of any colonial heritage bestowed upon independent Indonesia. We do not need to regret this.

The question of the grouping of the population into *bevolkingsgroepen* was no more linked to citizenship in the post-war Republic of Indonesia than it had been to *onderdaanschap* in the Netherlands Indies. These aspects will be considered at greater length in the second section of this chapter.

Fasseur was mistaken in his belief that Article 27 of the 1945 Indonesian Constitution "put an end to any form of racial classification before the law". When Soeharto's New Order government came to power in 1966, it formulated policies and laws with respect to the ethnic Chinese which, I have argued elsewhere, were manifestly ambivalent (Coppel 2001). Soeharto enunciated a policy of equal rights for all citizens, including those of Chinese descent, but in doing so he also instituted legislation which discriminated against them. In many respects, his anti-discrimination rhetoric was hollow, but in one respect, which is relevant to our present discussion, it showed more substance. Cabinet Presidium Instruction 31 of 1966 (issued on 27 December 1966) explicitly recited:

> That it appears that some colonial regulations continue to be in force to this day which are no longer in accordance with the level of struggle and status of the Indonesian nation, and which include rules about groupings of residents of Indonesia based upon descent or class.

It identified Articles 131 and 163 of the Indies Constitution of 1925 as the basis upon which the Civil Registration (*Catatan Sipil*, formerly *Burgerlijke Stand*) offices continued to differentiate between groupings of Indonesian residents ("Europeans", "Foreign Orientals" and "Natives"). Declaring that this division of the population was inconsistent with the achievement of a homogeneous and united Indonesian nation, it proclaimed that, henceforth, the only distinction to be made in the Civil Registration offices was that between Indonesian citizens and aliens. Unfortunately, there was as yet no Civil Registration Law which applied to the whole of the population, so a further Instruction 32 of 1966 (also issued on 27 December 1966) called upon the Minister of Justice to draft such a law.

It appears that that was as far as things went. More than three decades later, after the fall of Soeharto, lawyer and activist Frans Winarta argued that the colonial tripartite classification into Europeans, Foreign Orientals, and Natives was still in force and needed to be repealed (Winarta 1998).

"FOREIGN" NETHERLANDS SUBJECTS AND INDONESIAN CITIZENS OF "FOREIGN" DESCENT

So far we have only touched upon the history of another important strand in the classification of the population, namely, that of nationality and citizenship. In pre-modern times, the concept of a wider Netherlands nationality, as distinct from a local citizenship of, say, Amsterdam or Batavia, did not exist. By the middle of the nineteenth century, such a status (*Nederlanderschap*) had come into being, although it had little significance in practice. In the Netherlands Indies as well as in the Netherlands, the status of resident or inhabitant (*ingezeten*) was of more importance.

In 1892, a Dutch Nationality (*Nederlanderschap*) Law was passed which made it clear that only Netherlanders (but not Natives or those equated to them) held Dutch citizenship. It was less clear what the effect of this law was for the inhabitants of the Indies who were not Netherlanders. It was only in 1910 that a Dutch Subjecthood (*Nederlandsch Onderdaanschap*) Law was passed which clarified the national status of Natives (and "foreigners" equated to them who were born in the Netherlands Indies) to be "Netherlands subjects, non-Netherlanders". This legislation was prompted by the rise in nationalist sentiment among the locally-born Chinese population in the Indies, the enactment of the 1909 Chinese Nationality Law which claimed that all descendants of the Chinese, wherever they were born, were Chinese nationals, and the desire of the Chinese Government to open consulates in the Indies (Willmott 1961, chapter 2). It claimed as Netherlands subjects (*Nederlandsch Onderdanen*) all those born in the Indies of "foreign" (especially Chinese and Arab) parents who were domiciled in the Indies, as well as the indigenous Indonesian population and those who had been defined as Netherlanders in the 1892 law. After the passage of the 1910 law, many rights and duties which were previously attached to the status of "Netherlander" or "resident" now became attached to the status of "Netherlands subject".

From the point of view of international law, the status of "Netherlands subject" henceforth became the sole basis of rights, but in many ways the racial classification of the population discussed earlier continued to prevail. The status of "Netherlands subject" did not bring with it equality before the law.[9] The status of being a "subject" (*onderdaan* in Dutch, *kaulanegara* in Indonesian) of the Netherlands seemed to emphasize the colonial status of the Natives and Foreign Orientals, even if it was the case that the "Netherlanders" were, technically speaking, also "Netherlands subjects". The plausibility of this technical argument, which also rested on the common usage of the terms "subjects" in monarchies, and "citizens" in republics, was reduced because one category of "Netherlands subjects" — the Netherlanders — had a special, and higher, status in the colony. The significance of this could be seen in cases of naturalization. When a Chinese man sought naturalization (*gelijkstelling*) to European status, he applied to become a Netherlander, not a "Netherlands subject". Naturalization was open to all Chinese, whether foreign or locally born, provided they could meet the criteria. The fact that some Chinese who were already "Netherlands subjects" pursuant to the 1910 law thought it valuable to become Netherlanders makes it clear that discrimination on a racial basis continued (*Verslag* ... 1942, pp. 101, 137).

The combination of the Chinese Nationality Law of 1909 (based on *ius sanguinis*) and the Netherlands Subjecthood Law of 1910 (based on *ius soli*) gave rise to a problem of dual nationality among the ethnic Chinese who were claimed by the Dutch as "Netherlands subjects" under the 1910 law. At a practical level, this was resolved diplomatically through the consular convention of 1911, which — at least in formal terms — excluded Chinese who were "Netherlands subjects" from the jurisdiction of the Chinese consuls in the Indies or the Netherlands. The convention did not, however, extinguish their dual nationality, and the claim of the Manchu government that all descendants of Chinese, wherever born, were Chinese nationals was reasserted in the Nationality Act of the Republic of China in 1929. The dual nationality problem was, *pace* Fasseur, to prove to be another "colonial heritage bestowed upon independent Indonesia" and was to bedevil the situation of Chinese Indonesians for decades after independence.

Nor did the convention extinguish the demand among those Chinese nationalists in the Indies who had, without their consent and against their will, been defined by the 1910 law as "Netherlands subjects" that they should be given an adequate mechanism to reject that status. There was, of course, an absurdity in the colonial legal system which compelled them to be

"Netherlands subjects" but, at the same time, categorized them as "Foreign Orientals". Other Chinese were more concerned with seeking the same equal status with Europeans which had been achieved by the Japanese under the 1899 Japanese Law, and, in the case of those "Netherlands subjects" who saw their future as lying in the Indies, to secure special representation for the Chinese in the municipal councils and the People's Assembly (*Volksraad*). Although another, smaller group of Chinese chose to throw in their lot with the Indonesian nationalists, the political dynamics of the late colonial period, as well as the legal classifications of the colonial government, tended to separate the Chinese from the Indonesians, discursively as well as socially.[10]

The report of the Visman Commission nonetheless describes various attempts dating from the early 1930s to establish a kind of Indies citizenship (*Indisch Burgerschap*). As Fasseur cogently pointed out, "an Indies citizenship, linked with the exercise of political rights ... would have meant the end of the problem of racial differentiation in and before the law but also the end of Dutch political control of the Indies" (Fasseur 1994, pp. 53–54). Although the Visman Commission considered proposals for *Indisch Burgerschap*, unsurprisingly it did not recommend their implementation and in any case its report was completed just as the Japanese were occupying Indonesia (*Verslag* ... 1942, pp. 98–140).

Fasseur was therefore correct in saying that "the Dutch colonial state remained in fact a state without citizens", but his further statement that Article 27 of the 1945 Constitution of the Indonesian Republic "definitely put an end to any form of racial classification before the law" is open to question. It is true that Article 27 proclaims that all Indonesian citizens have the same legal rights and obligations in law and government, but reference to other articles gives a different picture. Article 26 provides that "citizens shall be persons who are native-born Indonesians (*orang-orang bangsa Indonesia asli*) and persons of other nationality (*orang-orang bangsa lain*) who are legalized by statute as being citizens". Thus, the Indonesian Constitution of 1945, which has had almost the quality of sacred text in Indonesia since its reintroduction by presidential decree in 1959, has enshrined within the fundamental law on citizenship a categorical distinction between "native-born Indonesians" and "persons of other nationality". In this sense, as I have written elsewhere, the distinction between Indonesian citizen and alien was also "a carrier of the colonial virus of racial separation" (Coppel 2001). The "native-born Indonesians" were those whom the colonial government had defined as Natives (*Inlanders*); if the ethnic Chinese were to qualify for Indonesian citizenship, their entitlement to it would depend upon the wording of future acts of Parliament which might (and did) change with the winds of political convenience.

Although the term "Indonesian citizen" (*Warga Negara Indonesia*, often abbreviated to *WNI*) applied, strictly speaking, to both categories of citizens referred to in Article 26 of the Constitution, in popular speech it has often been understood to refer only to *WNI keturunan asing* (Indonesian citizen of foreign descent). This synecdochic usage echoes the common but mistaken assumption in the late colonial period that it was only "non-Netherlanders" who were "Netherlands subjects". The use of the word *asing* ("foreign") in the term "Indonesian citizen of foreign descent" emphasizes the alienness in indigenous Indonesian eyes, even of the Indonesian citizen Chinese, just as in the late colonial era the Dutch classified as "Foreign Orientals" even those Chinese whom they defined as "Netherlands subjects, non-Netherlanders". The stain of "foreignness" which became attached to the ethnic Chinese under both the Netherlands Indies and Indonesian legal systems has become indelible, no matter how many generations ago their ancestors settled in the country.[11]

In another ironic parallel with (or is it continuity from?) the colonial past, Article 6 of the 1945 Constitution provided that "the President shall be a native-born Indonesian (*orang Indonesia asli*)". Whatever shifts might have taken place in the late colonial period away from the status of "Netherlander" to that of "Netherlands subject", the requirement that the Governor-General should be a "Netherlander" remained intact to the end of colonial rule. Thus, the Indonesian Republic has been no more willing to open its highest post to all of its citizens than the Netherlands Indies was to open its equivalent position to all "Netherlands subjects".

This is not the place to follow the twists and turns of Indonesian citizenship law as it affected the ethnic Chinese in the four decades after the proclamation of independence in August 1945. The attitude of the Indonesian Government towards the access of the ethnic Chinese to Indonesian citizenship has been at some times liberal and welcoming, at other times restrictive and rejecting. The ethnic Chinese themselves have been divided and inconsistent in their attitudes to Indonesian citizenship. The Government of China (after October 1949, the People's Republic of China) has likewise fluctuated in its attitudes towards the Chinese in Indonesia. Dramatic political changes in both Indonesia and China have also contributed to the ebb and flow of changes and uncertainties in the position of Chinese Indonesians. The implementation of the Chou-Sunario treaty of 1955, which was supposed to solve the longstanding problem of dual nationality, became embroiled in complicated debates about who were deemed to be dual nationals and who were to be exempted from having to reject their Chinese nationality if they wished to remain Indonesian citizens, while at the same time the Indonesian Citizenship Law was being radically amended. Even after its implementation was substantially completed in January 1962, the treaty had residual effects which were summarily curtailed by the Indonesian Government rescinding it in April 1969 following the suspension of diplomatic relations between the two countries in October 1967.[12]

Even those Chinese Indonesians whose Indonesian citizenship has not been in doubt have found that the equality of all citizens before the law supposedly guaranteed by Article 27 of the Constitution has not been honoured in practice. For example, although President Soeharto paid lip service to the principle of equal rights for all citizens, including those of Chinese descent, and condemned discrimination against *WNI* of "foreign descent", he singled out the ethnic Chinese for special treatment. They, but not the other citizens belonging to hundreds of indigenous ethnic groups, were called upon to abandon exclusiveness, to change their names, and to restrict the practice of their religion to the privacy of the home where it displayed elements of Chineseness. They, but not the Indonesian citizens of other ethnic groups, had their identity cards and passports marked with a special code, and were restricted in their access to state university student places. When special provision was to be made for members of what was euphemistically called "the economically weak group", all Chinese were assumed to fall outside this category, regardless of their individual circumstances.

In the post-Soeharto era, Chinese Indonesians have been emboldened to demand the dismantling of all legislation which discriminates on the basis of race and ethnicity. Soeharto's successors as President — B. J. Habibie and Abdurrachman Wahid — both pledged their support for such a reform, but little has been achieved. The habit of conceptualizing the population of Indonesia in racialized terms is rooted so deeply in its colonial past, as we have seen, that we should not expect the reform to be fully implemented in the near future.

Notes

1 The late Professor Wim Wertheim, who was one of the lawyers recruited in 1930, first alerted me to the story in his comments on a paper which I presented at a seminar at the Centre for Asian Studies, Amsterdam, in early 1996, and later published as Coppel (1997). We agreed that the issue deserved closer scholarly scrutiny, and he later published his version in Wertheim (1997a), and Wertheim

(1997b). The sections of the present chapter concerning "Foreign Orientals" are heavily indebted to these publications (and to his kindness in sending them to me); and to the discussion in Cees Fasseur's excellent essay (1992). These sections appeared in an earlier form in the paper I presented to the conference on "Law and the Chinese Outside China" held at the Australian National University, Canberra on 1–4 July 1998, and were later published in revised form in another anthology (Coppel 1999). I am grateful to Prof. Wertheim for his assistance and for that of Faye Chan and Rosy Antons-Susanto for respectively finding and commenting on relevant archival material. I also acknowledge the assistance of the Faculty of Arts at the University of Melbourne for its financial support.

2 According to Professor Wertheim, Fasseur erred in stating that indigenous Christians (*inheemsche christenen*) were equated with Europeans. A provision to that effect was suspended by the Governor-General, and they remained subject to *adat* law until the end of colonial rule.

3 These mitigations included the application of the Civil Code (*Burgerlijk Wetboek*), with respect to their family law and succession (*familie- en erfrecht*) to the Chinese of Java in 1917, and of the Outer Islands in 1925.

4 Emphasis in original. This is an abridged version of Fasseur (1992b).

5 This and the following two paragraphs are indebted to Fasseur (1992a).

6 Another leading Ethicus advocate of equalizing the Chinese was the lawyer P. H. Fromberg.

7 This distinction drew on a different classification of the population, which will be discussed in the second part of this chapter.

8 See, for example, P. L. G. [Phoa Liong Gie], "De rechtstoestand der Chineezen in Indonesië", *Chung Hwa Hui Tsa Chih* 5, no. 2 (October–November 1926); K. T. H. [Kwee Tek Hoay], "Gelijkstelling bagi bangsa Tionghoa", *Panorama* 29 (2 July 1927): 1–3; K. T. H. [Kwee Tek Hoay], "Boemipoetra dan gelijkstelling Tionghoa", *Panorama* 32 (23 July 1927): 1–4; C. T. Bertling, "Gelijkstelling van Chineezen met Europeanen", *Koloniale Studien* 11, no. 2 (1927): 44–71.

9 An example is the electoral law of 1925 referred to above, which was nominally based upon nationality, but in practice the differentiation between Netherlanders, indigenous Netherlands subjects (non-Netherlanders) and foreign Netherlands subjects (non-Netherlanders) essentially replicated the *bevolkingsgroepen* classification.

10 On the process of "racial and cultural separating out" in the late colonial period, see Wertheim (1959, p. 184), Doorn (1983, pp. 6, 13, 20), and Coppel (1997, pp. 574–75).

11 Americans or Australians whose forbears settled as immigrants in the early nineteenth century would find it incongruous to be categorized in law as "citizens of foreign descent".

12 In the 1980s, the Indonesian Government was to embark on a drive to encourage alien Chinese to become naturalized as Indonesian citizens, and the Chinese Government passed a Nationality Law in 1980 which acknowledged that Chinese

nationals who voluntarily acquired foreign nationality would automatically lose their Chinese nationality. These measures — which are reminiscent in their intent of the consular convention of 1911 — were a necessary prelude to the resumption of diplomatic relations between the two countries in 1990. For more information on the complicated history of national status and dual nationality of the Chinese in Indonesia, see Willmott (1961), Mozingo (1976), Coppel (1982), and Suryadinata (1985).

References

Albrecht, J. E. *Soerat Ketrangan dari pada hal Kaadaan Bangsa Tjina di Negri Hindia Olanda.* Batavia: Albrecht & Rusche, 1890.

BAKIN. *Pedoman Penyelesaian Masalah Cina di Indonesia* (3 volumes). Jakarta: Badan Koordinasi Masalah Cina — BAKIN, 1979–80.

Coppel, Charles A. "The position of the Chinese in Indonesia, the Philippines, and Malaysia". In *The Chinese in Indonesia, the Philippines and Malaysia,* pp. 1–9. London: Minority Rights Group, 1982.

————. "Revisiting Furnivall's 'plural society': Colonial Java as a mestizo society?". *Ethnic and Racial Studies* 20, no. 3 (1997): 562–79.

————. "The Indonesian Chinese as 'Foreign Orientals' in the Netherlands Indies". In *Indonesia: Law and Society,* edited by Timothy Lindsey, pp. 33–41. Leichhardt, N.S.W.: Federation Press, 1999.

————. "Chinese Indonesians in Crisis: 1960s and 1990s". In *Perspective on the Chinese Indonesians,* edited by Michael R. Godley and Grayson J. Lloyd, pp. 20–40. Hindmarsh, S. A.: Crawford House, 2001.

Doorn, Jacques van. *A Divided Society: Segmentation and Mediation in Late-Colonial Indonesia.* Rotterdam: Erasmus University, Faculty of Social Sciences, CASP, 1983.

Fasseur, C. "Colonial dilemma: Van Vollenhoven and the struggle between adat law and Western law in Indonesia". In *European Expansion and Law: The Encounter of European and Indigenous Law in 19th- and 20th-Century Africa and Asia,* edited by W. J. Mommsen and J. A. de Moor, pp. 218–42. Oxford & New York: Berg, 1992a.

————. "Hoeksteen en struikelblok. Rasonderscheid en overheidsbeleid in Nederlands-Indië". *Tijdschrift voor Geschiedenis* 105 no. 2 (1992b): 218–42.

————. "Cornerstone and Stumbling Block: Racial Classification and the Late Colonial State in Indonesia". In *The Late Colonial State in Indonesia: Political and Economic Foundations of the Netherlands Indies 1880–1942,* edited by Robert Cribb, pp. 31–56. Leiden: KITLV Press, 1994.

Fromberg, P. H. *Verspreide Geschriften.* Leiden: Leidsche Uitgeversmaatschappij, 1926.

Furnivall, J. S. *Netherlands India: A Study of Plural Economy.* Cambridge: Cambridge University Press, 1944.

Hooker, M. B. *Legal Pluralism: An Introduction to Colonial and Neo-Colonial Laws.* Oxford: Clarendon Press, 1975.

Hooker, M. B., ed. *Laws of South-East Asia, Volume II: European Laws in South-East Asia.* Singapore: Butterworths, 1988.

Kollewijn. "De Moderne Chinese Kodifikatie". *Indisch Tijdschrift van het Recht* 132 (1930): 323–40.

————. "Het moderne Chinese familierecht". *Indisch Tijdschrift van het Recht* 134 (1931): 107–111.

Marle, A. van. "De groep der Europeanen in Nederlands-Indië, iets over onststaan en groei". *Indonesië* 5 (1951–52): 500.

Mozingo, David. *Chinese Policy Towards Indonesia, 1949–1967.* Ithaca, N.Y.: Cornell University Press, 1976.

Prins, W. F. "De bevolkingsgroepen in het Nederlandsch-Indische recht". *Koloniale Studien* 17, no. 2 (1933): 679.

Suryadinata, Leo. *China and the ASEAN States: The Ethnic Chinese Dimension.* Singapore: Singapore University Press, 1985.

Verslag van de Commissie tot Bestudeering van Staatsrechtelijke Hervormingen ...: Deel II Indië's Wenschen. Batavia: Landsdrukkerij, 1942 (2nd printing).

Wertheim, W. F. *Indonesian Society in Transition: A Study of Social Change.* 2nd edition. The Hague & Bandung: Van Hoeve, 1959.

————. *De Status van de Chinezen in Vooroorlogs Nederlands-Indië: Zeer geheime documenten uit de jaren 1928–1932.* Research Report no. 97/1. Leiden: Van Vollenhoven Institute for Law and Administration in Non-Western Countries, 1997a.

————. "Political status of the Chinese in Pre-War Netherlands-Indies: Secret Documents from 1928–1932". *Indonesian Law and Administration Review* 3, no. 2 (1997b).

Willmott, Donald E. *The National Status of the Chinese in Indonesia 1900–1958.* Revised edition. Ithaca: Cornell Modern Indonesia Project, Monograph Series, Cornell University, 1961.

Winarta, Frans Tan. "RI Racist Laws Need to be Revoked". *Jakarta Post,* 13 August 1998.

6

CHINESE FAMILY FIRMS IN INDONESIA AND THE QUESTION OF "CONFUCIAN CORPORATISM"

Daniel Fitzpatrick

Just as some have given "Confucian capitalism" credit for much of East Asia's economic miracle, so have others blamed it for its apparent collapse. Thus, on the one hand, neo-Confucian values of frugality, diligence, group orientation, and respect for authority were said to have inspired the high savings rates, strong states, and corporate networks that fuelled economic growth.[1] Yet, on the other, the same values are now alleged to have fostered the crony capitalism and failure to force the exit of insolvent capital that triggered economic collapse.[2] In either case, the unexplored assumption is that culture is an independent variable in economic behaviour and performance, and is a common thread in overseas Chinese business networks and countries with Confucianist traditions.

As with economics, so too with law. Ever since Weber's study of China, orientalists have used culture to explain Asian legal behaviour and its relationship with formal law. A modern example is the notion of "Confucian corporatism", which posits that East and Southeast Asia have Western-style corporate laws, yet the foundations of these laws — separate legal entity and separation of ownership and control — are antithetical to neo-Confucian business customs founded upon personal relationships, intricate networks, and family-controlled firms. The result is said to be a clash of business culture and formal law, which then has the effect of rendering law either inappropriate or ineffectual.[3]

Yet, the role of culture in law and economic relations is not settled, and deserves greater analysis in the current economic and legal environment. To assume, without qualification, that culture is an independent variable risks legal reforms lacking in analytical justification. It is true, of course, that the traditional sociological view is that law is fundamentally rooted in culture: thus Weber viewed the Protestant work ethic as central to the rise of European capitalism and, ironically, Confucianism as historically obstructive of economic development in China.[4] Recent times have seen, however, the rise of economic theories asserting a limited role for "culture" in legal activity. Indeed, neo-classical law and economics posit no role for culture: all economic and legal behaviour is seen simply as a rational response to price signals in relevant markets.[5] For their part, the new school of institutional law and economics views culture as a dependent variable, a means by which rational self-interested entrepreneurs may prefer "private ordering" methods of contract enforcement, such as reputation, status and goodwill, to that offered by formal law.[6]

This chapter applies these differing models of culture and law to analyse the notion that Confucian culture is an independent variable in the operation of Southeast Asian corporate law. Its case study is Chinese family firms in Indonesia. The study is apt because these firms dominate the private commercial sector. They display many of the characteristics of "Confucian corporatism" — including strong family and group affiliation, highly diversified and networked conglomerates, and paternalistic and secretive styles of corporate management. Yet, they are subject to a Western-style company law which spectacularly failed to maintain, let alone improve, corporate governance in the run up to the economic crisis in late 1997.

Chinese Business Customs and Formal Law

Few authors, of course, ascribe East Asian economic behaviour solely to traditional Confucianism. After all, as Kim points out, the Confucian status system placed merchants alongside peasants in traditional society, and Confucian élites in China historically rejected trade with the West. Thus, it is "post", "neo" or "new" Confucianism that is said to have inspired rapid industrial development in East Asia.[7] In particular, this new Confucianism contained certain elements which, when combined with the Western-derived impetus for modernization and capitalism, created collectivist economic structures that were "better suited to the age of mass industrialisation".[8] These elements included family/group orientation, preference for personal relationships, benevolently autocratic leadership, and maintenance of harmony and industriousness. When applied to capitalist activity, they created business customs and corporate structures based around highly networked personal relationships, paternalistic management processes, growth rather than shareholder-oriented decision-making and stable careerism for employees: in short, the highly diversified conglomerates and networks of East and Southeast Asia.[9]

These values have moved from their original geographic source to dominate business organization in the region because of the preponderance of overseas Chinese in Taiwan, Singapore, and Hong Kong; the heavy influence of Chinese cultural traditions in Japan, Vietnam, and South Korea; and the economic dominance of ethnic Chinese minorities in Thailand, Indonesia, and Malaysia. They are also reinforced by the strength of intra-regional investment, the propensity of Japanese investment to form partnerships with local overseas Chinese businesses and the widespread adoption of Japanese organizational methods.[10]

The implication for law is that, in this culturalist conception, the dominance of neo-Confucian values in business inevitably renders formal commercial law of little influence. For example, contract law, with its fixed rights and obligations and assumption of court adjudication in the event of breach, means little where contractual relations are founded either upon family or group affiliations, or "*guanxi*" connections based on reciprocity and gift-giving. Rights and obligations in Confucian thought cannot be universalist as they are largely dependent on the personal relationships and status of the parties in question. It is face, status, and relationships which define commercial relationships, not the 100-page bond contract.[11] Hence, breach of contract is far less likely to be sanctioned by court enforcement than loss of "face" or status within a group or network.

Statements of this kind can be found littered throughout the literature of East Asian contract law. Now, similar culturalist reasoning is being applied in the area of insolvency law, a highly topical issue in the wake of East Asia's economic crisis. Thus, Tomasic and Little argue that cultural factors, particularly the notion of loss of "face", explain the limited use of insolvency laws in the East Asian region.[12] They reach this conclusion on the basis of overwhelming references to culture in interviewee responses in six Asian legal systems. The qualitative data indicate, in particular, that creditors are reluctant to push debtors into insolvency because of, firstly, strong personal relations with their debtors; secondly, the fact that the debtor may have a higher status, or be affiliated with a network important to the creditor; thirdly, fear that public exposure of a "bad debt" problem will damage the reputation and status of the creditor; and lastly, a cultural preference to solve conflict within the group rather than by reference to national courts.

Confucian Corporatism

We turn now to culturist analyses of East Asian corporate law. This is where the notion of "Confucian corporatism" is most relevant and requires some explanation. Modern Western corporate law is predicated fundamentally on two issues: separate legal entity, and the separation of ownership and control. Both allegedly create the rules and principles that sit at variance with Overseas Chinese forms of business organization.

The notion of separate legal entity separates corporations, for legal purposes, from their controllers. Hence, not only can a company hold property in its own name, but its liabilities are separated from the liabilities of its shareholders. This gives rise to the possibility of limited liability, which simply means that, if the company becomes insolvent, shareholders can only lose the extent of their capital contribution. It is, in turn, limited liability which has led to well-known legal rules on "lifting the corporate veil".

The separation of corporate ownership and control creates, in modern corporate theory, the possibility of investor risks: equity investor confidence depends on management acting in the interest of shareholders.[13] The result has been legal rules and institutions to constrain management actions. This is the basis of corporate law. Internally, management is supervised through shareholder rights, director duties, outside directors or a board of commissioners, disclosure requirements, and overriding powers of the general meeting. Externally, investor risks are minimized by capital markets (allowing both shareholder rights of exit and a market for corporate control), institutional investors, and prudential supervision.[14]

A number of scholars have argued, however, that this template model is incompatible with neo-Confucian forms of business organization. For example, Lawton has argued eloquently that Hong Kong's "corporate law regime is often little more than the formal clothing for, what in substance remains, essentially a familiar and personalistic Chinese organisation".[15] To similar effect, Tricker has stated that:

> Power and prestige in the Chinese business lies with the owner-manager. Responsibility for day-to-day activities of production and operations may be delegated to managers, but even then with frequent rearrangements and what would be considered, by Western executives, interference in delegated responsibilities. Responsibility for financial and personnel

> matters typically remains with the owner .... Furthermore, the notion of a board of directors with the responsibility to direct ... is contrary to the rubric of Chinese business thinking. The underlying perception of business in the Chinese mind is as a series of ad hoc deals, a succession of contracts or ventures, rather than a dominant strategy to provide a product and create a market.[16]

Tricker accordingly recommends that a special category of "dominated company" should be established in East Asian corporate law regimes to respond to the existing disconnection between formal law and business culture.[17]

Three particular consequences for corporate law may be distilled from this culturalist analysis. First, the concept of a separate legal entity is predicated on the Western perception of man as a distinct, individualized entity, whereas Chinese culture perceives individuals not as individuals *per se* but as one aspect of a connected and reciprocated network of relationships. Hence, Western-style corporate law has failed to prevent the persistent mixing of corporate and personal property in Overseas Chinese family firms.[18]

Secondly, the paternalistic and secretive management style associated with Overseas Chinese family corporations, which is said to stem from deep-seated Confucianism, is incompatible with formalized management processes based on transparency and shareholder accountability. It is thus said that Chinese family management has difficulties with legal corporate governance requirements.[19] They do not disclose accurate financial information, nor render accountability to minority shareholders, because Overseas Chinese company patriarchs prefer paternalism and family interests over market demands for protection of minority shareholders.

Thirdly, modern corporate law provides no assistance to the transformation of Chinese family firms in the second or third generation into long-lasting, professionally managed corporations. Indeed, this succession problem seems to be a particular phenomenon in the region. Because legal corporate governance requirements for public companies are so antithetical to Confucianist business culture, the transition to widely-held public companies is particularly difficult, and calls for a range of special legal responses.

Of course, more sophisticated versions of these arguments about law and culture include references to political and institutional factors. Lawton, for example, states that the commercial and political environments combine with culture to produce particular forms of corporate organization and behaviour. Similarly, a number of interviewees in Tomasic and Little's *Insolvency Law and Practice in Asia* also indicate that political factors play a role in the limited use of insolvency laws. However, the important point is that they all treat culture as an independent variable in economic relations and a direct source of the

Asian phenomenon of limited use of formal business laws. The following section criticizes this notion of culture as an independent variable. While it is not saying that culture is irrelevant to East Asian legal analysis, it suggests that culturalist explanations, on their own, fail to offer a structured model to explain and predict how culture combines with other factors to produce certain legal outcomes.

Culturalist Views of Law and the Overseas Chinese: A Critique

Because Overseas Chinese business networks have had such remarkable economic success, it is natural that cultural traditions have been the focus of analysis and explanation. Equally, much of the research on Overseas Chinese business cultures, particularly surveys of "coalface" practitioner attitudes, serves as valuable source material for the comparativist. Thus, for example, the family-dominated and networked nature of corporate structures does indeed provide challenges for corporate law. There is undoubtedly a disconnection between Overseas Chinese business practices and the principles of modern corporate law.

The following section argues that culturalist views of economic behaviour and their impact on law are flawed in a number of ways. First, "culture" has always been a reified sociological term, a static representation of dynamic group processes, associations, and institutions. To use it as an instrument of legal analysis tends to assume that cultural change can only occur as a result of external influences, rather than dynamic factors within a culturally distinct group. Hence, "culture" as an analytical tool overlooks the processes, including economic conditions, that induce and constitute that culture, and fails, particularly as societies become increasingly complex and social functions specialized, to provide a framework for analysis of political conflicts over law or cultural divisions within a group or society.[20]

Secondly, Savigny and Sumners' historically influential notion of law as fundamentally rooted in culture, with the result that law inconsistent with culture is destined to be inappropriate and ineffective, has long been discarded by modern sociological theories of law. This is due simply to the fact that most modern laws are instrumental: precisely because they are designed to affect social change they are, by definition at least, initially out of step with social practice. It follows that a bare assertion of a law's inconsistency with social or cultural practices only establishes the fact of inconsistency and does not necessarily prove that the law itself is inappropriate or ineffective.

Thirdly, the basic paradox that historical Confucian values militated against trade, but neo-Confucian values allegedly promote it, has never been satisfactorily explained.[21] It seems far more plausible to say that the fact of migration led many Chinese to turn their group and network orientations towards trade and material gain as a means of survival rather than as the result of any particular cultural imperative.[22] For example, in Indonesia, as with most Southeast Asian countries, the Chinese were prohibited from entering the bureaucracy and many of the professions, and were subject to substantial local social and cultural traditions. Moreover, they were encouraged by the colonialists to become commercial middleman in the colonial trading system. It followed almost inevitably that the Overseas Chinese grouped together in the pursuit of trade and business success. Yet, the precise effects of these practical socio-political imperatives on economics and law are not incorporated in the culturalist model.

Fourthly, not only do reified notions of culture fail to explain the internal dynamism of cultural traditions, they also fail to provide a structured explanatory and predictive model for the relationship between culture and other factors affecting legal and economic behaviour. Issues such as social and political marginalization, the prevalence of patrimonial states and the weakness of formal legal systems clearly need to be taken into account, yet the culturalist model fails to explain how they impacted on Overseas Chinese culture, let alone how they combined with cultural factors to affect economic behaviour and the role of formal law. It is not enough simply to say that politics and history interacted with culture to produce certain "legal" outcomes. What is required is a theoretical model that explains and predicts the way in which cultural factors interact with economic and political issues to produce these legal outcomes.

This final issue is a fundamental one. If, as the International Monetary Fund (IMF), World Bank and U.S. Treasury so clearly desire, transparent, predictable formal law is to play a greater role in post-crisis Asian economic relations, then a model which explains and predicts the interrelationship between cultural elements and institutional factors is clearly desirable. If economic and institutional factors are indeed significant, the implication is that economic changes to corporations, and political changes to states in East and Southeast Asia, will increase the role of formal law far more quickly than if law were governed by deeper cultural currents. Such a result, of course, would impact considerably on assessments of the region's future as an emerging market.

Law and Economics: A Model for Culture and Law?

One possible model, increasingly asserted for the region's legal future, is modern law and economic theory. It is a major source of efforts to reform

Asian economic law and governance, and is thus worthy of application to the question of law and Chinese family firms.

Neoclassical Law and Economics

Modern law and economics may be divided into neoclassical and new institutional schools of thought. Neoclassical law and economics assert that all law can be explained solely as a response to price signals in relevant markets. It assumes that all individuals act in a rational self-interested way to maximize wealth or other personal objectives. While all individuals may not adopt this rationalist cause of action, averaged out over time among a group, it will be the predominant pattern of behaviour. Given this assumption, individual responses to law can thus be explained and predicted on the basis of a cost/benefit analysis. At its simplest, law will be adhered to where it provides the most efficient route to self-maximizing objectives, but will be ignored, or contracted away, where it hinders efficient attainment of those objectives. It follows that culture *per se* has no influence on economic behaviour or the appropriateness of formal law because both are the rational products of accumulated self-interested decision-making by relevant individuals. "Culture", in this sense, cannot be an independent variable in explaining legal behaviour. It can only ever be an imprecise label applied to a conglomeration of rational decisions based on market signals.

Thus, Posner[23] applies law and economics to that most apparently "cultural" of institutions: customary law in primitive societies. In brief, he asserts that the "legal" features of traditional societies can be explained by high information costs. These include the close reliance on unpredictable forces of nature, and low levels of communication and transportation which, in the absence of other mechanisms for insurance, promote strong communal ties in order to spread risk. Similarly, the high cost of information relating to cause and effect in the natural world leads to reliance on supernatural retribution and justice as alternatives to rational "legal" instruments. Finally, because of the high costs of individualized case-by-case bargaining, and in the absence of other means for resolving disputes, there is an emphasis on status relationships to define rights and obligations.[24] A similarly egregious approach is that by Ramseyer[25] who analysed economic and legal behaviour in Japanese markets, such as that of geisha girls, to allege that traditional practices were not necessarily exploitative, or uniquely "cultural", but rational responses to relevant market characteristics.

However, the difficulty with neoclassical law and economics is that it fails as a model for law in practice, particularly because it fails to explain (1) the fact of differences in economic and legal organizations between countries, and (2) the persistent problems of market failures and imperfections. These points must be addressed by economic theories of law if they are to explain different economic and legal behaviour across a range of systems without using simplistic notions of "culture".

The failure of neoclassical law and economics to explain comparative differences may be illustrated by reference to corporate governance. Neoclassical law and economics would predict that, given the existence of some form of market behaviour and competition, legal rules and institutions will evolve over time into a more efficient state. In turn, and just as Posner argues that common law rules have evolved over time solely by reference to efficiency criteria, ultimately all legal rules and institutions would be expected to reach congruence across the world, a Teilhard de Chardin-like "omega point" for all law and law-based institutions. Yet as North[26] has pointed out, this efficiency theory of law and institutions fails to explain the prevalence and maintenance of inefficient laws and institutions throughout history, and the radically different performance of economies over time.[27]

Why is corporate governance so different in Germany and Japan compared with the United States and the United Kingdom (UK)? In Germany, bank representatives generally sit on the board of commissioners, and actively supervise and advise the board of directors. Similarly, in Japan, the "main" bank is usually a large shareholder in companies of its group, and supervises management through an informal web of influence. In the United States and the UK, however, banks have little influence and capital markets, institutional investors, and independent directors are the key instruments of corporate governance.[28] It could hardly be said that economic efficiency in these countries differs to a degree that is directly correspondent with these differences in legal and institutional corporate governance. All are developed mature economies, and the neoclassical assumption of institutional and legal evolution towards efficiency fails to explain how they could have such different systems of corporate governance. Nor, it must be said, do either neoclassical or culturalist theories explain why such culturally distinct countries as Germany and Japan could possess similar institutions of corporate governance.

The second issue is that neoclassical law and economics fail adequately to explain or address the persistent problems of market failures and imperfections. It is concerned with an ideal, a perfectly competitive market with perfectly informed participants. It is struggling with real world problems of imperfect markets. Thus, particularly during the 1980s, large numbers of international assistance programmes that promoted market activities through deregulation, privatization, and trade liberalization failed because the institutional underpinnings for market operations — property and contract laws, a reliable and competent judiciary, and a reasonably strong state — were not present.[29] Neoclassical law and economics have no answer for these problems because, in their conception, effective laws and institutions are market products rather than market requirements.

New Institutional Law and Economics

New institutional law and economics developed largely as a response to these defects in neoclassical law and economics. They are based on the notion that institutions — the constraints that humans devise to shape human interaction[30] — are central to economic development and transformation. Institutions for these purposes are said to consist of formal rules, informal norms and their respective enforcement characteristics.[31] Which institutions are applied, in a given circumstance, is based on "transaction costs". It is this "transaction costs" analysis that is relevant for our purposes, because it provides a means by which "cultural" and institutional elements may be integrated with other factors in the explanation of economic and legal behaviour.

Transaction costs are simply the costs of bargaining. They include not only common issues of identifying the parties, meeting them, bargaining, valuing, and enforcement,[32] but also difficulties associated with longer term contracting, in particular monitoring and insuring against potential opportunism or shirking by the other contracting party.[33] The important point, for us, is that parties to agreements will adopt different legal regimes in response to different transaction costs. This may even include "private ordering" mechanisms, such as reputation, status and goodwill, in preference to formal law. Such an outcome is all the more likely where cultural influences promote informal contracting and impose social costs on court actions, or strict reliance on fixed rights and obligations.

In other words, new institutional law and economics do recognize that "culture" may have an effect on law. However, it views culture as a dependent variable, not an independent analytical tool, but something that may reinforce or trigger rational decisions by parties to contracts. This means that East Asian conglomerates may prefer informal norms, rather than formal law, to govern their contracts because a range of institutional and cultural issues render informal contracting a more efficient response to the risks of bargaining than formal law. The crucial point, therefore, is that the limited use of formal law in the East Asian corporate context may be explained by analysing institutional rather than cultural issues. The significance, of course, is that if the conditions that make informal legal regimes in East Asia more attractive are changed, then formal law may become a more efficient response than informal norms. This opens up the possibility of more rapid change than if the deeper currents of "culture" were the defining variable.

The point may be illustrated by reference to corporate law. Why would East Asian conglomerates prefer informal norms to formal corporations law? First, informal norms are highly efficient where there is a tightly-knit commercial élite. This is because the close ties and repeat nature of transacting increase the costs of opportunism.[34] Thus, corporate misappropriation, or breach of contract, is more efficiently sanctioned within the commercial élite than by reference to formal rules or unreliable courts.

Secondly, when taking a commercial decision that affects members of a dominant élite, a rational director will simply weigh the risks of reputational loss, shareholder litigation, or prosecution with the risks of exclusion and punishment arising from alienation of the élite and the costs of ensuring a favourable judicial result. Equally, shareholder and prosecution agencies will weigh the benefits of litigation against the risks of alienating the élite. The result is that directors face few risks of legal sanction for breach of duty, and many incentives to act simply as an outgrowth of the commercial élite. In systems where the risks of formal sanction are minimal, and élite politico-commercial power is dominant, rational directors are far more likely not to act in the interests of their corporation but in favour of the dominant commercial élite. This is a pervasive rational decision in Indonesia. It flows from the fact that, in a system of crony capitalism, most commercial decisions and litigation will affect members of the commercial élite. Moreover, because of pervasive judicial corruption, any litigation or enforcement simply invites a judicial auction rather than rule-based decision-making.

Thirdly, the phenomenon of crony capitalism — close interconnections between commercial and political élites — may be explained, at least in part, by new institutional "transaction costs" analysis. Thus, where the state itself is a dominant economic force, government contracts are a primary source of recurrent business, and government officials possess significant incentives to obtain unofficial payments from contractors, then fundamental transaction costs include accessing government contracts, fostering relationships with government officials, and ensuring performance and periodic renewal of the contracting relationship. This involves a high degree of specialization of human capital as personal trust between the business person and relevant government official becomes paramount. Hence, the contractual governance structure which best deals with technically powerful patrimonialist states may well be rent-seeking agreements or joint ventures with state officials. Moreover, because political risk in this environment is itself a powerful transaction cost, a series of shifting inter-conglomerate alliances — a particular phenomenon in Indonesia — may be explained more as adaptive responses to political rather than purely commercial contingencies.

This analysis certainly appears to provide a structured means to explain the respective roles of culture, history, economics, and the state in economic and legal behaviour. Does it explain therefore, as an alternative to culturalist approaches, the apparent existence of "Confucian corporatism" characteristics in Indonesia, including the dominance of family-owned businesses, the highly diversified and networked system of conglomerates, the paternalistic and secretive forms of corporate governance, and the limited role of formal corporate law?

Chinese Family Firms in Indonesia

The above question can be assessed by reference to Chinese family firms in Indonesia. Hokkien Chinese traders have been trading with the Indonesian archipelago for well over 1,500 years and building settlements there since at least the fifteenth century. With the arrival of the Dutch East Indies company and its subsequent monopolization of trade, the Chinese evolved into domestic commercial intermediaries, initially as employees and lessees of monopoly rights and then as dominant distributors of imported goods, and collectors of export produce.[35] In 1856, their commercial activities were formally subjected to the colonial Dutch civil and commercial codes, although it appears that this was not seriously enforced until the Staatsblad of 1917. With the withdrawal of the Dutch, and then particularly under the Soeharto government's programmes of economic liberalization and patronage politics, they became the dominant force in large-scale commerce.

Does this mean that the Confucian corporatism analysis can be applied to Chinese firms in Indonesia? To be sure, Chinese-Indonesian firms do bear many characteristics of "Confucian corporatism". They are mainly family-owned or controlled, highly diversified and networked (particularly in larger concerns), and subject to paternalistic styles of corporate governance. Most importantly, they also appear to operate with little reference to formal Indonesian corporate law. Indeed, the extraordinary aspect of Indonesia's economic collapse was the remarkable absence of any role for formal law, particularly corporations law.

Reasoning similar to culturalist analyses is applied to Indonesian corporate law by the only two significant studies of its operation in practice: Nono Makarim's unpublished study, *Companies and Business in Indonesia*, and Carl-Bend Kaehlig's *Gesellschaftsrecht in Indonesien: Autonome und Nationale*

Gesellschaftsformen. In particular, both argue that Indonesian company law, then constituted by Articles 36–56 of the colonial Dutch Civil Code 1848, is dysfunctional in practice because its Western antecedents bear little relation both to autocthonous forms of business organization and the traditional Chinese *kongsi* business association.[36] Kaehlig, after considering both the *kongsi* and autocthonous forms of business organization, concludes that large Indonesian companies are characterized by their lack of proprietary capital, dependency on and interconnections with state control and patronage, unity of management, and ownership (usually in the form of one person or family control, and limited number of investors based on "very personal relationships").[37] Hence, he argues that Western-oriented company law in Indonesia is inappropriate and should be rejected in favour of modifying traditional production and profit-sharing contracts (*bagi hasil* and *bagi laba* agreements), as has been done with some success in the petroleum sector, so as to fit modern conditions.[38]

Makarim, for his part, argues that cultural and institutional factors led to *kongsi* continuing to operate under the cloak of Western corporations law.[39] In particular, Makarim contends that, as a result of centuries of social marginalization and arbitrary political power under colonial governments,[40] Chinese-Indonesian corporations are characterized by low average number of shareholders; wide use of bearer shares for anonymity; lack of independent directors or commissioners; low levels of authorized capital; disproportionate reliance on debt finance; high levels of issued and authorized capital held by one founder; and consistent meeting of large tax assessments with applications for bankruptcy. He then concludes that, because the hybrid liability features of the *kongsi* were not recognized by formal law, and because of the social and political marginalization of Chinese Indonesians, there were widespread abuses of the corporate form that were not satisfactorily addressed by Western-style corporate law.

Both authors assume, again, that mere disparity between business practices and formal law of itself renders law inappropriate or ineffective. This chapter argues that a more plausible explanation for the "failure" of corporate law in Indonesia is crony capitalism: the interconnection between family-based corporate ownership, corrupt, entrepreneurially-minded state officials, and weak legal and regulatory mechanisms.

Firstly, we consider the question of predominant family control. It is true that most large corporations in Indonesia are controlled by one or more Chinese-Indonesian families, and equally true that the succession problem identified by Lawton is apparent in the fact that almost no Chinese-Indonesian businesses have survived, or at least thrived, for more than two generations.[41] However, the fact of predominant family enterprises was apparent in England, Holland, and France in the late nineteenth and early twentieth centuries and, in those countries, the problem of succession to large professionally-run corporations was apparent to a greater or lesser degree.[42] Moreover, a number of indigenous Indonesian conglomerates — for example, the Djodjohadikusomo concerns — have arisen which are also large family-based enterprises.

Secondly, there is the question of networked connections between commercial and political élites. These may plausibly be explained by the fact that the state has had a central role in economic life through (1) its state-owned enterprise control over the "commanding heights" of the economy, (2) the pervasive need to obtain licences and permissions (official and unofficial) to engage in commerce, (3) the existence of lucrative state tendering opportunities in the areas of petroleum, manufacturing, mining, and infrastructure, and (4) the fundamental importance of receiving state bank credit (itself subject to state direction), at least until liberalization of the financial sector in the late 1980s. Furthermore, state officials under the Soeharto regime were extremely low paid and implicitly encouraged to seek unofficial levies. In these circumstances, the existence of good personal relations between an entrepreneur and relevant state officials is paramount, and it is not surprising that this would entail both closely held businesses in order not to dilute the personal relationship, and high political risks as suborned officials were replaced over time with new and unfamiliar decision-makers.

A related, and third issue is the fact that Chinese family firms in Indonesia have highly diversified and networked corporate structures. Do these arise because they are characteristics of the neo-Confucianist corporation? A more plausible explanation is the fact of high political risk and consequent existence of rent-seeking arrangements with state officials. Indigenous Indonesian conglomerates are themselves highly diversified and networked. Indeed, their rise mirror the earlier rise of Chinese conglomerates. All are politically well connected. All owe their success to government patronage, and all are highly diversified and have multiple joint ventures with Chinese-Indonesian-owned conglomerates.

This rise of networked indigenous Indonesian conglomerates has thus been a natural extension of the Indonesian patrimonial system. Because the state sector was so powerful, and senior officials controlled licence and contract allocation, the system moved inevitably from favours and kickbacks to direct or indirect financial stakes in contract recipients. Often, the private contractor would encourage the official or his or her relatives to take a financial interest as a means of locking in the relationship of preferential treatment. This process was most apparent in the rise of conglomerates controlled by the Soeharto family, encouraged by President Soeharto as a form of political protection for his children. Thus, Robison concludes that modern Indonesian economic structures take the form of "large conglomerates clustered around centres of politico-bureaucratic power".

A further point is that although diversified and networked conglomerates are a feature of East and Southeast Asian commerce, and hence in line with one aspect of the Confucian corporatist argument, in fact their corporate structures differ dramatically from country to country. Thus, the Japanese *keiretsu* are centred around a main bank and consist of a pyramidical hierarchical structure made up of first, second, and third-tier suppliers. There are interlocking share holdings, receding with the distance of the supplier, but generally without family management or control. The Korean *chaebol* are also pyramidical, with interlocking share holdings but they are family-owned and highly diversified. Taiwanese business groups usually consist of a number of families but are often loosely linked with large numbers of intermittently co-operating small to medium-sized enterprises. Finally, Indonesian conglomerates — both Chinese and indigenous — are similar to the *chaebol* in that they are diversified, pyramidical structures often centred around one family, but they are distinguished by the frequency and willingness with which they seek horizontal partners.[43] Hence, it is common for two or more Indonesian conglomerates to have a long history of co-operation (for example, the Salim, Lippo, and Widjaja groups) or to join forces for a particular project.

In sum, it is the neo-institutionalist, as opposed to culturalist, model that provides a better explanation for the apparently Confucian corporatist characteristics of Chinese family firms in Indonesia. In particular, in longer term contracting in Indonesia, the most relevant transaction costs are (1) accessing and maintaining government contracts and acquiring state government permissions, licences, and/or credit; (2) the contingency risks of opportunism and shirking by other contracting parties or by third-party state officials, and (3) information asymmetries between the politically powerful and foreign or other investors. In circumstances where the court system is inefficient and corrupt, cultural norms emphasize public harmony, and a tightly-knit élite controls large-scale corporate activity, the most efficient legal response to these transaction costs is not detailed formal contracts, arbitration, or litigation but relational contracting through the patrimonial élite. This relational contracting is best effected through highly diversified and networked corporate structures. Equally, in a corporate environment where management is not separated from ownership, and relevant agency costs are partner and state official risk, formal agency cost rules in the form of legal corporate governance requirements will have little practical relevance.

CONCLUSION

There is a school of sociological thought that analyses the "cultural embeddedness" of economic relations. Using its principles, some proponents have observed a connection between Confucian characteristics and forms of economic organization in East Asia. Put simply, many defining features of East Asian firms — including paternalism, hierarchy, family loyalty, diversification, and networking — can be explained by reference to Confucianist principles. In this way, "neo-Confucianism" has been used to explain both economic success and, perversely, recent failures. Indeed, the very features that allegedly propelled economic growth — a networked system of informal contracting, group-orientation, deference to authority — are now claimed as causes of the poor corporate governance that contributed to capital flight by investors.

These arguments have their legal resonances, particularly in the field of corporate law and corporate governance. The thesis is an alluring one. Just as formal contract law appears to have little relevance in a world of networks and connections, so too many underpinning principles of corporations law bear little relation to East Asian corporations. Modern corporate law is based on two fundamental principles: separate legal entity and separation of ownership and control. These principles generate common rules of corporate law: directors duties of accountability and disclosure, separation of corporate assets and liabilities within a corporate group, shareholder rights to information, equitable treatment, and approval of certain major decisions. Yet, of course, these principles are substantially inconsistent with patriarchal, networked, and family-controlled East Asian conglomerates.

This disconnection between East Asian corporate law and reality is a fact. It is a tempting step, therefore, to blame it for the "failure" of corporate law in East Asia. The argument simply runs that law which is too disconnected from reality has little hope of success. Expecting East Asian conglomerates to be transparent and accountable, to retain assets for corporate rather than corporate group purposes, and to refrain from self-dealing — simply because legislation requires it — is unrealistic. "Cultural" propensities to hierarchy, family loyalty, and group networks are far more likely to govern management actions — and to lead to these poor corporate governance results — than mere "black letter" provisions of law.

This chapter does not deny that "culture" is an element in East Asian legal behaviour. However, it does argue that culturalist explanations of comparative law, particularly economic law, reify notions of "culture" in a way that wholly fails to provide a structured and predictive model for analysis. The lesson is, of course, that cultural notions of neo-Confucianism need to be assessed with great care, whether it be in respect of economics or law. What is required is a model that analyses neo-Confucianist phenomena in the light of its institutional context and inputs. Such a model, at least in relation to corporate law, appears to be offered by new institutional economics.

Notes

1 For example, Hung-Chao Tai, "The Oriental Alternative: An Hypotheses on Culture and Economy", in *Confucianism and Economic Development: An Oriental Alternative*, edited by Hung-Chao Tai (Washington D.C.: Washington Institute Press, 1989); See also Cheah Hock Beng, "Towards a Sustained Recovery in the Singapore Economy and the 'New Capitalism'", *Southeast Asian Affairs* 1990 (Institute of Southeast Asian Studies, 1990), p. 317; Grace Goodell, "Another Way to Skin a Cat: The Spirit of Capitalism and the Confucian Ethic", *National Interest* 42 (1995): 66; and Mineo Nakajima, "'Confucian capitalism'; A challenge to the global economy", *Japan Close-Up* 7 (1993): 9.

2 For example, Christopher Lingle, "The Rise and Decline of the Asian Century: False Starts on the Path to the Global Millennium" (Barcelona: Sirocco, 1997); Christopher Lingle, "The End of the Beginning of the 'Pacific Century'? Confucian Corporatism and Authoritarian Capitalism in East Asia", *Pacific Review*, no. 3 (1996): 389.

3 Philip Lawton, "Berle and Means: Corporate Governance and the Chinese Family Firm", *Australian Journal of Corporate Law* 6 (1996): 348–79; R. J. Tricker, "Corporate Governance: A Ripple on the Cultural Reflection", in *Capitalism in Contrasting Cultures*, edited by S. R. Clegg and S. G. Redding (Berlin: Walter de Gruyter, 1990); and S. G. Redding, *The Spirit of Chinese Capitalism* (New York, Berlin: Walter de Gruyter, 1993).

4 Max Weber, *The Protestant Ethic and the Spirit of Capitalism*, translated by T. Parson, introduction by A. Giddens, 2nd edition (London: Allen & Unwin, 1976); Max Weber, *The Religion of China: Confucianism and Taoism*, translated and edited by H. H. Gerth, with an introduction by C. K. Yang (N.Y.: Macmillan, 1964). See also Timothy Brook. "Weber, Mencius, and the History of Chinese Capitalism", *Asian Perspective* 19, no. 1 (1995): 79.

5 Richard Posner, *Economic Analysis of Law*, 4th ed. (Boston: Little, Brown, 1992).

6 Oliver E. Williamson, *The Economic Institutions of Capitalism: Firms, Markets, Relational Contracting* (New York: Free Press; London: Collier Macmillan,

1990); and Oliver Williamson, "The Institutions and Governance of Economic Development and Reform", in *Proceedings of the World Bank Annual Conference on Development Economics* (Washington: World Bank, 1994).

[7] Kim Kyong-Dong, "Confucianism and Capitalist Development in East Asia", in *Capitalism and Development*, edited by Leslie Sklair (London, New York: Routledge, 1994).

[8] Hung-Chao Tai, op. cit. See also Kim Hyung Kook, "Between State and Market: Development Dynamics in East Asian Capitalism", *Asian Perspective* 18, no. 1 (1994): 57; Wellington K. K. Chan. "Chinese business networking and the Pacific Rim: The family firm's roles, past and present", *Journal of American-East Asian Relations* 1, no. 2 (1992): 171; and Murray Weidenbaum. "The Chinese Family Business Enterprise", *California Management Review* 38, no. 4 (1996): 141.

[9] Ibid.

[10] Richard Stubbs, "Asia-Pacific Regionalization and the Global Economy: A Third Form of Capitalism?", *Asian Survey* 35, no. 9 (1995): 785.

[11] Curtis J. Milhaupt, "The Market for Innovation in the United States and Japan: Venture Capital and the Comparative Corporate Governance Debate", *Northwestern University Law Review* 91 (1997): 865.

[12] Roman Tomasic, *Insolvency Law and Practice in Asia* (Hong Kong: FT Law & Tax Asia Pacific, 1997).

[13] Michael Jensen, and William Meckling, "Theory of the Firm: Managerial Behavior, Investor Costs and Ownership Structure", *Journal of Financial Economy* 3, no. 305 (1976): 312–33.

[14] Sally Wheeler, "Introduction", in *A Reader on the Law of the Business Enterprise*, edited by Sally Wheeler (Oxford: Oxford University Press, 1994).

[15] Lawton, op. cit., p. 362.

[16] Tricker, op. cit., pp. 204–5.

[17] Ibid., p. 210.

[18] Redding, op. cit., p. 41; and Lawton, op. cit., p. 356.

[19] Ibid., p. 362; cf. J. Child, *Management in China During the Age of Reform* (Cambridge: Cambridge University Press, 1994), pp. 152–53; S. Stewart, "China's Managers", *The International Executive* 34, no. 165 (1992): 176.

[20] R. Cotterrell, *The Sociology of Law: An Introduction* (London: Butterworth, 1992), p. 53.

[21] Ruth Mc Vey, ed., *Southeast Asian Capitalists* (Ithaca NY: Cornell University Press, 1992), pp. 161–90, especially p. 182.

[22] Rupert Hodder, *Merchant Princes of the East: Cultural Delusions, Economic Success and the Overseas Chinese in Southeast Asia* (Chichester, N.Y.: John Wiley & Sons, 1996).

[23] Posner, op. cit., pp. 25–30.

[24] Ibid.

[25] J. Mark Ramseyer, *Odd Markets in Japanese History* (New York: Cambridge University Press, 1996).

[26] Douglass Cecil North, *Institutions, Institutional Change, and Economic Performance* (Cambridge, New York: Cambridge University Press, 1990), p. 7.

[27] Ibid.

[28] Mark Roe, and Ronald Gilson, "Understanding the Japanese Keiretsu: Overlaps between Corporate Governance and Industrial Organisation", *Yale Law Journal* 102 (1993): 871–906; and Wheeler, op. cit., p. 14.

[29] Williamson, op. cit., p. 7.

[30] North, op. cit., p. 4.

[31] Ibid.

[32] Ibid., pp. 32–33; S. K. Datta and Jeffrey Nugent, "Transaction Cost Economics and Contractual Choice: Theory and Evidence", in *The New Institutional Economics and Development: Theory and Application to Tunisia*, edited by Mustapha K. Nabli and Jeffrey B. Nugent (Amsterdam, New York: Elsevier Science Publishers B. V., 1989), p. 37.

[33] Williamson, op. cit.; and Datta and Nugent, op. cit., p. 38.

[34] Datta and Nugent, op. cit., pp. 17–39.

[35] Nono Makarim, "Companies and Business in Indonesia" (Harvard University, 1979), pp. 56–60.

[36] Ibid., pp. 8–9; Carl-Bend Kaehlig, *Gesellschaftsrecht in Indonesien: Autonome und Nationale Gesellschaftsformen* (Hamburg: Institut for Asienkunde, 1986), p. 284.

[37] Ibid., pp. 283–84.

[38] Ibid., p. 284.

[39] Makarim, op. cit., p. 92–93.

[40] Ibid., p. 101.

[41] Richard Robison, "Capitalism and the Bureaucratic State in Indonesia" (Ph.D. dissertation, University of Sydney, 1977).

[42] Geoffrey Jones, and Mary Rose, *Family Capitalism*, edited by Geoffrey Jones and Mary Rose (London: Frank Cass and Company, 1993).

[43] Yuri Sato, "A Comparative Analysis of the Structures of Business Networks in East Asia", *Business News* (Jakarta), 10 May 1997, pp. 1B–6B.

7

CHINA'S CITIZENSHIP LAW AND THE CHINESE IN SOUTHEAST ASIA

Leo Suryadinata

This chapter deals with China's citizenship law and the Chinese in Southeast Asia during three periods, namely, the Qing (Ching) Dynasty, the Republican period, and the People's Republic (PRC) period. It examines the contents of these laws, why they came into being, how they were implemented, and what their impact was on the ethnic Chinese in Southeast Asia. The main emphasis will be on recent developments, that is, after the emergence of the PRC.

There are approximately 23 million Chinese in Southeast Asia, forming the largest Chinese community — about 80 per cent — outside China. Of the ten Southeast Asian countries, the Chinese in Indonesia are the largest in absolute numbers (about 6.2 million), followed by Malaysia (about 5.5 million), Thailand (about 5.2 million). The smallest number is in Laos (about 10,000).[1] In terms of percentage of the Chinese to the non-Chinese population, however, Singapore has the highest (about 77 per cent), followed by Malaysia (24.8 per cent) and Brunei (16 per cent). The lowest is still Laos (0.4 per cent).[2]

The majority of the Chinese who came to Southeast Asia before Western expansion was mainly *Huashang* (Chinese traders), and their number was relatively small. Only after Western colonization, because of the pull and push factors in China and Southeast Asia, did a large number of the Chinese arrive in the region — many were *Huagong* (Chinese coolies).[3] Of course, there were also traders but they formed a minority.

Although many Chinese in Southeast Asia were coolies, the most significant among them with regard to law was the commercial group. Thus, the Chinese came to be known as the "trading minority of Southeast Asia".[4] As time passed, the Chinese formed the middle class in their adopted countries — in Thailand, they even became both the economic and political élite.

In colonial Southeast Asia, the national status of the Chinese was not an issue until the nineteenth century when the Western powers imported Chinese coolies, and the Chinese overseas became politically important in the politics of mainland China. The ethnic Chinese were the source of both political and economic support. Not surprisingly, there was a tussle between the Western colonial powers and Qing China over control of the Chinese through the "nationality (citizenship) law."

Chinese citizenship law began with the Qing law of 1909, followed by the1929 law issued by the Guomindang (Kuomintang) government after it succeeded in unifying northern and southern China under the leadership of Chiang Kai-shek (Jiang Jieshi). Although the Communist Party of China came to power in 1949, the People's Republic of China only promulgated its nationality law in 1980.

THE QING NATIONALITY LAW (1909)

In traditional China, there was no concept of citizenship, only subject-ship. The emperor considered all people in the Qing territories his subjects (*chen min*). Owing to the small number of Mancu, the ethnic group that founded the Qing dynasty, the Qing emperor introduced a closed-door policy to minimize external contact.[5] This was meant to retard social change. However, in the nineteenth century the West defeated the Qing dynasty and succeeded in forcing the Chinese Government to be more open. As a result, a large number of Chinese went overseas. Initially, the Qing regarded the Chinese overseas (*Hua min*) as potential rebels, and hence called them forsaken subjects (*qi min*).[6]

Only towards the end of the nineteenth century, with the remarkable increase in the economic power of the Overseas Chinese, did the Qing government suddenly realize the value of these kinsmen. It therefore sought to control this population. However, the Chinese overseas were under the jurisdiction of the Western colonial powers. To have control over these Chinese, and also to deal with the foreign powers, the Qing government had to have a claim recognized in international law. This resulted in the birth of the first Nationality Law of China, on 28 March 1909. However, there is controversy on when and how this law was issued.

A Beijing publication maintains that the Qing Nationality Law was only a draft. Before it was officially announced, the 1911 Revolution took place and the law was not really implemented.[7] In fact, this is incorrect. The Qing Nationality Law was officially promulgated and implemented briefly. Nevertheless, the law that was passed is often called Da Qing Guoji Tiaoli (nationality regulations) rather than Guoji Fa (nationality law). According to Li Guilian, a law professor from Peking University, the law from its drafting to its promulgation took less than a month — a record in law-making history during the Qing dynasty as the Qing government was well known for its inefficiency.[8] In his view, this was due to pressures from the overseas Chinese in the Dutch East Indies. It started with a letter sent by a Chinese ambassador to the Netherlands. On13 October 1908, ambassador Lu Zhengxiang sent a letter to Chinese commercial associations (*Huaqiao Shangxiehui*) in Java warning them that the Dutch parliament was preparing a new nationality law which intended to claim residents of the Dutch colonies its subjects. Although the law was not meant for the ethnic Chinese *per se*, the Chinese would be most affected because they formed the minority.[9]

Lu's letter caused an uproar among the Chinese in Java. Chinese commercial associations in Surabaya, Yogyakarta, and Semarang called an emergency meeting in Surabaya and invited the Chinese Charge de Affairs in the Netherlands,Wang Guangxi, and the Qing special envoy, Wang Fengxiang. The meeting decided to boycott the Dutch Nationality Law by adopting the following strategies:

1. To appeal to China to establish a consulate in the Dutch East Indies and to issue a nationality law based on the principle of *jus sanguinis* immediately;
2. To publicize widely among the overseas Chinese the disadvantages of becoming Dutch nationals.[10]

The Chinese Chambers of Commerce in Shanghai and Xiamen supported the Surabaya Chinese appeal and pressured the Qing government to protect the overseas Chinese by establishing a consulate and issuing a nationality law. The Qing government thus responded to the appeal and issued the nationality law.

Because of this law, the Dutch also hurriedly issued the Netherlands *Onderdaanschap* (Dutch Subject-ship Law) in 1910, stipulating that all Chinese born in the Dutch East Indies (colonial Indonesia) were Dutch subjects. Therefore, both the Chinese and Dutch governments were claiming jurisdiction over these Chinese. Negotiations between China and the Netherlands, which had begun in 1908 but soon stopped, were now resumed in The Hague. The talks led to a Consular Treaty in 1911. The essence of the Treaty was that the Imperial Government of China acknowledged that the Dutch East Indies-born Chinese in the Netherlands and its territories were subject to Dutch law. However, they were free to choose either Chinese nationality or Dutch subjecthood when they left the Dutch territories. In return, the Dutch agreed to the establishment of a Chinese consulate in the Dutch Indies, which would primarily serve as a commercial agency.

China by no means abandoned its claim over the overseas Chinese, but merely agreed to the application of the Dutch Subject-ship Law to the *peranakan* Chinese when they were in the Indies. At that stage, the Dutch East Indies-born Chinese were holding *dual nationality*. It should be noted that strictly speaking, subject-ship was not really citizenship. Subject-ship held a lower status than citizenship or nationality. The Dutch East Indies-born Chinese were Dutch subjects. This was also the case with the Straits-born Chinese in Malaya and Singapore. They were British subjects, not British nationals. As in the case of the *peranakan* Chinese in Java, the Straits Chinese held dual "nationality" status.

The law adopted the principle of *jus sanguinis*, claiming that all persons of Chinese descent or legal or extra-legal child of a Chinese father (or a Chinese mother if the father was unknown) were Chinese nationals.[11] A married foreign male could apply for Chinese nationality through naturalization but a married woman whose husband was still alive could not apply unless it was through her husband. The law was biased against married women.

A male foreigner would be eligible to acquire Chinese nationality if he fulfilled the residential and property requirements. There was no mention of requirements pertaining to Chinese language and customs. A naturalized person was also limited in his rights. There were four categories of positions/ jobs which were denied to naturalized citizens (unless under special circumstances). These included "an office holder in the grand council, or in the privy council; the provincial officer of above the fourth rank; an officer or soldier in the army or a member of either house of parliament …".[12] These positions could only be held by natural-born citizens.

While it was not difficult for a foreigner to acquire Chinese citizenship, in theory, it was just as easy for a male Chinese national to renounce Chinese citizenship. According to the 1909 Law, any Chinese citizen who wanted to acquire foreign citizenship was required to obtain the permission of discharge from the Chinese Government. The permission of discharge would be given if he was not involved in a civil criminal case, not bound to military duties, did not owe taxes, and was not holding any governmental office or "vested with official rank". The phrase "not bound to military duties" did not make clear whether or not a male Chinese had to serve in national service before the permission was granted. In practice, it might not have been easy as the permission of discharge issued by China's Ministry of the Interior was required. Without this document, the national status of a Chinese could not be changed. The Qing government did not have much time to implement this new nationality law but it served as a basis for the subsequent nationality law in China.

THE NATIONALITY LAW OF THE REPUBLIC OF CHINA (1929)

It is not clear what happened to the Qing Nationality Law after the fall of the Manchu and the establishment of the Republic of China (ROC) in 1912. According to Johannes Chan, a law professor from the University of Hong Kong, after the fall of the Qing dynasty, the Republican government in Beijing issued a new nationality law, known as the 1912 Nationality Act, which was amended in 1914, and again in 1929.[13] However, Zhao Guochai, a law professor from Taiwan, only mentioned the Amended Nationality Law of 1914, issued by the northern warlords (Beiyang Zhengfu). Presumably, this is the amended version of the Qing 1909 Nationality Law.[14] I have come across the 1914 Amended Law, which does not mention the 1912 law.[15] Since I do not have access to the 1912 law, I shall assume that the 1914 law was an amended version of the 1909 Nationality Law. After the Kuomintang succeeded in staging the Northern Expedition in 1927 and unified South and North China, it issued a Nationality Law in 1929, which was based on the 1914 Amended Law.[16]

No matter whether the 1912 law existed or not, when we compare the 1909 Law, the 1914 Amended Law, and the1929 Law, there are many similarities. The laws all adopted the principle of *jus sanguinis*, claiming that all Chinese, regardless of birthplace, were under that law. Johannes Chan maintained correctly that the basic provisions of these laws on Chinese nationality remained. "No Chinese could divest himself of his nationality without first obtaining a certificate of denationalization from the Ministry of the Interior, and such a certificate was rarely gained".[17]

It should be noted that during the Republican period, even before the promulgation of the 1929 Law, the ethnic Chinese held dual nationality status. The principle of *jus sanguinis* in force before the 1929 Law was demonstrated in the case of Oen Keng Hian, a *peranakan* Chinese who worked for the Dutch East Indies government. He committed an offence against the Dutch law and escaped to China in 1926. On the request of the Dutch Consul, Oen was captured in Shanghai. This led to a dispute over Oen's nationality. The Dutch Consul maintained that he was a Dutch subject and therefore should be tried in Java. However, China asserted that Oen was a national of China according to the Chinese Nationality Law so that he could only be tried in China. The Oen case was heard in the Mixed Court in Shanghai, and China eventually won.[18]

As in the Qing Nationality Law, a naturalized citizen under the 1929 Law was not allowed to hold certain positions.[19] This time, however, there were seven instead of four groups of positions that a naturalized Chinese citizen could not hold (including Member of Parliament, military officer and ambassador). However, certain restrictions could be removed with the approval of the Ministry of the Interior.

Like the Qing Law, the Ministry of the Interior was powerful. To remove Chinese nationality, a permission of discharge had to be obtained from the Minister of the Interior but a person who had not served in national service could not be granted the discharge. In other words, if a person was unable to get the permission of discharge, he would remain a national of China despite having foreign citizenship. The same citizenship law is still used in Taiwan today but it is not enforced, as this is impossible.

A number of factors contributed to the *jus sanguinis*-based nationality law. Kuomintang China, like its predecessor, was aware of the value of the overseas Chinese. It intended to make the overseas Chinese remain culturally loyal to China. Chinese school education was supported throughout Southeast Asia, and Chinese nationalism was encouraged. However, as long as the Southeast Asian countries were colonial, Chinese nationalism, which was basically anti-Western colonialism, could co-exist with Southeast Asian nationalisms. (The exception was Thailand where there was a clash between Chinese nationalism and Thai nationalism).[20] Nevertheless, Chinese nationalism posed a challenge to Southeast Asian nationalism after independence.

THE PRC NATIONALITY LAW (1980)

The PRC was established in October 1949, but until early September 1980, there was no PRC Nationality Law. In the absence of a new law, it seems that the Kuomintang law was still in use, although it was modified.

Thirty-one years later, however, on 10 September 1980, suddenly the PRC Nationality Law was adopted by the Fifth National People's Congress.[21]

In discussing the 1980 law, Johannes Chan forcefully argued that it "reaffirms the principles of the *jus sanguinis* and non-recognition of dual nationality". On denationalization, it adopts a more liberal approach. "While maintaining the general principle of no denationalization without government consent, it allows, for the first time, automatic loss of Chinese nationality for those who have acquired a foreign nationality for those who have settled abroad and have acquired a foreign nationality of their own free will".[22]

In fact, the principles used in the 1980 law were practised by the PRC as early as 1955 when Premier Zhou Enlai (Chou En-lai) introduced his good-neighbour policy, which intended to solve the dual nationality problem. Aware of the suspicion of the new Southeast Asian governments, Zhou was willing to sign the dual-nationality agreement with Southeast Asian countries, which had sizeable Chinese populations. Once such an agreement was signed, the Chinese could only have one nationality. In other words, an ethnic Chinese was required to choose only one citizenship, and renounce the other. A minor would acquire the citizenship of his/her father; when the father's citizenship was unclear, he/she would adopt his/her mother's citizenship. A minor who had his/her father's citizenship would be allowed to choose either Chinese or Indonesian citizenship when he/she reached adulthood. Only Indonesia signed such a treaty. Beijing encouraged the Chinese to take up Indonesian citizenship and become integrated into the local society. The same appeal was made to the ethnic Chinese in other Southeast Asian countries. Beijing also urged the Southeast Asian governments to respect those Chinese who were Chinese nationals or who opted for Chinese citizenship.[23]

However, the 1965 coup led to the abrogation of the Sino-Indonesian dual-citizenship agreement by Jakarta unilaterally. The anti-communist Soeharto government felt that the dual-citizenship treaty was detrimental to Indonesian interests because the children of Chinese who had already opted for PRC citizenship were still given the opportunity to be Indonesian citizens when they reached adulthood. Since then, a foreign Chinese has to apply for Indonesian citizenship through naturalization. Soon after Soeharto came to power, there was a Cultural Revolution in mainland China and its foreign office came under the influence of the radicals. China's relations with the Southeast Asian governments tensed. The fall of the "Gang of Four" gave a chance to Chinese moderates to readopt a moderate policy towards the non-communist Southeast Asian governments. Malaysia, Thailand, and the

Philippines established diplomatic ties with the PRC in the mid-1970s. Joint communiqués establishing ties always included a clause that the signatories of the communiqué only recognized single citizenship.

The 1980 Nationality Law reflected this principle. Article 9 of the law stipulates that "any Chinese national who has settled abroad and who has been naturalized there or has acquired foreign nationality of his own free will, automatically loses Chinese nationality".[24] The phrase of "his own free will" is important because a Chinese national will not lose his nationality if the foreign nationality is forced upon him against his will.

The 1980 Nationality Law is more modern in the sense that it respects the "free will" of an individual and does not force any ethnic Chinese to remain a Chinese national when living overseas. Under the Kuomintang Nationality Law, a Chinese can only lose his citizenship with the approval of the Chinese Ministry of the Interior. In 1955, the PRC recognized that a Chinese of foreign citizenship would lose his Chinese nationality if there was a dual-nationality treaty between the country concerned and the PRC. The precondition of signing a dual-nationality treaty was later relaxed, and Zhou Enlai stated that an overseas Chinese who acquired foreign citizenship voluntarily would cease to be a Chinese citizen, but this was never put into law before 1980.

The announcement of the new Nationality Law did not mean much in reality because the ASEAN states had already introduced a one-nationality policy towards the Chinese. However, it helped internationally because the nationality of the Chinese in ASEAN was now made clear. The PRC has officially disclaimed the ethnic Chinese who are foreign citizens.

The 1980 Law is progressive in the sense that it respects free choice in resolving the problem of dual nationality. However, this principle has been abandoned in the case of Hong Kong. Beijing considered all Hong Kong residents who were British nationals (overseas, or BN[O]) or British overseas citizens (BOC), as Chinese nationals. However, in theory, these people were British nationals. Therefore, many scholars have maintained that these people were holding dual nationality. As Hong Kong is not part of Southeast Asia, the application of the1980 Law in the former British colony should not have been included in the discussion in this chapter. However, as the Hong Kong case may have wider implications on the Chinese nationality issue, a brief treatment can be justified.[25]

Hong Kong Chinese nationality is a complex subject. Suffice it to say that the British were suddenly concerned with the national status of the people in Hong Kong on the eve of Hong Kong's return to China. In 1990, the British authorities in Hong Kong hurriedly announced the British Nationality

Law, conferring the status of BN(O) or BOC on the inhabitants of Hong Kong. These British nationals/citizens, unlike the true British nationals, had no rights of abode in either the United Kingdom or other British territories. Nevertheless, they were given British passports and could travel using the passport.

However, after 1997, these Hong Kong inhabitants still had the BN(O) or BOC status and held their British passports, but the PRC Government insisted that these people were Chinese nationals and could only leave and enter Hong Kong by using PRC passports. In addition, these BN(O) and BOC had no diplomatic protection as China did not recognize the status. Although these Hong Kong inhabitants were not forced to give up their British national status, and hence were still "dual nationals", yet in practice, they were PRC nationals. One can therefore argue that this is not a case of dual nationality as the BN(O) status in Hong Kong after 1997 does not mean much.

Nevertheless, many legal experts on Hong Kong would argue that the BN(O) and BOC status is a reality. Beijing should hold the spirit of the 1980 Law and allow these "dual nationals" to choose. However, Beijing considers Hong Kong to be part of Chinese territory, and the 1980 Law does not apply.

Indeed, there is one hidden aspect in the 1980 Nationality Law with regard to renunciation of Chinese nationality, which is similar to the previous Chinese laws: voluntary application requires the approval of the Ministry of Public Security. According to one expert, "There are no published rules on how the Ministry description may be exercised, nor is there any system of appeal against refusal".[26] It was reported that those regarded as landlords, rich peasants, anti-revolutionaries, or 'unreformed bad elements' would be disqualified from renouncing Chinese nationality".[27] Since this is more relevant to the Chinese in the Chinese territories, no further discussion is required.

Although the 1980 Nationality Law was meant to allow ethnic Chinese to possess only single citizenship, its application in Hong Kong tended to deviate from the general rule. This is due to the fact that the law was meant to solve the Chinese problem in Southeast Asia rather than that in other areas.

The 1980 Law: Its Factors and Responses from Southeast Asia

The promulgation of the 1980 Nationality Law was apparently due to several factors. There was no doubt that international developments had much to do with it. The PRC leadership under the Deng Xiaoping (Teng Hsiaoping) group had been eager to gain the friendship of other countries, especially

ASEAN. It wanted to show that China was willing to follow international practices and win the confidence of other countries which had large numbers of ethnic Chinese. This was particularly significant when China was at odds with Vietnam and the Soviet Union, and when some of the ASEAN countries were suspicious of Beijing's overseas Chinese policy. In its efforts to break the perceived encirclement of the Soviet-Vietnamese alliance, Beijing wanted to woo the ASEAN states. It was, thus, not surprising that a new Nationality Law was promulgated after the 1979 Sino-Vietnamese war.

It was also possible that Deng's visit to Southeast Asia in 1978 convinced him that many Southeast Asian Chinese preferred to be regarded as Southeast Asians rather than *Huaqiao* (Chinese nationals overseas). His first-hand knowledge made him aware that many ethnic Chinese were not *Huaqiao*.[28] It is worth noting that after Deng's visit, the term *Huaren* (ethnic Chinese) began to be popularized in Chinese official documents. Previously, *Zhongguo ren* (Man of the Middle Kingdom), *Zhongguo xuetong* (Chinese blood) and *Huaqiao*, which were "more China-oriented" terms, had been used more widely.

When the 1980 Nationality Law was first announced, not much attention was paid to it in the ASEAN states because it did not alter the status quo. A few commentators in the ASEAN countries welcomed this new law because it gave a clear national status to the ethnic Chinese. However, the "domestic overseas Chinese" — a term meaning former Southeast Asian Chinese who had returned to China — particularly those in *Qiaolian* (Overseas Chinese Associations), were quite critical of the new law. Some expressed the view that if the Chinese Nationality Law inflexibly denied the dual-nationality status, this would affect the Overseas Chinese. They noted that there were many countries which recognized dual and multi-nationality status. They contended that in Hong Kong, for instance, there were many Chinese who held dual citizenship or multi-citizenship. They were critical of the decision made by the Chinese Government in not recognizing the dual-nationality status, being afraid of "offending" the governments of Southeast Asia where most of the overseas Chinese lived.

Hong Sisi, a representative of the Overseas Chinese residing in Beijing, who returned to China in 1950 after spending twenty years in Medan, Singapore, and Penang as a journalist, maintained that it was strange that the legislation of China should take into account whether or not it would offend a foreign government. If China, according to Hong, took this into consideration, then it should realize that it would also offend other countries by establishing a socialist state. Hong questioned whether China should abandon its efforts in promoting a socialist state. He further argued that it was not China that suffered "the sensitivity complex but it was others who suffer from this kind of disease".[29] Nevertheless, it was the Deng Xiaoping group, which was sensitive to the feelings of the ASEAN governments, that prevailed. It should be noted that many overseas Chinese leaders were not only old but also out of touch with the post-World War II situation in Southeast Asia. One wonders if they understand the ethnic Chinese who are living abroad.

In recent years, there was again discussion on Chinese nationality among the "domestic overseas Chinese". Although they no longer directly made demands for dual-nationality status, they urged the Beijing Government to make it easy for foreign Chinese to become Chinese nationals again.[30] They also argued that the Nationality Law had been issued at a specific time but that the centres of the ethnic Chinese were no longer concentrated in Southeast Asia but had expanded to North America and Europe.[31] With the rise of new "Overseas Chinese Centres" it was necessary for China to have a new policy towards the ethnic Chinese. However, there was no response from Beijing.

The Application of the 1980 Law

Would this Nationality Law provide an excuse for the PRC to intervene in the domestic affairs of other countries? It would if the country concerned were hostile to China and forced the ethnic Chinese to become its nationals on a large scale. Nonetheless, in many ASEAN states, it appears that the ethnic Chinese have been eager to become local citizens and there is no excuse for the PRC to intervene in this matter. A good example is the recent case of the Indonesian Chinese.

Indonesia was hard hit by the recent financial crisis in Asia, resulting in price hikes and widespread anti-Chinese riots across the country. As a result, many Chinese outside Indonesia criticized the government; some even suggested that Beijing should protect the Chinese there. However, Beijing refused to intervene. On 19 February 1998, Zhu Bangzao, the Chinese Ministry of Foreign Affairs' spokesman said, "We believe that the Indonesian government can control the situation, maintain social stability, and racial harmony".[32] Thus, Beijing considered this an Indonesian domestic problem.

Privately, a Chinese diplomat in the United States stated that Beijing would not be able to protest or send ships to Indonesia because "there is no good reason to do so as the majority of the Chinese in Indonesia are Indonesian citizens".[33] To do otherwise would mean intervention in Jakarta's domestic affairs, which would generate a negative reaction in other parts of Southeast Asia.

Some reports indicated that China's embassy in Jakarta would help, on a case by case basis, individual Chinese (presumably those who were non-Indonesian nationals) who encountered difficulty. Understandably, the embassy was cautious in doing so as this could affect Sino-Indonesian relations.

Beijing–Jakarta ties have been quite cordial since the re-establishment of ties in 1990 and Beijing has no desire to jeopardize the relationship. It is even reported to be willing to give economic assistance to ease Indonesia's economic crisis.[34] Even during the 13–14 May riots in Jakarta, when the ethnic Chinese were targeted by an organized group of provokers, resulting in lootings, raping, and killings, Beijing remained silent for a while. Only later, when the international Chinese communities launched protests against the gross violation of human rights, did the Chinese Government express its concern over the treatment of the ethnic Chinese. Beijing began to demand that the Indonesian authorities protect the legitimate rights of the ethnic Chinese. Nevertheless, there was neither open intervention nor public condemnation against the Indonesian Government.

The National Status of the Ethnic Chinese in Vietnam

Beijing's attitude towards Indonesia was very different from its attitude towards Vietnam in the late 1970s, when Hanoi forced the Chinese to become its nationals and moved them to special economic zones, and accused them of being capitalists. A large number of ethnic Chinese fled Vietnam. China protested strongly. However, deteriorating Sino-Vietnamese relations was essentially not caused by the Vietnamese treatment of the ethnic Chinese. It was Vietnam's decision to side with the Soviets to encircle Beijing. Hanoi's plan to force all Chinese to become Vietnamese nationals was also due to its suspicion of Beijing's intention towards the Chinese in Vietnam. But the 1979 Sino-Vietnamese War was largely due to the Vietnamese invasion of Cambodia — which was seen as an attempt of the Soviets to encircle China through its Vietnam proxy.[35]

Nevertheless, one of the issues of the Beijing-Hanoi conflict was the nationality of the ethnic Chinese in Vietnam. Although the nationality issue took place before the promulgation of the 1980 Nationality Law, it may have a bearing on the application of the law. Let us examine briefly the Vietnam case. In 1955, Beijing and North Vietnam signed an agreement on the national status of the ethnic Chinese in northern Vietnam. However, the agreement was not published. Only in the 1970s, when there was a dispute over the national status of the ethnic Chinese, did each side give its own version of the agreement.

According to Hanoi, the agreement stated that the "the Central Committee of the Chinese and Vietnamese parties agreed that Chinese residents in Vietnam were under the leadership of the Viet Nam Workers' Party and [would] gradually became Vietnamese citizens".[36] Hanoi implied that since Beijing had agreed to let the Workers' Party (the former name of the Communist Party of Vietnam) "manage" the ethnic Chinese in both North and South Vietnam, the result was that the majority of the Chinese in Vietnam became Vietnamese citizens. Hanoi argued that: "In South Vietnam in 1957, under the U.S. puppet regime, the large majority of the Hoa adopted Vietnamese citizenship and have been Vietnamese of Chinese descent for more than 20 years now. There remain only 3,000–4,000 Hoa bearing foreign residential status and the identity cards of Taiwan, Hong Kong, Macao, etc. Thus, following the complete liberation of Viet Nam, apart from the latter category … all the Hoa in Viet Nam have become citizens of the Socialist Republic of Viet Nam. Juristically, none of them are citizens of the People's Republic of China".[37]

However, the PRC gave a different version. According to Beijing, both governments agreed that "after a long and patient persuasion and education, the Overseas Chinese could become Vietnamese citizens",[38] but this should be done on a voluntary basis. According to the same source, Hanoi agreed to this, for the "ethnic Chinese to become Vietnamese citizens should be based on their own willingness. They should not be forced",[39] and that "those who do not want to become Vietnamese citizens will enjoy equal rights and will not be discriminated against. They will not be instructed and forced to become citizens nor will they be looked down upon".[40]

On the question of the ethnic Chinese in South Vietnam, Beijing argued that in the 1950s Hanoi agreed to settle the problem after the "liberation". When the Diem government promulgated in 1956 a retrospective decree declaring all Chinese born in Vietnam as Vietnamese citizens, the PRC initially noted its agreement. Later, Beijing staged a protest against the violation of international law because the Diem government had not given the people concerned any freedom of choice. According to the Chinese source, *Nhan Dan*, Hanoi's official organ, was in support of the PRC. The South Vietnam National Liberation Front also repeatedly stated in the documents issued in 1960, 1964, 1965, and 1968 that "all measures adopted by the American-backed regime on the Overseas Chinese will be abolished" and that "the Overseas Chinese have the right to choose their own nationality".[41]

Since the original documents are not available to this author, it is difficult to be sure which side was right. However, the fact is that the national status of the Chinese in Vietnam became a problem only after relations between Beijing and Hanoi deteriorated. Therefore, it was a political problem rather than a purely legal issue.

Here a question can be posed as to whether or not the 1980 Nationality Law of the PRC applies to the Chinese in Vietnam. In theory, it should apply to all ethnic Chinese in the world. A Chinese who has become a Vietnamese citizen will cease to be a Chinese national, but Beijing may argue that it only recognizes the Chinese who become Vietnamese of his/her own free will. Since many Chinese in Vietnam became Vietnamese nationals against their own free will, Beijing may still consider them to be PRC citizens, and the nationality issue can arise again. However, with the improvement of living conditions and democratization in Vietnam, one can argue that many Chinese may have willingly become Vietnamese citizens and Beijing should respect the will of these ethnic Chinese.

The above examples show that the 1980 Nationality Law made it more difficult for China to intervene on ethnic Chinese matters, but the possibility is still there if the government concerned is hostile to China, and if there is systematic and large-scale persecution of the Chinese in the country.

Chinese Citizens in Southeast Asia

As mentioned earlier, the PRC has encouraged the ethnic Chinese in Southeast Asia to be integrated into the local societies and take up local citizenship in order to release "the historical burden". The Southeast Asian governments have also prohibited prospective Chinese immigrants from entering their respective countries. As a result, the number of alien Chinese (read, Chinese nationals) has been drastically reduced. Nevertheless, it is difficult to define the ethnic Chinese and many Southeast Asian governments have not released figures on the ethnic Chinese in their countries. The figures in the table are therefore estimates.

TABLE 1
Numbers of Alien Chinese[42]
(c. 1990)

Country	No. of Ethnic Chinese	No. of Alien Chinese
Brunei	40,621	31,228
Burma/Myanmar	466,000	Minority
Cambodia	50,000	Minority
Indonesia	5,460,000	200,000
Laos	10,000	Minority
Malaysia	5,261,000	220,000
The Philippines	850,000	40,000
Singapore	2,102,800	48,200
Thailand	4,813,000	270,766
Vietnam	962,000	Minority

In recent years, because of globalization, a few Southeast Asian countries (Singapore and Thailand) began to relax their immigration policies towards the Chinese from mainland China, Taiwan, and Hong Kong. Many have been granted permanent residential status and some have even been granted local citizenship.

CONCLUSION

The Chinese Nationality Law emerged as a result of China's interaction with the West and also China's concern about its kinsmen overseas. Realizing the importance of the Chinese overseas, China declared all Chinese, regardless of his/her birthplace, as Chinese nationals. By this, China intended to woo the ethnic Chinese to remain loyal to the motherland and to control them. However, the colonial governments in Southeast Asia were equally determined to control the Chinese. Many declared the local-born Chinese as their subjects. This often resulted in people having dual-nationality status. This status was not a problem as long as the Chinese with dual-nationality status did not leave the colony. However, once away from the colony, China could claim jurisdiction over these Chinese. A clear example was the case of Oen Keng Hian, who fled from Java to China in 1926 after embezzling large sums of money. The Chinese Government had jurisdiction over him and hence he could not be extradited.

Generally, loyalty to China during the colonial period in Southeast Asia did not raise problems. However, when the Southeast Asian countries became independent and indigenous nationalism grew strong, the two types of nationalism tended to come into conflict.

Faced with many problems, including Southeast Asian nationalism, the PRC began to modify its policy. Beginning in 1955, it encouraged the ethnic Chinese in Southeast Asia to integrate into the local society. It even offered to conclude a "dual nationality" treaty with the Southeast Asian countries, in which local-born Chinese would be allowed to choose between local and Chinese citizenship. Their children under 18 years of age would also be allowed to choose their own citizenship when they reached adulthood. Each country would only recognize one nationality. However, only Indonesia signed such a treaty, and after the 1965 coup Jakarta unilaterally repudiated it, fearing that some "undesirable" Chinese children might become Indonesian citizens.

Nevertheless, in general, the PRC continued to encourage the ethnic Chinese to adopt local citizenship and recognized only one nationality. However, it continued to stress that the Chinese should not be forced to become a local national against his/her free will. This "free will" principle was only used against Vietnam in the 1970s. The nationality of the Chinese in Vietnam became a problem as both insisted that they were their respective nationals. In reality, the problem arose because of the Sino-Vietnamese political conflict. The ethnic Chinese were only used as pawns by both sides.

The 1980 Nationality Law of the PRC was a significant development in its policy towards the ethnic Chinese. The law clearly stated that an ethnic Chinese could only hold one nationality. A Chinese foreign citizen would automatically lose his/her Chinese citizenship. The touchy problem of citizenship was eventually solved.

However, the resurgence of China, the end of the Cold War, and economic globalization caused some Chinese to realize that many countries, especially immigrant states such as the United States, Canada, Australia and (possibly) New Zealand recognize dual nationality. Some of these "domestic overseas Chinese" began to advocate this concept and urged the amendment of the 1980 Nationality Law. However, in the foreseeable future, it is unlikely that countries in Southeast Asia, which are "indigenous states" will accept dual nationality for their ethnic Chinese population. Even Singapore, which is an "immigrant state", is a strong advocate of single nationality for its citizens. If China revises the 1980 Nationality Law and begins to introduce a dual-nationality policy, it will affect China's relations with Southeast Asian countries where the largest number of ethnic Chinese live.

APPENDICES

Appendix 1

Text of the Law on the Acquisition and Loss of Chinese Nationality (1909)

SECTION I
NATIONALITY BY PARENTAGE

Article I

The following are Chinese, whatever the locality may be in which they are born:

1. A child born of a father who at the time of its birth is Chinese.
2. A child born after the death of the father, if the father at the time of death was Chinese.
3. A child born of a Chinese mother, the father being unknown or without a determinate nationality.

Article II

A child born in China of parents unknown or of parents without a determinate nationality. An abandoned child without ascertainable place of birth takes China nationality, when found on Chinese soil.

SECTION II
NATURALIZATION

Article III

Any alien desiring to be admitted to Chinese nationality may apply for naturalization, provided he can comply with the following requirements:

1. That he has lived uninterruptedly over ten years within the limits of China.
2. That he has passed his twentieth birthday and is *sui juris* under the law of the country to which he originally belonged.
3. That he is of good moral character
4. That he possesses so much property or such sources of income or such ability as to enable him to live independently according to the circumstances of his place of residence.
5. That he shall, by the law of the country of which he is a subject be deemed to have lost the nationality thereof in consequence of his being naturalized abroad.

An alien without a fixed nationality may become naturalized if he is of full legal age and complies with the requirements enumerated in points 1, 3 and 4.

Article IV

The Waiwupu (Ministry of Foreign Affairs) and the Min-cheng-pu (Ministry of the Interior) can jointly propose to His Majesty to confer by a special decree the right of nationality on those foreigners, whether with or without a determinate nationality, who have rendered distinguished meritorious services to the Empire, even if they do not possess the requirements enumerated in points 1, 2, 3 and 4 of Article III.

Article V

The following persons, whether with or without a determinate nationality, are considered to have acquired Chinese nationality:

1. An alien woman who has married a Chinese.
2. An alien child living under the parental care of a Chinese step-father.
3. An illegitimate child born to and acknowledged by a Chinese father.
4. An illegitimate child born of a Chinese mother, when abandoned by the father and acknowledged by the mother.

Point 1 is confined to cases where registry of marriage has been duly made with the proper authorities; and points 2, 3 and 4 apply only to those persons who are either minors or unmarried women by the law of the country of which they were originally subjects.

Article VI

The Chinese nationality acquired by a man shall extend to his wife and his minor children; but if, by the law of his country, they do not thereby lose the nationality thereof, they shall be deemed to remain aliens. In case, however, the wife desires to acquire Chinese nationality, or the nationalized person desires to have his minor children possess Chinese nationality they may separately apply for certificates of naturalization, even when they do not fulfil the requirements enumerated in points 1, 2, 3, and 4 of Article III.

Major children of a naturalized person, when residing in China, may also apply for naturalization without being required to fulfil the requirements enumerated in points 1, 2, 3 and 4 of Article III.

Article VII

A married woman cannot alone apply for naturalization during the life of her husband.

Article VIII

A naturalized subject is incapable of becoming:

1. An office holder in the Grand Council or in the Privy Council.
2. A provincial officer of above the fourth rank.
3. An officer or soldier in the army.
4. A member of either house of parliament or of a provincial council.

The Ministry of the Interior may propose to His Majesty the removal of this disability from those persons to whom the right of nationality has been conferred by a special decree, when they have resided in China for a period of ten years reckoning from the date of their naturalization; and from those who are naturalized under the ordinary procedure, when they have resided in China for a period of 20 years reckoning from the date of their naturalization.

Article IX

An alien who applies for naturalization must make and file a petition setting forth that, on his becoming naturalized, he will be faithful to the Constitution and obey the law of China and relinquish absolutely and forever whatever privileges and rights may attach to the nationality of the country to which he, at the time of filing his petition, may belong; and his petition is to be accompanied by a written joint guarantee of two respectable members of the gentry of his locality as to his faithful adherence to the declaration in the petition.

Article X

The petition for naturalization, together with other papers, is to be addressed to the first officer of that locality in which the petitioner resides. This officer examines the petition and, if satisfied that it is in a proper form, submits it to the highest provincial authority with the request that the latter transmit it to the Ministry of the Interior. The Ministry of the Interior decides upon the petition and posts its decision on the notice-board, and if the petition were granted, issues a certificate of nationality to the petitioner.

The naturalization shall take effect at the moment of issuance of the certificate of nationality. Persons who have become naturalized in pursuance of Article V must register with the first officer of that locality under whose jurisdiction they reside; and this officer shall submit such registry to the provincial authority with the request that it be forwarded to the Ministry of the Interior. Likewise such persons, when residing abroad, must register at the Legation either directly or through a consulate; and the Legation shall forward such registry to the Ministry of the Interior.

SECTION III
LOSS OF NATIONALITY

Article XI

Any Chinese subject intending to acquire an alien nationality must first obtain permission of discharge.

Article XII

The permission of discharge shall be accorded only when the petitioner at the time of filing his petition

1. is not involved in any pending civil or criminal case,
2. is not bound to military duties,
3. is not in arrears with any state or communal tax, and
4. is not holding any governmental position or vested with official rank.

Article XIII

The following persons shall be deemed to have lost Chinese nationality:

1. A Chinese woman who has married a foreigner.
2. A Chinese child living under the parental care of an alien step-father.
3. An illegitimate child born to an acknowledged alien father.
4. An illegitimate child born of an alien mother, when abandoned by the father and acknowledged by the mother.

Point 1 is confined to cases where registry of marriage has been duly made with the proper authorities. If by the law of her husband's country she does not acquire its nationality through marriage, she shall be deemed to remain Chinese.

Points 2, 3, and 4 shall apply to those persons only who are either minor children or unmarried women under the law of China.

Article XIV

The discharge acquired by a man extends to his wife and to his minor children, unless the wife desires to retain Chinese nationality or unless the discharged man desires his minor children to retain Chinese nationality, in which case they remain Chinese on petition to the authorities.

Article XV

A married woman during the lifetime of her husband cannot alone apply for a discharge. All persons who, according to the law of China, are either minors or not *sui juris* likewise cannot alone apply for discharge.

Article XVI

Any Chinese who has divested himself of national status as a Chinese subject shall not enjoy any of the special privileges enjoyed by Chinese in the interior.

Article XVII

Any person who applies for discharge must make and file a written statement declaring that he fulfills the requirements enumerated in Article XII and is free from any secret crime.

Article XVIII

The petition for discharge is to be addressed to the first officer of that locality in which the petitioner resides. This officer examines the petition, and if satisfied that it is a proper form, submits it to the provincial authority with the request that it be forwarded to the Ministry of the Interior. The Ministry of the Interior decides upon the petition and posts its decision upon the notice-board.

In case the petitioner resides abroad, his petition is to be addressed to the Legation either directly or through a consulate; and the Legation shall forward the petition to the Ministry of the Interior for final decision.

The discharge shall not take effect until the sanction of the Ministry of the Interior has been granted and posted on the notice-board; and all persons who have not filed a petition and whose petition is not granted remains Chinese for all purposes.

SECTION IV
READMISSION

Article XIX

A Chinese woman who has become an alien by or in consequence of marriage may apply for readmission to Chinese nationality provided she has been judicially divorced from her husband or has become a widow.

Article XX

The wife of a discharged person may, when the marital relations have been terminated by divorce or death, also recover Chinese nationality on petitioning the Chinese authorities. Any person, who, while a minor, became an alien through discharge of his father, may after he has attained his majority, likewise reacquire Chinese nationality on petitioning the Chinese authorities.

Article XXI

Any Chinese subject who has become an alien with permission of the Chinese authorities but who has since lived uninterruptedly in China for a period of more than three years may petition for readmission to Chinese nationality if he can fulfil the requirements in points 3 and 4 of Article III. This provision, however, does not apply to any naturalized subject.

Article XXII

Any person seeking readmission shall furnish in support of his petition a written joint guarantee of two respectable members of the gentry of his original native province as to the validity of his claim; and the procedure of forwarding the petition and securing its sanction should be the same as is provided in Article X. In case the petitioner resides abroad the guarantee shall be signed by two Chinese residing in the locality and addressed to the Legation of the Interior. The readmission shall take effect at the moment when the sanction is granted and posted on the notice-board.

Article XXIII

No person who has reacquired Chinese nationality can, previous to the completion of five years' residence in China, become one of the officers enumerated in Article VIII except by special decree of the Emperor.

Article XXIV

This law shall go into effect immediately on obtaining the Imperial sanction.

SUPPLEMENTAL PROVISION

1. Any Chinese subject who, prior to the operation of this law, has become naturalized in a foreign state without permission from the Chinese authorities and has since resided abroad must, on returning to China, report at the first port to the consul of the country of his acquired nationality and request the latter duly to communicate his naturalization and the date thereof to the local Chinese authorities, and such communication shall be deemed sufficient proof of his renunciation of his national status as a Chinese subject.
2. Any Chinese subject who, prior to the operation of this law, has become naturalized as an alien subject without permission of the Chinese authorities and has since resided in the settlement of a Chinese treaty port, must within one year of the enactment of this law make known his alienation to the local Chinese authorities who, before recognizing his expatriation, shall first ascertain from the consul who represents his acquired nationality, the time at which such naturalization was effected.
3. Whosoever does not prove the loss of his Chinese nationality in pursuance of the preceding two provisions shall be deemed to have remained a Chinese subject.
4. Any Chinese who, prior to the operation of this law, has acquired an alien nationality without permission of the Chinese authorities but who has since resided, traded and owned immovable property in the interior and enjoyed such special privileges and rights as Chinese are entitled to enjoy shall be deemed to have remained always a Chinese subject.
5. Any Chinese who, prior to the operation of this law, has acquired an alien nationality without permission of the Chinese authorities and yet has since held or is still holding some government position shall be deemed to have remained always a Chinese subject.
6. Any Chinese subject who, prior to the operation of this law, has become an alien may at any time petition for readmission to the Chinese nationality in pursuance of Article XXII of this law without being subject to Articles XXI and XXIII.
7. Any Chinese subject who, prior to the operation of this law, has long resided abroad in consequence of his birth and yet is desirous of retaining Chinese nationality shall be deemed to be a Chinese.

8. Any person who has lost Chinese nationality in accordance with this law shall not reside in the interior under penalty of expulsion, and shall be required to sell and give up within one year after naturalization all immovable property and all other interests which he has hitherto acquired and enjoyed as a Chinese, failing which all such property and interests shall be sequestrated.
9. Where a person who has expatriated himself in accordance with this law is discovered at a later time not to have fulfilled all the requirements of Article XII, or to have been involved in a criminal act before or at the time of his expatriation, the permission of alienage already issued to him shall be rescinded and he shall be liable to the prosecution and punishment authorized by Chinese law.
10. Where any person obtains permission of expatriation under pretense of acquiring an alien nationality or knowingly makes false statements in his declaration, the permission of expatriation shall be rescinded and he shall be liable to imprisonment for not less than six months nor more than one year.

Source: *American Journal of International Law* 4 (1910): 160–66.

Appendix 2

Text of the Nationality Law of the Republic of China (1929)

SECTION I
NATIONALITY BY PARENTAGE

Article I

The following persons have Chinese nationality:

1. A child born of a father who at the time of its birth is Chinese.
2. A child born after the death of the father, if the father at the time of death was Chinese.
3. A child born of a Chinese mother, the father being unknown or with an indeterminate nationality.
4. A child born in China of parents unknown or with an indeterminate nationality.

SECTION II
ACQUISITION OF CHINESE NATIONALITY

Article II

The following persons are considered to have acquired Chinese nationality:

1. An alien woman who has married a Chinese, excluding those who retain their own nationality in accordance with the law of their original country.
2. An illegitimate child born to and acknowledged by a Chinese father.
3. An illegitimate child born to and acknowledged by the Chinese mother while the father of the child is unknown or does not acknowledge the child as his.
4. An alien child who is adopted by a Chinese stepfather.
5. A person who is naturalized.

Article III

An alien or a stateless person can be naturalized after receiving permission from the Ministry of the Interior. An applicant should fulfill the following requirements.

1. That he has lived in China.
2. That he has passed his twentieth birthday and is considered capable by both Chinese law and the law of his original country.
3. That he is of good moral character.

4. That he possesses considerable property and skills which enable him to make a living.

When a stateless person applies for naturalization, the condition stipulated in Point 2 of this Article is based on Chinese law.

Article IV

The following aliens who now reside in China can be naturalized although they have not fulfilled the five-year residential requirement:

An alien whose father or mother is a Chinese.

1. An alien whose wife is a former Chinese.
2. An alien who was born in China.
3. An alien who has lived in China interruptedly for more than ten years.

An alien who fulfills the requirements in Points 1, 2 and 3 will not be permitted to be naturalized if the person has not lived in China for more than three years uninterruptedly. But an alien who fulfills the Point 3 requirement and his father or mother was born in China will not be in this category.

Article V

An alien who is currently residing in China, if his/her father or mother is a Chinese, will be allowed to be naturalized although he/she does not fulfil Points 1, 2 and 4 of Article III.

Article VI

An alien who has rendered extraordinary and distinguished meritorious services to China can be naturalized upon the permission of both the Ministry of the Interior and the Government, even when he does not fulfil the requirements stipulated in Point 2 of Article III.

Article VII

Naturalization becomes effective on the date it is announced in the State Gazette.

Article VIII

The Chinese nationality acquired by a man shall extend to his wife and his minor children, but if by the law of his country, they do not thereby lose the nationality thereof, they shall be deemed to remain aliens.

Article IX

An alien who has been naturalized, as well as his naturalized wife and children, are not entitled to become the following:

1. Chiefs of various councils in the national government, heads of various ministries and chairmen of the national government committees.
2. Committee members of the legislature and control commission.
3. Ambassadors or envoys.
4. Officers in the army, navy, and air force.
5. Provincial and district officers.
6. Special municipal governors.
7. Officers in autonomous districts.

Nevertheless, the naturalized person under Article VI can petition the Ministry of the Interior five years after he has acquired the nationality, while other naturalized persons require ten years to have the above restriction removed.

SECTION III
LOSS OF NATIONALITY

Article X

A Chinese who is in the following categories loses his/her nationality of the Republic of China:

1. A Chinese woman who has married a foreigner and has requested to renounce Chinese nationality and has permission of the Ministry of the Interior.
2. A child born to and acknowledged by an alien father.
3. A child born of an alien mother when abandoned by the father and acknowledged by the mother.

Points 2 and 3 shall apply to those persons who are either minor children or unmarried women under Chinese law.

Article XI

Any Chinese national intending to acquire an alien nationality must first obtain permission of discharge from the Ministry of the Interior. This applies only to those who have passed their 20th birthday and are considered capable according to the Chinese law.

Article XII

The permission of discharge shall not be accorded when the petitioner at the time of filing his petition:

1. Is at the age of national service but has not fulfilled it.
2. Is in the national service.
3. Is currently holding a civil or military position.

Article XIII

The following person, although he/she has fulfilled the requirements of Articles X and XI, does not lose his Chinese nationality:

1. A suspect or accused in a criminal case.
2. A person who is still serving his sentence because of a criminal act.
3. An accused in a civil case.
4. A person who is serving his obligatory sentence.
5. A person who has been declared bankrupt and has not been restored.
6. A person who has not paid a tax or who has been penalized because of a tax problem which is still not yet settled.

Article XIV

A person who loses his Chinese nationality will be treated as an alien and hence loses his privileges as a Chinese national. His property acquired under the privileges which were accorded to him before he lost his nationality will be given to the State Treasury if it is not transferred to a Chinese national within a year commencing from the day he loses his Chinese nationality.

SECTION IV
READMISSION

Article XV

A person who loses her Chinese nationality under Point 1 of Article X may apply for readmission to Chinese nationality when her marital relations have been terminated by divorce or death. She will reacquire her Chinese nationality upon permission of the Ministry of the Interior.

Article XVI

A person who lost his Chinese nationality under Article XI may apply for readmission to Chinese nationality if he resides in China and has fulfilled the requirements enumerated in Points 2, 3 and 4 of Article III. But this does not apply to his wife and children who lost their nationality.

Article XVII

The condition in Article VIII shall also apply to Articles XV and XVI.

Article XVIII

A person who has reacquired Chinese nationality is not allowed to hold any of the positions listed in Article IX until after a period of three years.

SECTION V
SUPPLEMENTAL PROVISIONS

Article XIX

The implementation regulations of this Law are announced separately.

Article XX

This Law becomes effective on the day it is promulgated.

Source: *Zhonghuaminguo fagui huipian 3* (Shanghai: Zhonghua Shuju, 1934): 66–69. This translation was done by Leo Suryadinata after consulting the English version of the 1909 Chinese Nationality Law. The official English translation is not available to this author.

Appendix 3

Text of the Nationality Law of the People's Republic of China (1980)

Article I

This Law is applicable to the acquisition, renunciation and restoration of the nationality of the People's Republic of China.

Article II

The People's Republic of China is a unified, multinational country. Persons belonging to any of the nationalities of China have Chinese nationality.

Article III

The People's Republic of China does not recognize dual nationality for any Chinese national.

Article IV

Any person born in China whose parents are Chinese nationals or one of whose parents is a Chinese national has Chinese nationality.

Article V

Any person born abroad whose parents are Chinese nationals or one of whose parents is a Chinese national has Chinese nationality. But a person whose parents are Chinese nationals and have settled abroad or one of whose parents is a Chinese national and has settled abroad and who has acquired nationality on birth does not have Chinese nationality.

Article VI

Any person born in China whose parents are stateless or of uncertain nationality but have settled in China has Chinese nationality.

Article VII

Aliens or stateless persons who are willing to abide by China's constitution and laws may acquire Chinese nationality upon approval of their applications provided that:

1. they are close relatives of Chinese nationals; or
2. they have settled in China; or
3. they have other legitimate reasons.

Article VIII

Any person who applies for naturalization in China acquires Chinese nationality upon approval of his or her application; no person whose application for naturalization in China has been approved is permitted to retain foreign nationality.

Article IX

Any Chinese national who has settled abroad and who has been naturalized there or has acquired foreign nationality of his own free will automatically loses Chinese nationality.

Article X

Chinese nationals may renounce Chinese nationality upon approval of their applications provided that:

1. they are close relatives of aliens; or
2. they have settled abroad; or
3. they have other legitimate reasons.

Article XI

Any person whose application for renunciation of Chinese nationality has been approved loses Chinese nationality.

Article XII

State functionaries and army men on active service shall not renounce Chinese nationality.

Article XIII

Aliens who were once of Chinese nationality may apply for restoration of Chinese nationality provided that they have legitimate reasons; those whose applications for restoration of Chinese nationality are approved shall not retain foreign nationality.

Article XIV

The acquisition, renunciation, and restoration of Chinese nationality, with the exception of cases provided for in Article IX, shall go through the formalities of application. Applications for those under the age of 18 may be filed by the minors' parents or other legal representatives.

Article XV

The organs handling nationality applications are local municipal and county public security bureaus at home and China's diplomatic representations and consular offices abroad.

Article XVI

Applications for naturalization and for renunciation or restoration of Chinese nationality are subject to examination and approval by the Ministry of Public Security of the People's Republic of China. The Ministry of Public Security issues a certificate to any person whose application is approved.

Article XVII

The nationality status of persons who have acquired or lost Chinese nationality before the promulgation of this law remains valid.

Article XVIII

This law comes into force from the day of promulgation.

Source: *Xinhua News Agency*, 15 September 1980.

Notes

[1] See Leo Suryadinata, "Ethnic Chinese in Southeast Asia and their Economic Role", in *Chinese Populations in Southeast Asian Societies: Identities, Interdependence, and International Influence*, edited by Jocelyn Armstrong, Warwick Armstrong and Kent Mulliner (London: Curzon Press, 2001), pp. 55–73.

[2] Ibid.

[3] Wang Gungwu has discussed various patterns of Chinese migration, including *Huashang* and *Huagong*. See Wang Gungwu, *China and the Chinese Overseas* (Singapore: Times Academic Press, 1991), pp. 3–21.

[4] W. F. Wertheim, "The Trading Minorities in Southeast Asia", in *East-West Parallels: Sociological Approaches to Modern Asia* (Chicago: Quadrangle Books, 1965), pp. 39–84.

[5] Zhuang Guoto, *Zhungguo fengjian zhengfude huaqiao zhengce* (Xiamen: Xiamen daxue chubanshe, 1989), pp. 99–100.

[6] Yuan Ding, *Wan Qing qiaowu yu Zhongwai jiaoshe* (Xi'an: Xibei Daxue, 1994), p. 5.

[7] Mao Qixiong and Lin Xiaodong, *Zhongguo qiaowu falu fagui gaishu* (Beijing: Zhongguo huaqiao chubanshe, 1994), p. 79.

[8] Li Guilian, "Wan Qing 'Guojifa' yu 'Guoji Tiaoli'", *Faxue Yanjiu*, no. 70 (May 1990): 76–79. I would like to thank Prof Li Guilian of Peking University for drawing my attention to his article.

[9] Ibid., p.78.

[10] Ibid.

[11] For the text of the 1909 law, see Appendix 1.

[12] Ibid.

[13] Johannes Chan, "Nationality", in *Human Rights in Hong Kong*, edited by Raymond Wacks (Hong Kong: Oxford University Press, 1992), p. 488. I would like to thank Prof Johannes Chan of the University of Hong Kong for providing me this article.

[14] See *Xinhai Geming yu Nanyang Huaren Yantaohui Lunwenji* (Taipei: Guoli Zhengzi Daxue [National Chengchi University], 1986), p. 402.

[15] *Zhonghua minguo faling daquan bubian* (Shanghai: Shangwu Yinshuguan, 1914), section 5, internationl affairs, p. 1.

[16] Ibid.; but I have not been able to get hold of the 1914 China Nationality Law.

[17] Chan, op. cit., p. 488.

[18] For a discussion of the Oen case, see Leo Suryadinata, *Peranakan Politics in Java, 1917–1942*, 2nd edition (Singapore: Singapore University Press, 1981), pp. 26–27.

[19] For the text of the 1929 Nationality Law, see Appendix 2.

[20] Supang Chantavanich, "From Siamese-Chinese to Chinese-Thai: Political Conditions and Identity Shifts among the Chinese in Thailand", in *Ethnic Chinese as Southeast Asians*, edited by Leo Suryadinata (Singapore: Institute of Southeast Asian Studies, 1997), pp. 232–59.

[21] For the text of the 1980 Nationality Law, see Appendix 3.

[22] Chan, op. cit., p.489.

[23] For a discussion of the dual nationality treaty, see Leo Suryadinata, *Pribumi Indonesians, the Chinese Minority and China: A Study of Perceptions and Policies* (Kuala Lumpur and Singapore, 1978), pp. 119–27.

[24] See Appendix 3.

[25] On the application of the 1980 Law to Hong Kong, I have relied heavily on Johannes Chan's article (1992) cited earlier in this chapter.

[26] Chan, op.cit., p. 493.

[27] Ibid.

[28] For a discussion of Deng's visit, see Leo Suryadinata, *China and the ASEAN States: The Ethnic Chinese Dimension* (Singapore: Singapore University Press, 1985), pp. 83–88.

[29] Ibid., p. 87.

[30] Mao Qixiong and Lin Xiaodong, *Zhongguo qiaowu*, pp. 328–40.

[31] Ibid.

[32] *Lianhe Zaobao* (Singapore), 25 February 1998.

[33] Ibid.

[34] *Lianhe Zaobao*, 13 April 1998; and *Straits Times*, 13 April 1998.

[35] For a discussion of the Sino-Vietnamese war, see Suryadinata, *China and the ASEAN States*, pp. 43–58.

[36] See Huong Nam, "On the Hoa issue in Viet Nam", *Supplement to Vietnam Pictorial*, No. 234 (June 1978). See also "Statement by the Ministry of Foreign Affairs of the Socialist Republic of Vietnam on the issue of Hoa People in Vietnam", *Vietnam Courier*, No. 74 (July 1978): 3.

[37] Ibid.

[38] Li Haobei, *Guoji wenti de bijiao yanjiu* (Beijing: Shangwu, 1981), p. 243.

[39] Ibid.

[40] Ibid.

[41] Ibid., p. 244.

[42] It is difficult to obtain the numbers of ethnic Chinese who have settled in Southeast Asia but are still holding alien status. Most governments do not release these figures. Therefore, the above information is based on estimates or calculated guesses. See Leo Suryadinata, *Chinese and Nation-Building in Southeast Asia* (Singapore: Singapore Society of Asian Studies, 1997), p. 13. For the figure on Thailand, see National Statistical Office, Office of the Prime Minister, *Statistical Yearbook, Thailand*, no. 43 (1996): 49.

INDEX